SOME LIKE IT HOTTER

The Official Cookbook of the Galvanized Gullet

Geraldine Duncann

101 PRODUCTIONS

Publisher	Brete C. Harrison
Associate Publisher	James Connolly
Editors	Susanne Fitzpatrick and Annette Gooch
Proofreader	Carolyn Chandler
Director of Production	Steve Lux
Composition	ProImage
Cover Photographer	Michael Lamotte
Photographic Stylist	Sara Slavin

Text copyright © 1985, 1988, 1992 The Cole Group
Illustrations copyright © 1992 The Cole Group

Printed and bound in the USA
Published by 101 Productions/The Cole Group
4415 Sonoma Highway
PO Box 4089
Santa Rosa, CA 95402-4089

A B C D E F G
2 3 4 5 6 7 8 9

Distributed to the book trade by Publishers Group West and gift/gourmet trade by Max Burton Enterprises, Inc.

Library of Congress Catalog Card Number in progress
ISBN 1-56426-503-X

To my father, Gerald Duncann Wenker, who laid the solid foundations for my love of hot foods, good beer, and people.

FOREWORD

Out of this world is out of this world, whether in the creative kitchen or on the printed page. There is an affinity between having a jalapeño-Vesuvius erupt on your tongue and having an explosive idea erupt in your consciousness. Each can be a startling and, in reflective savoring, a very great pleasure.

Some Like It Hotter says it for me. Every recipe I've sampled from this marvelous collection is a delight. But then I suffer withdrawal symptoms if you keep me away too long from capsicum; not to mention horseradish, mustard, and ginger—all of which I grow in my garden whenever possible because the fresher, the hotter, the better.

My exploratory ventures into chili seasoning started while I was living in a mountain village called *Tlalpujahua* deep in the heart of Mexico. This is where I began research into the early history of the spice trade, an essential background for building the worlds of *Dune*. At the time, Mexico was a haven for the poor writer, a guarantee that even if you had little money you would not starve in a garret.

Market day in this tiny Michoacán village was Wednesday, and the array of different chiles was an invitation to experiment.

Geraldine once counted 37 different varieties of chiles in a Mexican market. Not to play one-upmanship with her, but I have counted more than 40 varieties in the Toluca market, and the number was even greater if you counted fresh and dried separately, which you should do because the flavor definitely is different.

Mexican friends say the variations are much greater if you factor in the time of harvesting. Some chiles are considered best if picked immature; others (they say) must be allowed to ripen on the vine.

Those of us with galvanized gullets owe a great deal to the evolution of food preferences in that band around the globe about ten degrees north and south of the equator, a cummerbund of human development that I refer to as "the capsicum belt." The spiced foods of this region, *picante* as hell, often will make you sweat—which is what they are supposed to do because the reaction serves as air-conditioning for the body in the hot climate. Chili-spiced foods also are very high in Vitamin C, and if the chiles are grown in the proper soil, they contain essential minerals.

The general rule is "If it doesn't clear your sinuses, it's not hot enough."

It's not difficult to acquire an addictive taste for these foods. If they are new to you, start slowly. Turn to page 144 where Geraldine has placed my recipe for Pre-Dune Fried Rice. Go easy on the ginger at first. Later, you will want to increase it and, perhaps, add more freshly chopped green onions, a bit more chile and garlic, and hot mustard on the side. (That hot mustard you get in Chinese restaurants is best made with stale beer, a trade secret from San Francisco's Chinatown.)

After reviewing all of the recipes in this collection and finding many old friends here, I can recommend this without reservation as a wonderful introduction to the world of the galvanized gullet. And when you go into the kitchen to prepare these delicious foods, remember how to greet all intruders who would have you soften the blow: "If you're not here for the heat, get out of my kitchen."

—Frank Herbert
Science fiction writer,
author of *Dune*
Somewhere in Space
(where we all are)

CONTENTS

PREFACE

THE GALVANIZED GULLET

This book was born in Berkeley at the home of an Anglican priest. Father Green and his family hosted "Sunday Supper" every week for years. It was a potluck communion of friendship for Christian and non-Christian alike. One Sunday, Father Green's contribution was a dish that was definitely beyond most people's tolerance for hot foods. To his great joy and delight, about six of us came back for bowl after bowl of his delightful fiery pottage, bypassing the other, more traditional potluck contributions of lasagna, tuna and cream-of-mushroom-soup casserole, macaroni salad, and pineapple upside-down cake.

Through Father Green's creativity, those of us sharing a love of robust foods found each other. We decided to make a pilgrimage to an almost unknown restaurant in San Francisco serving Hunan food. The excursion proved so successful that we arranged to get together for a potluck of nothing but hot, hot foods. Twelve people participated in that first extravaganza. The contributions ranged from chili to seviche. Jars of kimchee and jalapeño jelly were present as just a little something extra to nibble on.

My ex-husband, who can't even tolerate a little black pepper on his morning eggs, bit into a slice of chile-cheddar corn bread and, with tears in his eyes, exclaimed, "You guys must have galvanized gullets to be able to eat this!" An organization was born.

When the Galvanized Gullet meets, dishes include couscous and *wat* with *injera*, curries, Sichuan stir-fry, a Thai rice and shrimp concoction that is pure ecstasy, and, of course, a reputable selection of the world's fine brews.

Who were these strange few imbued with such unusual tastes? Joel is a wine maker. David and Ernie are priests. Gail is an insurance adjuster. Ardis is a jeweler. Michael is a football coach. Pete is head of a high school mathematics department. Ellen sings in the San Francisco Opera chorus. Another David is an attorney. The list includes computer programmers, musicians, dancers, a psychologist, an electrical engineer, a union negotiator, a probation officer, a police officer, a trucker, a lab technician, two business executives, a restaurateur, a rock concert producer, a falconer, a classical music radio announcer, several science fiction authors (including Frank Herbert and Poul Anderson), an ex-Mousketeer, and me.

Galvanized Gullets crop up in the strangest places. How's 30,000 feet in the air for strange? During a transatlantic flight, I struck up a conversation with a flight attendant. We discovered that we both delighted in hot foods and eagerly launched into a discussion of our favorite dishes. Another member of the crew was hailed, who likewise confessed to being a hot-food junkie.

A while later the captain came to my seat and said, "I understand you collect recipes for hot foods. I just happen to have a few . . ." Seating himself next to me, he plunged into what was obviously a favorite subject of his—unfortunately, he explained, one not shared by his wife. He bestowed upon me five fine recipes, gathered from far-flung places he had visited during his career as a pilot (including the one for Nasi Kuning Lengkap on page 142) before he grudgingly went back to relieve the co-pilot. I was richer by five excellent recipes and several new friends and Galvanized Gullet members.

If the concept of the Galvanized Gullet tantalizes you, why not found a branch? The rules are simple. Get together with friends to eat fine hot, zesty foods, drink good beer, and engage in brilliant conversation.

I would like to give thanks to the following people and organizations, without whose help I might not have been able to complete this project: to the patient staff at the Bancroft Library, University of California, Berkeley; to numerous people at the University of California at Davis; to Graham Proud, barman extraordinaire, for sharing his knowledge about the great brews of Britain; to the helpful staff at the Turf Tavern, Oxford, England; to Fritz Maytag, Anchor Brewing Company, San Francisco; to the staff of the Mexican Tourist Board. And a most special thanks to the ground and flight crews of British Airways, who on numerous flights have gone out of their way to accommodate me and my research materials.

—Geraldine Duncann

EATING HOT STUFF

Those of us who revel in the tingling delights of chiles, the lusty joy of ginger, and the warm pleasures of horseradish can be a sorely misunderstood lot. More-timid souls, possessed of paltry palates, can never fathom the ecstasies we share. "When you've burned out all your taste buds with chiles and horseradish, there isn't any way you can taste anything at all," say the uninitiated. They mistakenly believe that we exemplify some unique cult of S and M—that we are displaying undue bravado, machismo to the maximum. It is their true belief that we are indulging for the pain alone.

The fact is that in dishes designed to be hot, the heat-producing elements enhance the total sensation of the combined flavors. Anatomists tell us that the human tongue is able to distinguish four flavors: sweet, sour, bitter, and salty. And that is only the foundation for the gustatory glories available to the human palate. We can tell the difference between crab and lobster and distinguish among fat and succulent Pacific oysters, delicate, firm oysters from the coast of Louisiana, and belons captured off the western coast of France. We are able to distinguish between a 1979 Hacienda Chenin Blanc and a 1980 Stevenot Chardonnay. I love to tell doubters that one of the few people I have ever met who had a tolerance for hot foods that equaled my own is the wine maker at one of California's most prestigious premium wineries. His is a job that requires a sensitive palate. If his sensitive palate can revel in tingling ecstasies—if he can like it hotter—anyone else can, too.

GERALDINE'S MAJORITY-OF-ONE PHILOSOPHY OF COOKING

When using this book, please consider that any cookbook should be only a guideline that helps you develop your own creativity. Do not let a cookbook dictate to you, least of all this cookbook. If you don't want food to be so hot, don't make it so hot. If you want it to blow off the top of your head, be my guest and add the optional volcanic intensifiers. If you dislike garlic, (oh horror of horrors) then don't use it. Actually, if you don't like garlic—or chiles for that matter—you had better put down this book now. The point is that the amounts of seasonings specified in any recipe are guidelines. I almost always use a heavier hand with seasonings than is called for in this book, but subtlety is not in my vocabulary.

You'll see a lot of my own background and interests throughout the book. I talk about my family, the history of cooking, and people I've shared recipes with around the world. Cooking has been an integral part of my California-frontier family history for generations. The recipe for Son-of-a-Bitch Stew (see page 92) is one example. My mother first learned Mexican cooking from a Mexican woman who lived on my great-grandfather's cattle ranch in the San Joaquin valley in California, and Chinese recipes from the Chinese cook who was the supreme commander of that kitchen. My father learned from Jack London how to prepare oysters using seaweed and Anchor Steam Beer.

The hearty farmhouse fare of the last century tells us as much about the people who prepared and ate it as microwave gourmet food tells us about today's mobile society. The history of cooking has become fascinating to me and drawn me to develop many recipes, including Yogurt Ice (see page 164), which is the sort of dish that Saladin and Richard Coeur de Lion would have eaten during the Crusades.

A study of humankind is a study of food, and vice versa. I have gathered recipes from a Mexican trucker who stopped at the side of the road near Topolabampo to help me clean my fuel pump; from members of the houseboat community in Sausalito, California; and from a garlic vendor in the marketplace in Chartres. The best apple pie I have ever eaten was made by an 87-year-old political activist in Berkeley, who was given the recipe by Henry Miller. I have collected recipes from science fiction writers (see Pre-Dune Fried Rice, page 144), from jazz musicians (see New Orleans Beans and Rice, page 140), and from airline pilots (see Clams With Rice, page 48). Every culture has its own kind of soul food. I find the eating habits of any society and the social and economic elements that created them among the most compelling aspects of history.

In this book I have not included recipes for standard Indian curries or the Mexican foods that have become incorporated into American cuisine. I have omitted a recipe for chili con carne. Everyone in the United States who makes chili knows his or her recipe is the best. Even my friends in England have chili recipes. There are no recipes for tacos, quesadillas, and the like. These are foods that anyone can sling together for a quick and easy snack. Instead, I focus on excellent dishes that are less standard fare, drawn from cuisines around the world, dishes that are probably not in your culinary repertoire.

To me cooking is not a science but an art, with the exception of certain kinds of baking where the success of a recipe is determined by a specific chemical reaction. I believe that recipes and cookbooks are sometimes not in the best interests of fine food. On the one hand there is the philosophy that cookbooks are designed to give readers information that makes it possible to reproduce recipes consistently, and saying "a dollop" or "some" or "bake until done" is inadequate. At the risk of being considered a Dolloping Gourmet, I dislike recipes with specific quantities, particularly for seasonings (see Broth, page 10), and since I am unfamiliar with your stove, how can I tell you how long to cook something? Nevertheless, I have formulated my recipes in teaspoons and minutes.

For me, reproducing a dish exactly is necessary only in the restaurant and catering businesses, where cooking becomes a commercial science. Good food in the home is an art. Why can't a dish be a one-time experience, something that is special and unreproducible? How many *Mona Lisas* are there in the world? Are any two productions of *La Bohème*

identical? Did Isadora Duncan dance to a formula? Is the sunrise the same each morning? No one in his or her own kitchen should ever worry about making a dish come out the way it "should" taste. Trying to cook a dish the "right way" is not fun. So please consider my instructions to be guidelines, not commandments, unless otherwise stated.

When I feel a particular instruction is vital to a recipe, I tell you. One example is the tedious way you need to add the first half of the oil when making mayonnaise (see page 152). Another is the necessity to mince vegetables very finely for Cajun Boudin (see page 96). Note: I said *very finely mince*; I did not say *make into mush*. Therefore, if you have a quick thumb on the button and can make a food processor produce a pile of nice, fluffy, finely minced vegetables, not baby food, then by all means use it. If not, then put the machine away and use a good knife, a very sharp knife. You will probably have to resharpen it several times during the process. Is all this clear?

A kitchen can be much more than a place where you prepare the requisite daily nutrition or even wonderful food. A kitchen

can be the workshop and studio where your creative talents are unleashed in full glory. It can also save you many a trip to the therapist. Opening a coconut (see page 12), kneading bread (see page 146), or thwacking a chicken apart with a cleaver (see Intoxicated Fowelle, page 29) can be a great way to let out your pent-up aggressions.

The kitchen is also the social nexus for family and friends. Parties are born in the kitchen and often wind up there. How many times have you designed a party with candles on a buffet table, dimmed the lights, and turned on appropriate music, only to find guests congregating in the kitchen under the bright lights picking at the turkey carcass?

Although I don't think much of a party where the refreshments consist of a bag of pretzels and a six-pack, I nevertheless feel strongly that you need to enjoy your party as much as the guests do. Good food and drink are elemental to a good party, but you should also be able to enjoy the party yourself. If the number of guests happens to exceed the food supply, do not worry. In the chapter on Party Nibbles (see page 15), you will find many recipes designed to get you out of the kitchen with as little fuss as possible, while allowing you to amaze and mystify guests with your culinary prowess.

As long as I am on my soapbox, I'll address another culinary concept that makes me gnash my teeth: leftovers. I struck the word from my family's vocabulary years ago. There is no such thing as leftovers; there are only "planned overs," or "ingredients" as my daughter terms them. "But my family hates leftovers," you say. "I'm not so sure," I respond. Do you throw out the leftover chocolate cake or apple pie? I'll bet your freezer contains a partly consumed carton of ice cream. That's a leftover. How come last night's roast beef is not a leftover but last night's brussels sprouts are? Now, admittedly, a leftover collapsed soufflé is less than appetizing. I am not fond of leftover omelets, and leftover dumplings should be buried in the backyard. But consider that it takes both natural resources and human resources—that is, your time—to prepare food, and often it is far more conserving of both if you purposefully prepare more food than can be eaten at one meal. The

modern kitchen, with its myriad miracle machines, is designed to aid you in making yesterday's food into today's delight. I do not ask my family to eat turkey soup the week after Thanksgiving. I store the remaining turkey in the freezer. In February, turkey soup is a real treat—which brings me back to the subject of this book because many cultures use capsicums and other bold seasonings as an artful way to make leftovers into planned overs.

WHY HOT?

Over the centuries many cultures have developed cuisines based on hot food. What almost certainly began as culinary necessity gradually was refined into some of the most sophisticated cooking in the world. You can hardly say that people eat fine, hot Hunan, Sichuan, Ethiopian, Thai, or Ceylonese food just for the pain. Like any distinctive gastronomic experience, these exciting cuisines are based on careful blendings of elements that have evolved over generations, sometimes centuries.

The cultures that originally developed hot foods probably

did so out of need. These cultures were often located in hot climates, and, before mechanical refrigeration, food tended to spoil quickly. Evidence indicates that heavy seasoning of foods retards spoilage. In the early Middle Ages, people discovered that adding a lot of black pepper to sausages made them into good travelers. Black pepper is still a major ingredient in sausages that are intended to keep.

The contribution of heavy seasoning in retarding spoilage was minor compared with its use as a cover-up for food that had already spoiled or was at least off-tasting. It is possible to kill most toxins that attack elderly victuals by recooking them for a prescribed length of time. It is not possible, however, no matter how long that stew is boiled, to disguise the repugnant flavor that results from decomposition. It probably won't make you sick, but it isn't much fun to eat. The addition of heavy, pungent seasonings masked the unsavory aspects of food kept too long. In Eastern cultures pepper, mustards, cloves, anise, fenugreek, cinnamon, and turmeric were well known for their powers of camouflage.

When the West began significant intercourse with the East (usually considered to be at the time of the Crusades), Westerners discovered that they no longer had to endure the flavors of tainted foods. So the race to discover safer and more economical routes to the spice-producing lands was on.

For people living in hot climates, there is another benefit to consuming zestily seasoned foods. Eating hot foods produces sweat, which is beneficial in hot weather. As the moisture on skin and garments evaporates, the body is cooled by natural "air-conditioning."

HOT STUFF: AN ANNOTATED LIST

The foods that are most often used to produce the sensation of heat are garlic, onion, ginger, mustard, horseradish, pepper, and chiles. "Don't forget chili powder and curry powder," you say. Remember, though, that they are manufactured. Chili powder and curry powder are born when you invite garlic, dried ground chiles, ginger, pepper, and other spices and ingredients to jump into the same little can. Chili powder was invented in the Southwest of the United States. In my experience, all brands are good as long as they are used fresh. Curry is a blending of spices and other flavoring agents; as few as 5 or as many as 30 can be mixed in a single curry. There are myriad types; my favorite is labeled *Madras-style*.

Onions and Garlic

Some people consider onions and garlic to be hot. They possess an acid that may seem unpleasantly harsh when they are eaten raw. Although some people today feel they have been poisoned if they are asked to eat anything with garlic in it, the English during the Middle Ages and the Renaissance ate it with great gusto. After all, it warded off the plague, guaranteed that your firstborn would be a male, and kept away witches and vampires.

For those who love the flavors of onion and garlic but wish they weren't so pushy, despair not. The longer either vegetable is cooked, the more the acid breaks down and the harshness is dissipated, leaving a delightful flavor. Therefore, when preparing a dish that requires long cooking, such as a stew, roast, or casserole, you can put in as much garlic as you like. Lamb shank stew from Turkey uses 30 to 40 cloves of garlic (see Leyla's Lamb Shank, Garlic and Pepper Casserole, page 74). The meat, vegetables, and garlic are slowly cooked in the oven for five hours. The result is a rich, delicious concoction, strong in personality but easy to get along with.

For dishes that require little or no cooking, controlling the effect of garlic is somewhat more difficult but not insurmountable. In preparations such as a delicate omelet, or quiche, where the flavor of garlic is desirable but should not destroy the essence of the dish, you can cook the garlic first. I often mince the garlic, then slowly simmer it in enough water to almost cover, or I gently sauté it in butter or a mixture of butter and white wine. This civilizes the garlic and makes it ready to introduce into polite society.

Mustard

The seeds of the mustard plant are hot. Prepared mustards run the gamut from the yellow goo we spread on hot dogs at the ballpark to various cultural adaptations including fiery Chinese mustard and the subtle, multiflavored concoction known as Dijon mustard.

Mustard is common in wine-producing regions since it is often used as a regenerative cover crop planted between rows of vines. In the Côte d'Or of France, as in the Napa and Sonoma valleys of California, winter and spring are made glorious by the brilliant yellow of the flowering mustard plants stretching acre after acre among the noble vines.

Horseradish

This cousin of mustard is hot and heady, makes the eyes cross, and clears the sinuses. Freshly grated horseradish can bring the most robust member of the Galvanized Gullet to his or her knees.

If fresh horseradish root is available (or you grow it yourself), you are in for a new dimension in heat. Whereas the heat of chiles rests on the tongue and tingles the lips, horseradish reaches the nose. The instant the fumes of freshly grated horseradish touch your tongue, they race up your nose and lodge in the sinus cavity behind your eyes.

Bottled products labeled simply as *horseradish* are usually quite hot; however, to my tastes, products labeled *horseradish sauce* are a little mild. The recipes in this book are formulated for bottled horseradish. If you grate your own horseradish, disregard the amount given in a recipe and begin by adding and tasting a bit at a time or else you are going to be in big trouble.

Ginger

Ginger is delightfully hot and has the unique characteristic of being compatible with both sweet and savory foods. I use it in all its forms: fresh, ground, Asian pickled, sweet-and-sour dried strips, sweet and preserved in jars, and, of course, candied. Go into an Asian market sometime and discover the great variety of ginger products available. Ginger is one of the foods that Asian cultures consider to be essential in the cleansing of both the body and the soul.

Pepper

Black or white, fine or coarse, pepper is hot and imparts a particular flavor that cannot be reproduced. There is no substitute for freshly ground pepper.

I would like to shatter a myth. How many recipes have you seen that call for several whole peppercorns to be added to a soup or stew? James Beard once did an experiment: He put a handful of whole peppercorns in a kettle of water and boiled them for an hour, after which he discovered that there was no measurable change in the flavor of the water. Pepper will not release its flavor unless it's ground or cracked.

I use black pepper even when I am not making something particularly hot. I can't imagine cooking without it. I seldom add salt at the table, but I always find I want more pepper and feel deprived when a waiter at a restaurant comes to the table carrying a gigantic peppermill and, with great flourish, allots me a penurious twist or two.

Pepper is not only one of the elements in any hot cuisine—it has been a pretty hot item throughout history. The spice merchants were among the wealthiest men of medieval Europe. A pound of ginger bought a sheep; a pound of cloves purchased three cows in milk with their calves or the finest well-trained stud horse. Kings gave gifts of pepper to the pope. Taxes and debts could be paid with peppercorns.

It was the quest for spices, not the lust for gold, that sent the first cumbersome wooden vessels across thousands of miles of turbulent uncharted seas. The newly discovered continent never did fill the Old World coffers with the sought-after cinnamon, nutmeg, ginger, and cloves. The Old World benefited instead by the introduction of tomatoes, potatoes, and chiles.

When Sir Francis Drake sailed up the western coast of the New World in 1579, he replaced all the bags of Devonshire sand, which had been placed on the hold of the *Golden Hind* for ballast, with gold and silver bullion pillaged (or liberated, depending on your point of view) from Spanish strongholds. Yet the pepper and cloves he later added to his trove as he circumnavigated the globe were considered to be the greatest part of his bounty.

Chiles

For centuries, Europeans obtained their spices through trade with Eastern cultures reached by overland travel. When the first enlightened few perceived that the world was round and you really wouldn't fall off the edge, they conceived the idea of sailing west to reach the lands where the coveted spices grew. What they hadn't reckoned with was a very large continent in their path. When they landed in the Americas, thinking they had reached their destination, they naturally wondered, "Where's the pepper?"

Upon being served dishes containing chiles and experiencing the bite they produce, these visiting merchant-adventurers decided that they could make their fortunes back home by selling them as pepper. Just as the name *Indian* came to be applied to Native Americans, so *chiles* became interchangeable with *peppers*. But not in this book. To avoid confusion, I refer to black and white pepper as *pepper* and to chiles as *chiles,* or *capsicums*—what you call chiles if you are scientifically inclined. Incidentally, a variation of only one gene determines whether a member of the genus *Capsicum* is hot or sweet. If it's sweet, it's a bell pepper. Cayenne pepper is finely ground red pepper made from a variety of dried red capsicums.

The Wide World of Capsicums

I do not call for specific varieties of chiles in the recipes in this book because names and descriptions can be misleading. Instead, here are some guidelines for choosing which chiles to use, followed by a glossary for those of you who want to try to name and order the confusing world of the capsicums.

There are dozens of varieties of chiles. In one marketplace in Mexico I counted 37 varieties at one stall. Although the varieties have individual names, I do not use them in this book. On one hand, the same chile is often sold in different markets under a variety of names; on the other hand, a single name may be used for a number of different chiles. Finally, your market may carry only one kind of chile, and that one may not be labeled with the name I would use. So rather than shop for a specific chile, you'll want to work with what's available to you, adjusting the recipe as necessary.

Many elements influence the heat of a chile. The variety usually determines hotness, but within a single variety there may still be a range. The type of soil in which a chile was grown and how much water the chile received during its growing period affect the intensity of the heat. Cross-pollination can also have an impact. So even if in your experience the light yellow chiles are not quite as hot as the bright red ones, don't always count on it. Bell peppers—green, red, or yellow—are always sweet and mild, as are fresh pimientos.

Chiles that are light green, long (5 to 6 inches), and twisted in form are mild. They are quite similar to the green bell pepper, but not always. I've been buying these chiles for years, and they have always been mild and a little more flavorful than standard bell peppers. But I did once buy one that turned out to be extraordinarily hot. The very

dark green, heart-shaped chiles, about 4 inches long, are usually slightly hot and very flavorful. Remove the seeds and they are quite mild indeed, most of the time.

Next are the little chiles about the size of a thumb. In general, the dark green ones range from hot to quite hot. Remove the seeds, and they should be tolerable even for a beginning Galvanized Gullet. The yellow wax chiles can be hotter, some of the time. Remove the seeds, and the flesh is usually tolerable to most people. The bright blood-red chiles range from quite hot to hand me a beer quick! Taking out the seeds doesn't change the intensity.

The hottest chiles I have ever experienced were about the same length as the three mentioned above, but only about half as thick, and tapered to a very slim point. They ranged from dark forest green to bright red, with a few mottled ones. I bought them in Southall, near London, and one—I repeat one—was enough to make a bowl of guacamole made with six avocados hotter than I normally make it when using five chiles.

It's hard to describe a chile.

Taste-Testing Chiles

If you have a choice of fresh chiles, taste-testing—the only sure-fire way to determine their heat—will allow you to calculate how much of what kind to use in a recipe. Here's how to taste-test chiles. Put 3 table-spoons of cottage cheese in each of several small bowls, one for each kind of chile you are testing. Mince the chiles and put 1 teaspoon of each into a bowl of cottage cheese; mix. Let sit for about 5 minutes. Label each bowl with the kind of chile it contains. Then, a glass of lager in hand, start tasting down the line and make your own designations as to the degree of hotness of each chile. You might want to do this with all of the hot ingredients used in this book. Try fresh chiles both with and without seeds. Try crushed dried chiles, cayenne pepper, Tabasco sauce, as well as various mustard products such as horseradish, dry Chinese, English, German, and Japanese wasabi. By doing this you can define the parameters of your taste.

In any of the recipes in this book, I recommend using fresh chiles because fresh are better. Dried chiles can be used in place of fresh in roughly the same amounts, but the flavor will be slightly different. Dried chiles can produce the same level of heat but not the same complexity of flavor. (You can also use dried chiles in addition to fresh, to increase the heat.)

If you live in an area where fresh chiles are unavailable, don't pass up recipes that call for them. Just use another product, adding it gradually until it suits your taste. You can substitute about 1 tablespoon of chopped or minced bell pepper (available almost everywhere) for each chile. This gives the flavor of a fresh chile. Then add the heat with crushed dried chiles or cayenne pepper. To get maximum heat from dried chiles and cayenne, use them when they are new. If you don't expect to use them up in a month, store them in the freezer in a tightly closed, moistureproof container. Tabasco sauce is a condiment with a flavor all its own, which often is desirable, but it is not interchangeable with fresh chiles.

A note on working with chiles: While handling them, remember not to touch your eyes or mouth with your fingers because the oils can burn. Some people feel comfortable wearing rubber gloves, but I don't because I think the risk of cutting off a finger due to loss of dexterity is greater than that of getting burned by the oil. If the oil of chiles, onions, or garlic burns mucous membranes or exposed skin, flood liberally with water.

Glossary

Most of the dried chiles used in this book are small, whole dried red chiles, the same chiles in their crushed form, and cayenne pepper. All the other chiles are fresh, except for canned peeled green chiles and pickled jalapeño chiles. The following glossary of fresh chiles is to be used as a general guide. You will find that the names of chiles are far from standard in the market, and as I explained earlier, a given type or variety may not maintain its degree of hotness from individual chile to individual chile.

Anaheim Sometimes called New Mexico chile, Rio Grande chile, long green chile, or California chile. Light green, about 6 inches long, 1 to 2 inches wide. Mild.

Bell Pepper Red, green, and yellow, 4 to 5 inches long, often almost as wide. Sweet and mild.

Cayenne A hot red chile usually dried and ground to produce cayenne pepper. Sometimes ground cayenne is a blend of several ground dried chiles.

Creole or Louisiana Bright green or red, small and slender, 1 1/2 to 2 inches long. Hot.

Frying Bright green or red, smooth skinned, 6 to 7 inches long, tapering and slightly twisted. Usually mild but with a little more flavor than the standard bell pepper.

Guero Sometimes called *yellow wax* (see page 10) or New Mexico chile. Pale smooth yellow to yellowish green, 3 to 4 inches long, 2 to 2 1/2 inches in diameter, slightly curved and tapering. Mild to hot.

Italian Deep forest green, 4 to 5 inches long, heart shaped. The flesh is somewhat bitter and a bit on the tough side. Usually medium hot, but don't count on it. This is the only chile I have experienced whose flesh is just as hot as its seeds.

Jalapeño The quintessential chile. Yellowish through grass green, smooth skinned, 2 inches long. Hot.

Paprika Dark red, heart shaped. Smaller and sweeter than red bell peppers.

Pasilla Dark green to near black, narrow with wide shoulders, about 6 inches long. Moderately hot.

Pequin Bright red or green, tiny, usually no more than 1/2 inch long. Very hot.

Pimiento Very similar in appearance and taste to the paprika.

Poblano Sometimes called *ancho*, especially when dried. Dark green, similar to Italian chiles. Changes from green to dark brick red in several weeks off the vine, about 5 inches long. Medium hot to hot.

Serrano Smooth, bright green chile, 2 to 3 inches long and tapering. Hot and flavorful.

Sichuan Small, round, brown speckled, uniquely flavored. Medium hot to hot.

Thai Green or red, very narrow, 2 or 3 inches long. Very hot.

Yellow Wax Whitish yellow, turning somewhat red after picking. Almost translucent, smooth skinned, about the size and shape of your thumb. Hot.

OTHER INGREDIENTS

Here is a selection of other ingredients that appear in this book, with comments on use and methods of preparation where appropriate.

Bean Curd

In Asian non-Japanese recipes this ingredient is usually called *bean curd*. In Japanese and all other cuisines, it is called *tofu*. In the interests of consistency, this book refers to the ingredient as tofu.

Broth

Wherever you see this ingredient, you have at least three options: commercial canned beef or chicken broth; homemade broth; or powdered bouillon, augmented with a few other ingredients. Commercial broths are adequate, but I never use them because they are expensive. I resent paying a lot of money for a product whose main ingredient is water.

If you have the time, the ideal choice is to make your own stock. It is not nearly as difficult as people seem to think. To produce stock, use any of a variety of ingredients: bones and meat scraps from cooked steak, roasts, chicken, or turkey, or raw bones and trimmings. When chickens are on sale, I buy a dozen at a time, remove the breasts and freeze them in one package to use for stuffed chicken breasts or stir-fry dishes. I pack the wings, legs, and thighs for frying, roasting, or making teriyaki. The livers and giblets make another package. The necks and backs go into the stockpot.

I do not use an exact recipe for stock. Sometimes I mix poultry and red meat but not fish or smoked products. I put the bones and trimmings into a heavy pot and add enough water to cover. I add an onion cut in half, a head or two of garlic cut in half crosswise, and either a bouquet of fresh herbs or some mixed dried herbs (see page 13). Whenever I make stock, soups, or stews, I put the dried herbs into a tea ball and then toss the tea ball into the pot. Another excellent flavoring agent for stock, soups, and stews is a teaspoon or more of mixed pickling spices put into a tea ball and boiled with the bones.

Bring the pot to a boil, then reduce the heat; cover and cook at a rapid simmer for at least 2 hours. If the level of the liquid drops below the level of the bones and scraps, add enough boiling water to cover again. When finished, strain the broth through a colander, then through a fine sieve or piece of soft muslin; defat and store.

The third method starts with, dare I say it, powdered bouillon. I find that powdered bouillon is less salty than cubes, and I am able to make a perfectly reasonable broth by mixing the powder about 20 percent weaker than called for on the package. Low-salt powders are also available. For each quart of bouillon, I add half an onion, 5 or 6 cloves of garlic, and a bouquet garni made of fresh parsley, leaves from the center of a head of celery, a small bay leaf, and fresh dill if available.

If you do not have fresh herbs, add 1/2 teaspoon mixed dried herbs (see page 13). I also add 1/4 cup of cream sherry and 1 tablespoon of butter. Simmer the mixture for 1/2 hour, strain, and use as you would any other stock.

The ideal method for storing stock is to pour it into ice cube trays, freeze, then pop out the frozen cubes and store in plastic bags in the freezer. This way stock is ready to use at all times. You can just chuck a fistful into the pot.

Cilantro

When I say *cilantro*, I mean cilantro, not parsley. Parsley and cilantro are not interchangeable. Their flavors are as different as Chardonnay and Zinfandel, Swiss cheese and Cheddar, yogurt and sour cream—each pair is related but not interchangeable. (In Asian markets and recipes, cilantro is called *fresh coriander* or— mistakenly—*Chinese parsley*.) If cilantro is unavailable, make the dish, with no substitution. Without cilantro it just won't have quite the depth.

Clams, Mussels, and Oysters

Clams, mussels, and oysters are bivalves. One aspect of eating bivalves is the problem of "red tide," a discoloration of the ocean water caused by an increase in certain microscopic organisms.

Bivalves feed on these organisms and concentrate the resulting poisins in their bodies. On the West Coast, the red tide occurs every year, usually during the summer months. Eating the affected bivalves at this time may cause paralysis or death. There is only one sure method for telling when a bivalve is safe to eat on the West Coast. Call your local office of the State Department of Health to find out exact dates of the quarantine.

Incidentally, red tide is not a new phenomenon. Before Sir Francis Drake landed in California, the coastal Indian nations set up sentries along the trails to the beaches during the dangerous period to warn Indians from inland regions.

Coconut Milk

For recipes requiring coconut milk, you may choose canned coconut milk, homemade coconut milk, the liquid from the nut, or any combination to make the amount you need. The ingredients list of each recipe in this book that uses coconut milk gives the amount of coconut and boiling water to use when making homemade. When using canned coconut milk, if you want a rich consistency, shake the can vigorously before opening to incorporate the cream. If you want a thinner consistency, do not shake the can before opening it; open the can carefully and skim the "cream" from the top. Save the cream for another use.

To produce homemade coconut milk, you must first open the coconut. Now this can present a problem. There are three vulnerable points of entry—the eyes. Armed with a very large nail or a screwdriver, pound the sharp implement into two of the eyes. Let the liquid drain out through the resulting holes. Reserve the liquid to add to coconut milk or to use if the recipe calls for it specifically.

When the liquid is drained, crack the nut. If this isn't where the term "a hard nut to crack" came from, it should have been. After years of maiming myself with saws, pry bars, and sledgehammers, I have found a safe and workable method of cracking a coconut. Stand on the top step of your front porch and slam the coconut on the concrete walkway with all your strength. With luck it will crack. You can also use a hammer to tap sharply all around the "equator" and split the coconut in half.

Pry out the meat with a clean screwdriver. If you use a knife, you are begging for a trip to a hospital emergency room. The meat comes away from the shell easily if you freeze the coconut first. Grate the meat of the coconut on the large holes of a grater. It's not necessary to remove the brown skin.

Put the grated coconut into a bowl and pour boiling water over it; use the amount specified in the particular recipe. Let sit until cool. Line another bowl or a colander with a clean damp muslin cloth (cheesecloth is not fine enough) and pour coconut mixture into it. Gather up ends of cloth and squeeze to strain all liquid. Use the resulting milk immediately or refrigerate. If you refrigerate the milk, a layer of coconut cream may rise to the top; if it does, mix it back into the milk. The pulp can be toasted and used for cakes and cookies.

Crabs

Getting on intimate terms with these tasty crustaceans is an exceedingly personal matter, and everyone has his or her own ideas about preparing crabs. (The instructions for cleaning, given here, are for crabs that are already cooked, whether you buy them that way or cook them yourself. I don't like to kill them so I buy them already cooked, but if you wish to cook them yourself, crustaceans die instantly when plunged into a large pot of rapidly boiling water.) Many people will skip this section and simply say to the fishmonger, "Two large crabs, please. And, oh yes. Clean them. Thank you very much." For this service they most likely will pay more money per pound. That seems a shame to me since they will forfeit one of the best parts—the crab butter. You can have the delicious crab butter if you buy the crab cooked but clean it yourself.

To learn how to clean a crab and save money at the same time, buy a cooked whole crab. Set it in a clean sink and scrub thoroughly under cold running water with a vegetable brush. Pick up the crab and determine which is the front and which is the rear. The large claws and eyes are at the front. Turn the crab around and, holding it firmly, put your thumbs between the two shells, one thumb on the top shell and one thumb on the bottom. Then pull off the top shell, leaving the body with legs attached.

Set top shell aside. The white fibrous elements in rows down each side of the body are the gills. These and the shell are the only inedible parts. They won't make you sick, but you won't enjoy eating them. I also throw away the white squiggly part that is the intestinal tract.

Lying in a layer over the body and in the corners of the top shell is a rich substance ranging in color from creamy white to ocher and in texture from liquid to fairly solid. This is the butter, and it is delicious. The light-colored solid part is,

to my taste, better than the darker liquid. The butter has many uses. I save the liquid if I am making a soup, stew, or chowder within two hours; otherwise I discard it. For these dishes, I also save all of the solid butter. For preparations such as cracked crab or crab salad, I do not use the butter, but I remove the solid part and freeze it until I have enough for dips. It's excellent mixed with sour cream.

After removing the butter, rinse the body of the crab under cold running water and set it upside down to drain. Wash the top shell and drain it if you are going to make stuffed crab or use it for decoration. When serving whole crab I clean and wash the body, leaving the legs and claws attached, and place it on a large platter with the top shell sitting in its proper place.

Shelling the crab is done in two phases. First remove the legs and claws. Using a nutcracker, gently crack the shell, then remove the meat, usually in one piece. The sweet, delicate body meat is ingeniously enclosed in little honeycomb chambers made of a substance similar to celluloid. It isn't difficult to get at, just tedious and time-consuming. I break the

body into halves, then proceed to disassemble each half, chamber by chamber, removing the white meat as I go. The meat can be shredded or left whole for use in soups, salads, sandwiches, quiches, omelets, soufflés, and myriad other dishes.

Mixed Dried Herbs

I often use a good basic blend of herbs such as thyme, rosemary, sage, and savory. Mixed herbs and Italian seasoning are basically the same and are marketed by a variety of distributors. All are good blends, and I find it much more convenient to use 1/2 teaspoon of commerically prepared mixed dried herbs than to measure out 1/8 teaspoon of each single herb.

Oil

Unless otherwise stated in a recipe in this book, any light-flavored vegetable oil will do. Use a brand you like and can afford. Generic oils are fine. However, if I specify olive oil, peanut oil, or sesame oil, I do so because the flavor of the oil is essential to the flavor of the dish. For frying, in particular deep-frying, I use the least expensive oil I can find because I discard used oil frequently. If you must have special oils for special dietary reasons, choose what is best for you.

Some recipes instruct you to use half olive oil and half light-flavored oil, or half butter and half light-flavored oil. The flavor of the olive oil or butter is essential to the recipe, but they tend to burn easily; adding plain vegetable oil allows them to stand up to heat better.

Salsa

Salsa is as basic to hot foods as soy sauce is to Chinese cuisine or as tomato sauce is to Italian cuisine. Salsa is a staple in our house. It sparks up many a quick meal, such as a tortilla or piece of pita bread filled with any appropriate ingredients currently in the refrigerator. If cheese, tortillas, lettuce, and salsa are in the refrigerator, no one feels as if the larder is bare. Other quick foods are cottage cheese with salsa and an omelet garnished with salsa. My kids toss chuck roast or chicken into a pan, pour salsa over it, and pop it into the oven. Good, healthful, and

quick. Salsa is also good as a base for dips, salad dressing, or a marinade, and to zest up leftover meats.

My family uses so much salsa that making it is more economical than buying it ready-made. There are three recipes for salsa in this book: Salsa Cruda, an uncooked version (see page 158); Salsa Diablo, a smooth version (see page 158); and Salsa Son-of-a-Gun, a chunky version, (see page 157) which is my favorite. Use your own version if you prefer.

If you don't make your own, use any good commercial product, fresh, frozen, or canned. What brand? What type? Brand is irrelevant. I have tasted generic salsa that is excellent and brand name salsa that is not. Many markets carry fresh salsas in the refrigerated section, most of which are quite good. The advantage of fresh is that it contains the incomparable flavor of herbs, and fresh chiles. The disadvantage is that freshness is lost if you do not use the salsa shortly after buying it. Also, I have yet to find a fresh salsa that is as hot as some of the canned varieties. La Victoria, a pioneer in quality commercial salsas, for years won the salsa competitions in the Southwest. A proliferation

of products, inspired by the growing popularity of hot food, has given the company some stiff competition.

Salt

I rarely give a specific amount of salt in recipes and instead call for salt to taste. In my opinion, salt is way up there on the public enemy list with drugs, alcohol, tobacco, and caffeine. I feel it is important to monitor salt intake for health reasons; I do use salt, but sparingly. Remember, however, that there is no substitute for salt. If you are on a salt-free diet, then don't add salt. Please don't use a salt substitute.

Sugar

I often use sugar in cooking, but not in amounts large enough to make a dish sweet. Sugar brings out the flavor of the other ingredients, as do flavor enhancers containing monosodium glutamate, but sugar isn't nearly as harmful. I find that adding a bit of sugar takes a dish with the grace of a street urchin and makes it behave as if it had gone to finishing school.

PARTY NIBBLES

The hors d'oeuvre, or party nibble, is one of my favorite foods. The possibilities are limited only by your creativity. I have a repertoire of several hundred such recipes. Choosing a scant handful for this book has put me into the agonies of indecision.

Because there is no way to know how far a dish will go at a party, the yields for some of the recipes in this section state the amount made rather than the number of servings. Unlike a dinner, a party isn't intended to provide a complete meal. The food at a party is meant to enhance the total experience and can be entertainment as much as it is sustenance. Not everyone will eat some of everything, and you do not have the responsibility of offering every guest a full meal. If the turnout exceeds the guest list and you run out of food, don't worry. A party is for enjoyment, yours as well as everyone else's. Just serve forth a variety of delightful dishes you feel like preparing, and have a good time.

DIP IT

With few exceptions, dips have been an American phenomenon. I enjoy sharing my culinary concoctions with friends abroad. Years ago, when I made guacamole from two precious avocados smuggled through customs at Heathrow, my English friends insisted on putting a handful of crisps (potato chips) on their plates, spooning the guacamole over them, and eating the pile with knifes and forks. At a more recent party in Oxford, the guests eagerly scooped up guacamole from the bowl with chips I had made from Indian *pappadams,* since tortillas were unavailable.

In France, my friends have always been willing to scoop up my dips with the thin slices of toasted French bread I prepare, but they refuse to do it casually before dinner while having drinks and indulging in chitchat. Instead, the bowl of dip and basket of bread are placed in the middle of the table, and we all sit about diligently dipping and eating until the first course is served.

Dips are a godsend to the host. They have a glorious quality: They can be made well in advance, leaving you free to enjoy your party and your guests.

One-Step-Beyond Guacamole
California-Mexican Cuisine

In my book, guacamole is the dip supreme, the king of dips, a dip worthy of sainthood. Now I realize that to a lot of you guacamole is only mashed avocados with a little lemon juice and pepper chucked in. I happen to think that a good guacamole should have a lot more going for it than that. However, if you want to continue to live with mashed avocados and a squirt from a plastic lemon, be my guest, but be warned! The ghost of Montezuma may smash all your pre-Columbian artifacts and a feathered serpent may swoop down and curdle your Margaritas. So for those of you who are rather fond of your pre-Columbian artifacts and like a good Margarita, here is a delightful alternative.

In addition to serving guacamole as a dip, it is good stuffed inside crisp tacos or spooned on top of an omelet or a burrito. Or try alternating slices of avocado, tomato, and cucumber on a bed of romaine lettuce. Spoon guacamole over the top and garnish with chopped pitted black olives.

3 very ripe avocados
Juice of 2 to 4 lemons
1 large tomato, finely diced
1 large yellow onion, minced
1 stalk celery, minced
4 green onions, minced
1 bell pepper, seeded and minced
4 to 6 cloves garlic, finely minced
3 or 4 small fresh hot chiles, seeded and finely minced
1/4 cup minced fresh parsley
1 teaspoon finely minced cilantro
1 teaspoon sugar
1/8 teaspoon ground cumin
1/4 teaspoon coarsely ground black pepper
1/3 cup vegetable oil
Salt and cayenne pepper or Tabasco sauce, to taste (optional)
Assorted chips, sliced baguette, and raw vegetables, for accompaniment

Scoop avocados into a bowl and mash thoroughly with a fork. Add lemon juice a bit at a time, tasting after each addition, and stir well. Add remaining ingredients except salt and cayenne and mix. Add salt and cayenne to taste (if desired). Serve with your choice of accompaniments.

Makes about 2 cups

Gobba Ghanouj
Turkey

No, the typesetter didn't make a mistake on this one. *Baba ghanouj*, as described in most cookbooks, is a rather nondescript eggplant purée. My culinary guru and friend, Leyla, taught me to make this delightful concoction that will never be accused of being a bore at a party. Because this Turkish dish contains chunks and gobs of many delightful things, my sons christened it Gobba Ghanouj. In the Middle East this dish is served with leaves of romaine lettuce for scooping. I like to accompany it with potato chips, tortilla chips, slices of French bread, and assorted raw vegetables as well.

1 large eggplant
1 large tomato, minced
2 stalks celery, minced
1 large yellow onion, minced
3 or 4 green onions, including tops, minced
1 each green and red bell pepper, seeded and minced
3 or 4 small fresh hot chiles, seeded and minced
8 to 10 cloves garlic, minced
1/4 cup minced fresh parsley
1/3 cup freshly squeezed lemon juice
1 1/2 teaspoons sugar (optional)
1/2 teaspoon coarsely ground black pepper
2/3 cup olive oil
Salt, sugar, and cayenne pepper, to taste
Romaine lettuce, assorted chips, sliced French bread, and raw vegetables, for accompaniment

Preheat oven to 350° F. Using a barbecue fork, hold eggplant over hot coals or a gas flame and turn slowly until skin is blistered and singed in places. Rub off loose skin, leaving a bit of burned skin, which is necessary for the unique flavor of this dish.

In an ovenproof baking pan, bake eggplant until soft (30 to 45 minutes). Remove from oven and cool until it can be handled. Cut off stem and, with your hands, thoroughly mash flesh in a bowl. Continue kneading until lumps are gone and skin is broken up. Remove large chunks of skin that will not incorporate.

Add tomato, celery, yellow and green onions, bell peppers, chiles, garlic, parsley, lemon juice, sugar (if desired), and black pepper. Mix thoroughly. Gradually drizzle oil into bowl, and knead mixture with your hands until oil has been completely incorporated. Mixing oil into other ingredients will make a homogeneous substance that is not at all oily.

Add salt, sugar, and cayenne to taste (if desired). Traditionally, this dish is almost sweet-and-sour in addition to hot. Make it as mild or mighty as you wish by adding extra cayenne. Serve chilled, accompanied with romaine leaves, assorted chips, sliced French bread, and raw vegetables.

Makes about 3 cups

Ceylonese Sweet-and-Sour Curry Dip
Sri Lanka

I usually suggest drinking beer with hot foods, but this dish from Sri Lanka goes exceedingly well with either Gewürztraminer or champagne. As accompaniment, try a selection of whole strawberries, small bunches of grapes, pineapple spears, melon balls on picks, and slices of peach, orange, pear, apple, and nectarine. For a fancy presentation, spoon the dip into the hollowed-out half shell of a pineapple or a jagged-cut melon.

Continued

1 cup (8 oz) sour cream
1 can (8 1/2 oz) crushed pine-
    apple, drained
1 stalk celery, trimmed and
    finely minced
1 small fresh hot chile, finely
    minced
1 tablespoon minced red onion
1 tablespoon frozen orange
    juice concentrate
1/4 to 1/3 cup brown sugar
2 tablespoons cider vinegar
1 tablespoon Madras-style curry
    powder
1/2 teaspoon cayenne pepper
1 cup (1/2 pt) whipping cream
Mint sprigs and orange slices,
    for garnish
Assorted fresh fruit, for accom-
    paniment
1/2 lemon, cut into wedges

In a bowl thoroughly combine all
ingredients except cream, garnish, accompaniment, and lemon.

Whip cream to stiff peaks and
gently fold into dip mixture.
Chill thoroughly. Transfer to a
serving bowl and garnish with
mint and orange.

Place bowl in center of a
platter and surround with a
selection of fruit. Squeeze lemon
juice over cut fruit to prevent it
from turning brown.

Makes about 2 cups

Garden-Fresh Herb Dip
Family Recipe

Too many people think of hot
foods as being heavy and
overcooked, an assumption that
this recipe delightfully refutes.
For accompaniment, try sugar
peas, whole mushrooms, slices
of yellow and red bell pepper,
broccoli and cauliflower florets,
red onion rings, slices of chayote
and jicama, and pieces of fennel.
Leaves of romaine lettuce and
red cabbage also make good
scoopers.

2 cups (16 oz) cottage cheese
1/2 cup minced fresh basil
    leaves
1/4 cup each minced fresh
    chives, minced fresh mint,
    and minced red onion, and
    minced green onions,
    including tops
1 teaspoon minced cilantro
3 cloves garlic, minced
1/3 cup hot chunky salsa, com-
    mercial or homemade (see
    Salsa Son-of-a-Gun,
    page 157)
Salt and coarsely ground black
    pepper, to taste
Tabasco sauce, to taste
    (optional)
Assorted raw vegetables, for
    accompaniment

In a bowl toss together all ingredients except accompaniment
and chill. Put dip into a serving
dish, set on a large platter or
flat basket or tray, and surround
with vegetables.

Makes about 3 cups

Bagna Cauda
Italy

A garlic lover's delight, this hot
anchovy dip hails from the Pied-
mont region of Italy. It exempli-
fies the northern Italian finesse
at producing dishes that are
simultaneously stimulating and
refined. To keep the dip warm,
set serving dish over a heat
source such as a candle warmer,
electric hot tray, or spirit lamp.
Celery sticks, cherry tomatoes,
mushrooms, cucumber, red bell
pepper, and green onions are
excellent for dipping.

4 tablespoons butter
1/2 cup minced mushroom
    stems
3 tablespoons finely minced
    garlic
8 anchovy fillets, drained and
    minced
1 cup (1/2 pt) whipping cream
1 cup grated mozzarella
1/8 teaspoon cayenne pepper

1/4 teaspoon sugar
1/8 teaspoon coarsely ground
    black pepper
Salt, to taste
Assorted raw vegetables, for
    accompaniment

In a frying pan over low heat, melt butter and gently sauté mushrooms and garlic but do not brown. Add anchovies and stir constantly for about 1 minute. Add remaining ingredients except accompaniment and cook over very low heat, whisking constantly, until cheese is melted.

Pour dip into a serving dish. Accompany with a basket of crisp, chilled raw vegetables.

Makes about 1 1/2 cups

STUFF IT

Take two foods that are tasty, put one inside the other, and you have something even tastier. Since we are celebrating the genus *Capsicum* in this book, I'll begin this section with two delicious recipes for stuffed chiles, one Sichuan and cooked, the other Ethiopian and uncooked.

Sichuan Fried Chiles
China

Although this recipe calls for hot chiles, you may feel free to use milder ones. Mixing various colors—green, yellow, red—gives the dish added visual excitement. Each chile should be about as long as your thumb.

24 small fresh hot chiles
Sichuan Chile Stuffing
    (recipe follows)
Sichuan Chile Batter
    (recipe follows)
Oil, for deep-frying
Sichuan Chile Sauce
    (recipe follows)
Lemon slices and watercress or
    parsley sprigs, for garnish

Cut off stem end of each chile and remove seeds and pulp, being careful not to break skin. Bring a large saucepan of water to a boil and drop in chiles. Leave until water comes to a boil again, then immediately plunge chiles into cold water. When cold, drain.

Make Sichuan Chile Stuffing. Gently place stuffing into chiles, again being careful not to tear skin. Set aside and make Sichuan Chile Batter.

In a deep, heavy pot, heat oil to deep-frying temperature (375° F). Dip chiles in batter and shake off excess. Fry three or four at a time until golden brown (about 5 minutes). Drain thoroughly on paper towels.

Make Sichuan Chile Sauce.

To serve pour sauce into a small bowl and place on a serving platter. Surround with deep-fried chiles. Garnish with lemon slices and watercress sprigs.

Makes 2 dozen Stuffed Chiles

Sichuan Chile Stuffing

1/2 pound ground pork
1 egg
1 medium onion, minced
1 stalk celery, minced
6 cloves garlic, minced
1 1/2 teaspoons grated fresh
    ginger
1/4 teaspoon five-spice powder
1/8 teaspoon cayenne pepper
1 tablespoon soy sauce
1 1/2 teaspoons sugar
1/2 teaspoon coarsely ground
    black pepper

In a bowl mix together all ingredients.

Sichuan Chile Batter

1 egg
1 cup unbleached all-purpose flour
1 cup ice-cold water
1/4 teaspoon baking soda
1/2 teaspoon rice vinegar
Pinch each salt and sugar

In a bowl beat together vigorously all ingredients; set aside until ready to use.

Sichuan Chile Sauce

1/4 cup soy sauce
1 tablespoon tomato paste
1/4 cup brown sugar
1/4 cup rice vinegar
4 cloves garlic, finely minced
1 teaspoon finely grated fresh
   ginger
1/4 teaspoon cayenne pepper
2/3 cup water

In a blender purée all ingredients until smooth. Strain into a small saucepan and simmer over low heat for 5 minutes. Sauce may be served hot or cold.

Kifto-Stuffed Chiles with Berberé
Ethiopia

This mixture is essentially steak tartare, spiced up by the hot Berberé Sauce.

1 medium onion, finely minced
2 small fresh hot chiles, seeded
   and finely minced,
6 green onions, including tops,
   finely minced
1 bell pepper, seeded and finely
   minced
6 cloves garlic, finely minced
1 teaspoon finely grated fresh
   ginger
1/4 teaspoon each ground cardamom, ground cinnamon,
   and coarsely ground black
   pepper
1 cup Berberé Sauce
   (see page 157)
2 tablespoons freshly squeezed
   lemon juice
1/4 teaspoon grated lemon rind
1 teaspoon sugar
Salt, to taste
1 1/2 pounds top-grade lean
   beef, trimmed of fat and
   finely chopped or coarsely
   ground
12 large long, fresh mild chiles,
   halved and seeded
Watercress or parsley sprigs
   and lemon wedges, for
   garnish

Pat minced onion, hot chiles, green onions, bell pepper, and garlic, in a bowl, and add ginger, cardamom, cinnamon, black pepper, 1 tablespoon of the Berberé Sauce, lemon juice, lemon rind,

sugar, and salt to taste. Add beef and mix well.

Stuff mild chiles with the meat mixture.

To serve put the remaining Berberé Sauce into a serving bowl and place in the middle of a large platter. Arrange stuffed chiles around it and garnish with watercress sprigs and lemon wedges.

Makes 1 dozen Stuffed Chiles

Stuffed Drumsticks with Capsicum-Ginger Glaze
Family Recipe

To prepare these drumsticks, you will need an exceedingly sharp knife, a bottle of good wine, and the patience of a saint. The knife hopefully goes inside the chicken leg and the wine goes inside you, to help you achieve that saintly patience.

12 small chicken drumsticks
1/2 pound each ground pork
   and ground lean ham
1 medium onion, minced
4 cloves garlic, finely minced
1 1/2 teaspoons minced candied
   ginger
1/8 teaspoon ground cinnamon
1/2 teaspoon cayenne pepper
1/4 teaspoon coarsely ground
   black pepper

1 tablespoon brown sugar
Salt, to taste
1 recipe Capsicum-Ginger Glaze
   (see page 156)

Holding a drumstick by the wide end, stand it on a firm surface. Cut and scrape meat away from bone. The process gets easier when you have exposed enough bone at wide end to grab hold of drumstick. Continue until all but about 1 inch of bone is free. Meat will have almost turned inside out. Using a pair of poultry shears, cut off freed bone, leaving the last inch which is attached to meat at narrow end. Turn empty leg right side out.

Preheat oven to 350° F. In a bowl mix well all remaining ingredients except the Capsicum Glaze, using your hands. Stuff mixture into each empty chicken leg. Pull skin up and close opening with a wooden toothpick, shaping skin and stuffing into the form of a chicken leg. Make Capsicum-Ginger Glaze.

Place drumsticks on a rack over a baking pan and bake for 25 to 30 minutes, coating often with Capsicum-Ginger Glaze. Remove toothpicks and serve hot.

Makes 1 dozen Stuffed Drumsticks

Diablo Mushrooms
Family recipe

This dish only whispers an acquaintance with capsicum, boasting instead of its relationship with garlic and fresh basil. If you have leftover meat stuffing or basil-flavored topping, you can spread it on French bread and toast it in the oven. I designed this recipe for very large mushrooms. You can't find gargantuan or huge mushrooms? Then big will do—well, even not so big. Okay, so you have to use small. It's a pain, and of course you will need a bunch more of them, probably about 3 or 4 dozen. But it's worth it.

12 large mushrooms
2 tablespoons butter
2 tablespoons cream sherry
4 cloves garlic, minced
3 tablespoons minced onion
1/2 teaspoon minced fresh hot
   chiles
1/2 cup chicken livers
1/2 cup ground pork
1/2 teaspoon sugar
1/8 teaspoon freshly ground
   black pepper
1 egg
Salt, to taste
1 tablespoon shelled pine nuts
Diablo Mushroom Topping
   (recipe follows)
1/2 cup grated Swiss cheese

Fill a 3- to 4-quart pan with water and bring to a boil. Remove stems from mushrooms and finely mince stems. Set aside. Preheat oven to 350° F.

When water boils, drop in mushroom caps. When water returns to a boil, boil 1 minute longer, then immediately drain mushrooms and place under cold running water until they are cold. Drain.

In a large skillet over moderate heat, melt butter with sherry. Add garlic and gently sauté for 3 or 4 minutes. Adjust heat to keep garlic from browning. Add onion, chiles, mushroom stems, chicken livers, and pork. Continue cooking, stirring to break up meat, until pork is no longer pink but not yet browned. Livers should still be slightly pink inside.

Put mixture into a blender or food processor and add sugar, pepper, egg, and salt to taste. Purée until smooth. Scrape out into a bowl with a rubber spatula and stir in pine nuts.

Put a dollop of mixture into each mushroom cap. Set aside. Make Diablo Mushroom Topping.

To assemble, top each filled mushroom cap with a dollop of topping and sprinkle with grated cheese. Put on a baking sheet and bake until cheese is melted and slightly bubbling. Serve piping hot.

Makes 1 dozen Stuffed Mushrooms

Diablo Mushroom Topping

1 tablespoon vegetable oil
1 tablespoon olive oil
4 cloves garlic, crushed
1/4 teaspoon minced fresh hot
  chiles
1 cup chopped fresh basil
  leaves
1/4 cup whipping cream
1/4 teaspoon sugar
Salt and coarsely ground black
  pepper, to taste

In a blender purée all ingredients until well blended.

I once judged a dolmas competition. When biting into one of the entries, I chipped a tooth. The contestant who had created the dish looked astounded and said, "But the recipe didn't say to shell the pine nuts." In the interest of dental health, please shell all nuts.

Chicken Necks Diablo
Family Recipe

Served on a bed of watercress or other attractive greens, these capsicum-stuffed chicken necks are equally tasty hot or cold. If you want to dress up this dish a bit more, place cherry tomatoes and a few wedges of lemon atop the serving platter.

24 chicken necks (see Note)
2 cups cooked long-grain white
  rice
1 egg
1 large onion, finely chopped
1/2 bell pepper, seeded and
  chopped
1 stalk celery, finely chopped
1 tablespoon minced fresh hot
  chiles
6 cloves garlic, minced
1/4 cup minced fresh parsley
1/2 teaspoon mixed dried herbs
  (see page 13)
1/4 teaspoon coarsely ground
  black pepper
1 teaspoon sugar
Salt, to taste
Vegetable oil, for frying
Watercress sprigs or lettuce
  leaves, for accompaniment

Remove skins from chicken necks and set skins aside. Cover necks with water and boil until tender. When cool enough to handle, pick meat from bones and put into a bowl. Add remaining ingredients except reserved skins, vegetable oil, and accompaniment, and mix thoroughly with your hands. Fry a bit to test for seasoning, and adjust seasoning to taste.

Carefully stuff skins with mixture. Skewer each end shut with a wooden toothpick. In a cast-iron or other heavy skillet, over medium-high heat, warm about 1/2 inch of vegetable oil and fry stuffed necks until crisp and golden brown all over (about 3 minutes on each side). Drain on paper towels. Pat off excess oil with paper towels and serve on a bed of watercress.

Makes 2 dozen Chicken Necks

NOTE—When purchasing necks, make sure skins are attached. You may have to place a special order with the butcher.

Horseradish Beef Rolls
England

Not all hot foods contain capsicum, as these beef rolls from England attest. Prepared horseradish is hot, but fresh root is especially hot. Boy oh boy, is it hot! If using a grated fresh root, add a bit at a time and taste as you go.

4 ounces cream cheese
1/4 to 1/3 cup prepared horse-
radish, to taste
2 tablespoons minced fresh
chives
1 tablespoon minced red bell
pepper
2 cloves garlic, minced
1 1/2 teaspoons minced fresh
dill or 1/2 teaspoon dried dill
1 generous tablespoon chopped
ripe olives
1/3 cup minced red onion
1/4 teaspoon coarsely ground
black pepper
Salt, to taste
24 thin slices medium-rare lean
roast beef
Watercress sprigs, for garnish

In a bowl blend well all ingredients except beef and garnish.

Spread cheese-horseradish
mixture onto each slice of beef
so that it is thicker than butter
on bread. Roll firmly and secure
with a cocktail pick. Stuff a watercress sprig in one end of each
roll and place on a serving platter. Chill before serving.

Makes 2 dozen Rolls

Lumpia
The Philippines

Lumpia are Philippine egg rolls.
In this version the Lumpia are
stuffed with chicken, pork, and
potato. Philippine cuisine is a
delightful blend of Asian,
Polynesian, and Spanish cuisines,
which are evident in this tasty
treat.

2 tablespoons vegetable oil
1/4 cup water
1 medium onion, minced
6 cloves garlic, minced
1 tablespoon finely minced
seeded fresh hot chiles
1 scant teaspoon grated fresh
ginger
1/2 pound ground pork
1/2 bell pepper, preferably red,
minced
1/2 cup chopped fresh bean
sprouts
1/2 cup finely shredded napa
cabbage
1/4 cup minced celery
3 green onions, including tops,
minced
1 tablespoon minced fresh
parsley
1/2 teaspoon dry mustard
2 tablespoons soy sauce
1 1/2 teaspoons sugar
Salt and coarsely ground black
pepper, to taste
1 cup finely shredded cooked
chicken

Cayenne pepper, to taste
(optional)
1 cup mashed potatoes
2 eggs, lightly beaten
1 package (approximately 20)
egg-roll wrappers
Oil, for frying

In a wok over high heat, heat
the 2 tablespoons oil and the
water. Add onion, garlic, chiles,
and ginger, and stir-fry for about
2 minutes. Add pork, bell pepper, bean sprouts, cabbage, celery, green onions, parsley, mustard, soy sauce, sugar, and salt
and pepper to taste. Stir-fry until
vegetables are wilted (2 to 3
minutes). Remove from heat.
Add chicken. Taste mixture. If
you want Lumpia to be hotter,
add a bit of cayenne to mashed
potatoes. Stir eggs into mixture.

Lay an egg-roll wrapper on a
flat surface. Spread it thinly and
evenly with mashed potatoes,
leaving a 1/2 inch margin
around edges. Place about 1 1/2
tablespoons of vegetable mixture
in a line along edge nearest you.
Lift wrapper edge near you and
begin rolling. When you have
rolled half the wrapper, fold
sides inward. Continue rolling
until you reach end. Set aside,
seam edge down. Continue until
you run out of wrappers or
stuffing.

Continued

In a heavy skillet heat about 1 inch of oil until it reaches deep-frying temperature of 375° F (it should be hot but not smoking). Place two or three rolls at a time in hot oil and fry on both sides until golden brown. Remove from pan with a slotted spoon and drain thoroughly on paper towels.

Makes about 20 rolls

GRILL IT!

The need for maximum mobility prompted nomadic peoples to develop the technique of grilling. Following their herds from one pasture to another, desert nomads could not easily transport such cumbersome gear as stoves and a vast array of cooking implements. Grilling small pieces of meat also required less fuel than did roasting large joints of meat, as became the custom in northern Europe where fuel was more plentiful. In addition, grilling required little water for cleanup, an important concern in a climate where water was at a premium.

The following recipes, although designed for an open grill, are also tasty if cooked under the broiler or on a rack in a hot oven.

Shish Kabob
Middle East

Any dish that keeps the cook out of the kitchen is a welcome addition to any party. Since the preparation of this recipe is mostly chopping and arranging, it minimizes kitchen time and maximizes party time. Note, however, that lamb should be marinated for 2 hours.

Shish Kabob Marinade
(recipe follows)
2 pounds lean boneless lamb,
cut into bite-sized pieces
1 large onion, cut into wedges
1 small eggplant, cut into bite-sized pieces
12 small fresh mild to hot chiles
2 or 3 ripe but firm tomatoes,
cut into wedges

Prepare Shish Kabob Marinade. Place remaining ingredients in a large bowl. Cover with marinade, and toss gently to coat evenly. Refrigerate for at least 2 hours, stirring occasionally.

Thread meat and vegetables alternately onto skewers and grill about 4 inches from heat. Turn frequently and baste with marinade from bowl during cooking. Cook to desired doneness. Serve hot.

Makes 16 to 24 skewers

In the Middle East, foods prepared for events where alcohol will be served often contain a lot of olive oil. The theory is that the oil coats the intestinal tract and retards the absorption of alcohol into the body, thereby helping to prevent intoxication.

Shish Kabob Marinade

1/4 cup olive oil
1/2 onion, minced
8 cloves garlic, finely minced
1/4 cup freshly squeezed lemon juice
3 teaspoons minced fresh dill or 1 teaspoon dried dill
1 teaspoon minced cilantro
1/2 teaspoon each crushed dried hot chiles and dry mustard
1/8 teaspoon ground cinnamon
1 teaspoon sugar

In a bowl mix together all ingredients.

Seafood Shish
Middle East

You don't have to cook this marvelous dish yourself. Let guests do their own grilling—if, that is, they are not the type who will seize all the prawns and leave nothing but swordfish for the next guy. Remember to use clams and mussels in the correct season only (see page 11). The fish should marinate for 2 hours.

Seafood Shish Marinade
(recipe follows)
2 pounds assorted firm-fleshed
fish and shellfish such as
swordfish, shark, giant
prawns, scallops, shucked
clams or mussels
1 lemon, cut in half

Make Seafood Shish Marinade. Add fish to marinade and stir to coat. Refrigerate for at least 2 hours before serving.

Thread fish onto skewers and grill about 4 inches from heat. Fish are best when cooked lightly. Squeeze lemon juice over fish during grilling.

Makes 12 to 16 skewers

Seafood Shish Marinade

1/4 cup olive oil
1/4 cup freshly squeezed lemon
* juice*
3 teaspoons minced fresh dill or
* 1 teaspoon dried dill*
3 cloves garlic, minced
1 medium onion, minced
2 bay leaves, crushed
1/2 teaspoon or more crushed
* dried hot chiles, or more to*
* taste*
1/8 teaspoon dried thyme
1/2 teaspoon sugar
1 teaspoon paprika
1/4 teaspoon coarsely ground
* black pepper*

In a large bowl mix together all ingredients.

Beef Teriyaki
Japan

In good Japanese teriyaki the edges of the thin meat are singed and barely crisp, and the center remains quite rare. The contrast of textures is part of the essence of this dish. You can let guests cook their own to their individual preference.

2 pounds top-grade lean bone-
* less beef*
1 recipe Hot Teriyaki Sauce
* (see page 157)*

Put beef in freezer and leave until it is firm but not frozen solid (1 to 2 hours). Make Hot Teriyaki Sauce. With an exceedingly sharp knife, cut beef as thin as possible. Slice sheets into strips about 1 inch wide and 3 to 4 inches long. Place in Hot Teriyaki Sauce and marinate for at least 1 hour.

Thread strips of meat onto short bamboo skewers. On a barbecue or a hibachi over glowing coals, grill very quickly about 4 inches away from the coals. Turn frequently.

Makes 16 to 24 skewers

Kabob means quickly cooked meat and refers to a method of cooking that seals the outside, preserving all the flavors and juices on the inside. In the Middle East many kabob are large pieces of meat that are cooked in an oven or on top of the stove in a dutch oven. *Shish* refers only to one variety of kabob: meat that is cooked quickly on a shish, or skewer.

Onion Bhujjias
India

Crisp on the outside and steamy on the inside, these seasoned tidbits have become a regular dish in my culinary repertoire.

4 onions, grated
8 cloves garlic, finely minced
2 tablespoons minced seeded
*   fresh hot chiles*
1/4 cup minced fresh parsley
1 scant teaspoon grated fresh
*   ginger*
1 teaspoon minced fresh
*   cilantro*
1/8 teaspoon each ground cori-
*   ander, fenugreek, ground*
*   cumin, cayenne pepper, and*
*   ground cinnamon*
1/2 generous teaspoon sugar
1/4 teaspoon coarsely ground
*   black pepper*
Salt, to taste
2 eggs
1/2 cup unbleached all–purpose
*   flour*
Oil, for frying
Flour, for dusting (optional)

In a bowl mix well all ingredients except the oil and flour. In a skillet fry a small patty in oil to test for seasoning. Add salt and more cayenne if desired. Divide mixture into 16 to 20 equal portions and form into balls. You may need to dust your hands lightly with flour to prevent sticking.

In a deep skillet or wok, heat 4 inches of vegetable oil 375° F (oil should be hot but not smoking). Fry one ball first and break open to make sure it is done on inside. If it gets too brown on the outside before it is done on inside, reduce heat slightly and test again. Fry remaining balls, a few at a time, until golden brown (3 to 4 minutes). Drain thoroughly on paper towels and serve hot.

Makes 16 to 20 fritters

MIX IT

Part of the fun of preparing foods for a party is that you can be creative not only with the recipes but also with the menu. Here are several mix-and-match party nibbles.

Steak Tartare
Family Recipe

This dish, which does not require cooking, is a help for the harried host, and is good for a hot day. Guests can make their own combinations of cool fresh meat and crisp condiments.

Accompany Steak Tartare with a basket of rye crackers, poppy seed crackers, or thin slices of baguette. I always provide additional salsa and lemon slices, Tabasco sauce, and a pepper mill.

8 to 12 leaves curly endive
2 pounds freshly ground top-
*   grade beef*
1/2 cup mild or hot chunky
*   salsa, commercial or home-*
*   made (see Salsa Son-of-a-Gun,*
*   page 157)*
1 egg
1 large red onion, minced
1/2 cup minced green onions,
*   including tops*
4 small fresh hot chiles, minced
1 tablespoon minced garlic
4 hard-cooked eggs, minced
2 tablespoons capers, drained
1 can (4 1/2 oz) chopped black
*   olives, drained*
1/4 cup minced fresh chives
2 tablespoons minced cilantro
Lemon slices, for garnish
Assorted crackers and sliced
*   French bread, for*
*   accompaniment*
Salsa, Tabasco sauce, and
*   additional lemon, for*
*   accompaniment*

Line a serving platter with curly endive. Mound beef in center. Make a well in middle of beef. Pour in salsa and break egg into middle. Place red onion, green onions, chiles, garlic, hard-cooked eggs, capers, olives, chives, and cilantro in small piles around beef and garnish with thin slices of lemon. Chill before serving.

Serves 16 to 20 as an appetizer, 8 as an entrée

Sashimi with Three Sauces
Japan

A plate of tuna, salmon and prawn sashimi accompanied by these three zesty sauces makes an appetizer to remember. Sets of disposable wooden chopsticks are the perfect utensils to set alongside.

1/2 pound fresh raw tuna
1/3 pound fresh raw salmon
1/3 pound raw prawns, peeled and deveined
1/4 cup grated daikon
1/4 cup minced green onion tops
1/4 cup finely shredded carrot
Sashimi Sauce No. 1 (recipe follows), for accompaniment
Sashimi Sauce No. 2 (recipe follows), for accompaniment
Sashimi Sauce No. 3 (recipe follows), for accompaniment

With a very sharp knife, slice tuna and salmon as thin as possible. Split prawns in half lengthwise.

Chill a serving plate. Along one side of plate make lines of the daikon, green onion, and carrot. Arrange thin slices of fish and prawns in an attractive pattern beside vegetables. Refrigerate while you prepare sauces.

To serve set out platter of sashimi with bowls of sauces alongside.

Serves 8 to 12

Sashimi Sauce No. 1

1/4 cup soy sauce
1 1/2 teaspoons dry mustard
1 teaspoon sugar

In a small bowl mix together all ingredients.

Sashimi Sauce No. 2

3 tablespoons soy sauce
1 tablespoon rice vinegar
1 1/2 teaspoons sugar

1/2 teaspoon finely grated fresh ginger
1/2 teaspoon peanut oil
4 cloves garlic, finely minced
1/8 teaspoon cayenne pepper

In small bowl mix together all ingredients.

Sashimi Sauce No. 3

2 teaspoons wasabi
3 tablespoons soy sauce

Mix wasabi according to manufacturer's instructions or with enough water to make a smooth paste. Place in a mound in the center of a small flat bowl. Pour soy sauce around it to form a moat.

Marinated Vegetables
Family Recipe

These vegetables can be eaten a few hours after stirring in the marinade, but are best if refrigerated for two to three days. The dish will keep for two to three weeks in the refrigerator. However, I have never had a crock of these veggies last more than twenty minutes after I set it on the table.

Continued

2 quarts water
1/2 head cauliflower, cut into florets
2 large carrots, peeled and cut on diagonal
20 green beans, cut in half
1/2 pound broccoli, cut into florets
12 small boiling onions
Zesty Marinade (recipe follows)
1 each red and green bell pepper, seeded and cut into strips
12 small fresh mild chiles, seeded
2 stalks celery, washed, trimmed, and cut into 2-inch pieces
1 red onion, cut into rings

In a large saucepan bring the water to a rapid boil. Add cauliflower and leave in only until the water returns to a boil. Drain immediately and put under cold running water until thoroughly cold. Repeat blanching, draining, and cooling process for carrots, green beans, broccoli, and boiling onions. Blanching times differ: After the water returns to a boil, leave carrots and green beans in the water for 2 to 3 minutes; broccoli for 1 minute; and onions just until they can be pierced with the tip of a sharp knife.

Prepare Zesty Marinade. In a large bowl or a crock, combine blanched vegetables with bell peppers, chiles, celery, and red onion. Pour marinade over vegetables and stir gently, being careful not to break vegetables.

Serves 12

Zesty Marinade

2 cups water
2 cups cider vinegar
1/2 cup sugar
1/3 cup salt
20 cloves garlic, coarsely chopped
1 teaspoon crushed dried hot chiles
1/2 tablespoon pickling spices
3 teaspoons fresh dill or 1 teaspoon dried dill
1/4 teaspoon anise seed
1/4 cup olive oil

In a saucepan bring all ingredients except oil to a boil. Reduce heat to simmer and cook for 5 minutes. Remove from heat, add oil, and let cool.

Aaron's Hallelujah Garlic
Family Recipe

When this dish is ready, the garlic is soft and sweet, its harshness dissipated by long, slow cooking. It is named for my younger son, Aaron, who is a dedicated garlic fan. We set it in the middle of the table and gather around to tear off chunks of bread, dip them in the butter, and spread with the mushy garlic.

20 cloves garlic, peeled
1/8 teaspoon cayenne pepper
1/2 cup butter
1 baguette, for accompaniment

Put garlic, cayenne, and butter in a small heatproof serving dish. Set dish inside a steamer and steam for 45 minutes, adding water to steamer when necessary. When ready garlic will be soft and sweet. Serve with a baguette.

Serves 4 to 6 as an appetizer

Garlic was held in such high esteem in Egypt that vows were sworn on it.

An inscription on the Great Pyramid of Cheops records that 1,600 talents of silver were spent on onions and garlic for the workers in 2900 B.C.

Intoxicated Fowelle
Elizabethan England

We have some Goodwife late in the sixteenth century to thank for this extraordinarily delicious and simple dish. The original recipe called for "One Elderly Fowelle." As for the other ingredients, the inclusion of the New World capsicum dates the recipe sometime after Sir Francis Drake's circumnavigation of the globe in 1577–80. Ginger had been known in England since the Crusades. Spanish sherry—or sack as it was also called—was very popular at the time. English merchant-adventurers had taken home great quantities of the sherry after their sack of the Spanish town of Jerez where the wine was produced. The word *sherry* was as close as the English tongue could come to duplicating the Spanish word *Jerez*. Note that the dish should marinate in the refrigerator for at least 2 days.

1 frying chicken
*10 small fresh mild or hot
    chiles (selection of red, yel-
    low, and green, if available)*
20 cloves garlic
2 cups cream sherry
*1 tablespoon slivered fresh
    ginger*

*1/2 teaspoon cracked black
    pepper*
1 teaspoon pickling spices
*1 1/2 teaspoons minced fresh
    dill or 1/2 teaspoon dried dill*
Salt, to taste

Cut chicken in half. With a heavy, sharp cleaver, chop into 2-inch chunks, any way the cleaver happens to fall.

Rinse chicken pieces under cold running water and put in a saucepan with enough water to cover. Bring to a boil, then reduce heat to simmer and continue cooking until tender (45 minutes to 1 hour). Drain (save broth for another use). Rinse chicken pieces and put into a crock or jar large enough to hold them comfortably.

With a small knife, slit each chile. Slightly crush garlic. Add chiles, garlic, and remaining ingredients to chicken. Refrigerate for at least 2 days before serving, stirring occasionally to make sure all the fowelle is well "intoxicated."

Serves 8 to 12

Sterling's Popcorn Diablo
Family Recipe

My older son, Sterling, created this recipe. Our family was playing with popcorn flavors long before commercially prepared seasonings became fashionable. A great way to prepare popcorn for a hungry horde is to put hot popped popcorn and seasoning in a paper bag and shake. Serve right out of the bag. Children love it, and there are no dishes to wash.

1 cup butter
1 teaspoon curry powder
*1/4 teaspoon each chili powder
    and cayenne pepper*
Garlic salt, to taste
6 cups hot popped popcorn

In a small saucepan over low heat, melt butter with curry powder, chili powder, cayenne, and garlic salt. Drizzle over popcorn and serve hot.

Makes 6 cups

SOUPS

I adore soup: soup with a meal, soup as a meal, soup thick or thin, hot or cold. I do not like soup from a can, either over my noodles with a can of tuna, or as an accompaniment to a salad.

The word soup comes from sop *or* sops, *the chunks of stale or dry bread that were always served in the Middle Ages for sopping up broth. Spoons were a luxury not found in all households. Almost everyone ate broth in the Middle Ages. It was an economic necessity. The quality of the broth was judged by the quantity of the* sops *provided to accompany it. Geoffrey Chaucer, while in the employ of John of Gaunt, recorded an incident involving a French dignitary who left a dining hall in high dudgeon because the broth had not been accompanied by* sops. *John of Gaunt, being quite urbane and living in comfortable circumstances, provided his guests with spoons, thus making the serving of* sops *unnecessary. The Frenchman didn't see it that way and thought he had been slighted.*

By the end of the fourteenth century, almost every-one had spoons. People began to look to the quality of the broth itself, or soup, as it had become known. Soup became a fad. People of fashion would show their chefs out of the kitchen and create their own soups. Monastic chefs were equally enthusiastic. The Archbishop of Canterbury decreed that only one soup could be served per course in certain monastic orders because the members were spending far too much time in the kitchen.

Fourteenth-Century Broth and Sops
England

This soup is a relic from English monasteries. It is hot and heady with garlic and mustard, not chiles, which hadn't yet been brought over from the New World. The original recipe called for turnips, because potatoes also had not yet been imported from the New World.

1 quart rich beef broth
40 cloves garlic
1 1/2 teaspoons dry mustard
1 large potato, peeled and
    diced
2 large leeks, including 4
    inches of green tops, well
    cleaned and chopped
1 large onion, chopped
1 teaspoon sugar
1/2 teaspoon mixed dried
    herbs (see page 13)
6 tablespoons butter
Salt and freshly ground black
    pepper, to taste
3 tablespoons cream sherry
1 cup shredded mustard greens
6 to 8 slices (1 in. thick)
    French bread
1/3 cup grated Swiss cheese

In a 2 1/2- to 3-quart saucepan, put broth, 20 of the garlic cloves, 1 teaspoon of the mustard, potato, leeks, onion, sugar, herbs, and 2 tablespoons of the butter. Simmer until vegetables are tender. Let cool a bit, then purée in a blender in two or three batches. Rinse out saucepan and return broth to it. Add salt and pepper to taste.

Crush the remaining garlic cloves. In a small saucepan over low heat, gently cook crushed garlic, sherry, the remaining mustard, and the remaining butter until garlic is soft (6 to 7 minutes). If it begins to brown or oxidize, add a few more drops of sherry. When garlic is soft, purée in a blender.

Preheat oven to 400° F. Bring broth to a simmer. Add shredded mustard greens and continue to simmer until greens are only slightly wilted (no more than 5 to 7 minutes). Pour broth into a heatproof serving dish and keep warm.

Toast bread, spread with garlic-mustard butter, and float bread on top of broth.

Sprinkle cheese over top and bake in oven until cheese is melted and beginning to bubble and brown. Serve immediately.

Makes about 4 cups, serves 6 as an appetizer, 4 as a meal

Asopao de Camarónes
Puerto Rico

The bright reds and greens of capsicums make this Puerto Rican shrimp soup a hot dish for the eye as well as the palate.

2 tablespoons oil
1 onion, finely chopped
1 onion, cut into thin rings
1 red bell pepper, seeded and
    cut into thin strips
2 small fresh hot green chiles,
    cut into thin strips
3 tomatoes, chopped
6 to 8 cloves garlic, minced
1/4 cup tomato paste
6 cups chicken broth
1 cup cooked long-grain white
    rice
2 pounds shrimp, peeled and
    deveined
1 cup fresh or thawed frozen
    green peas
Salt and coarsely ground black
    pepper, to taste
Tabasco sauce, to taste
    (optional)
1/3 cup slivered cooked lean
    ham, for garnish
2 green onions, minced, for
    garnish
1 jar (2 oz) chopped pimientos, for garnish

In a heavy skillet or wok, heat oil. Do not let it smoke. Add chopped onion, onion rings, bell pepper, chiles, tomatoes, and garlic. Stir-fry until vegetables are tender.

Remove to a 2 1/2- to 3-quart pot and add tomato paste and broth. Stir until paste is dissolved. Add rice and bring to a boil, then reduce heat to simmer. Add shrimp and peas and simmer for 15 minutes. Season to taste with salt, pepper, and Tabasco (if desired).

To serve, ladle into a large heated tureen and sprinkle with ham, green onions, and pimientos.

Makes 6 cups, 4 to 6 servings

Peanut-Chile Soup
South Africa

This recipe proves that I don't put garlic into everything. It is a tasty dish that stands on its own without the help of what has been called the stinking rose.

2 large leeks, including 4 inches of green tops, thoroughly washed
4 cups chicken broth
1 large onion, chopped

1 cup cooked long-grain white rice
3 small fresh hot chiles, cut into rings, seeds included
1 red bell pepper, seeded and cut into thin strips
1 cup roasted salted peanuts (not dry roasted)
1 cup fresh or canned okra
Salt, freshly ground black pepper, and cayenne pepper, to taste
1/4 cup finely chopped roasted salted peanuts, for garnish

Cut leeks into thin rings and set aside 1/2 cup. In a heavy 2- to 3-quart saucepan over high heat, bring broth, onion, and the remaining leeks to a boil, then reduce heat to low and simmer until vegetables are tender (25 to 30 minutes).

Remove from heat and purée in a blender. Return soup to saucepan, reserving 1 cup. Add rice, chiles, bell pepper, and reserved leeks and bring to a boil. Reduce heat to simmer and cook for about 15 minutes.

Meanwhile, in a blender purée reserved soup and peanuts. Stir into soup on stove and continue cooking for the remainder of the 15 minutes. If using fresh okra cut into rings and boil until tender (about 5 minutes). Drain and rinse thoroughly. If using canned

okra drain and rinse. Add okra to soup, stir, and remove from heat. Season to taste with salt, pepper, and cayenne.

To serve, ladle into a heated serving dish and lightly sprinkle top with chopped peanuts.

Makes 5 to 6 cups, 4 to 6 servings

Soto Ayam Kuning
Indonesia

Three bulbs of garlic guarantee that this chicken noodle soup is far from chickenhearted.

1 frying chicken, quartered
1/2 teaspoon crushed dried hot chiles
3 bulbs garlic, halved and loose outer skin removed
2 large onions, quartered but not peeled
2 stalks celery, coarsely chopped
4 or 5 thin slices fresh ginger
1 small bay leaf
1 star anise pod
1/2 teaspoon ground turmeric
1/2 teaspoon sugar
2 ounces cellophane noodles (see Note)
1 medium onion, cut into thin rings

Continued

1 medium leek, including 2 inches of green tops, thoroughly washed and cut into thin rings

1 red bell pepper, seeded and cut into thin strips

1 large, long mild fresh chile, cut into thin rings

1/4 pound snow peas, trimmed of strings

1/4 pound mushrooms, thinly sliced

Oil, for coating skillet

1 egg, beaten

Salt and freshly ground black pepper, to taste

Cayenne pepper, to taste (optional)

2 green onion tops, chopped into thin rings, for garnish

In a large, heavy pot, put chicken, dried chiles, garlic, quartered onions, celery, ginger, bay leaf, anise, turmeric, and sugar. Add enough water to cover chicken. Bring to a boil, then reduce heat to a rapid simmer and continue to simmer until chicken is tender but still on the bones (about 45 minutes). When chicken is cool enough to handle, lift from pot, drain, and remove skin. Remove all meat from bones. Return skin and bones to pot, cover, and continue to simmer for another 45 minutes to 1 hour. Cool. Cut meat into thin strips and reserve.

While broth is simmering, put noodles into a bowl and cover with cold water. Leave until soft.

When broth is ready, strain through a fine sieve. Discard remains, rinse pot, and return strained broth to pot. When noodles are soft, drain them and add to broth. Add onion rings, leek, bell pepper, fresh chile, snow peas, and mushrooms. Bring to a boil, immediately reduce heat to simmer, and cook for 5 minutes.

Lightly oil a skillet; preheat over medium heat. Pour in egg and swirl to coat pan evenly. Cook until surface is almost dry (not more than 1 minute). With a pancake turner, begin to roll egg. Leave for just a bit longer to ensure that it is dry inside, then turn out onto a cutting surface. With a sharp knife, shred finely.

Taste broth for seasoning. Season to taste with salt, black pepper, and cayenne (if desired).

To serve, ladle soup into a heated serving dish and add slivered chicken and stir. Sprinkle egg and green onion over surface and serve immediately.

Makes 5 to 6 cups, 4 to 6 servings

NOTE—Sometimes called long rice, bean threads, glass noodles, or Chinese vermicelli, cellophane noodles are available in Asian markets as well as many large supermarkets.

Menudo
Family Recipe

Tripe Soup

In the 1930s my dad spent many a night in a small-town jail for informing the farm workers of California's San Joaquin Valley of their right to strike. The recipe that follows is one he enjoyed at the home of a Mexican farm worker he had marched with. A great dish, menudo shows what ingenuity can produce when you can afford only the stomach and feet of the pig. My friends tell me it is also an excellent remedy for a hangover.

2 pounds tripe, cut into thin
    strips 3 to 4 inches long
2 pig's feet, split
4 quarts beef broth or water
4 onions, coarsely chopped
1 bay leaf
1/2 teaspoon cracked black
    pepper
6 small dried hot chiles
10 cloves garlic, crushed
1/2 teaspoon each dried
    oregano and ground cumin
1 can (14 oz) hominy
4 tomatoes, chopped
1 each green and red bell
    pepper, seeded and cut into
    thin strips
Salt and freshly ground black
    pepper, to taste
Flour tortillas, heated, for
    accompaniment.

In a 6-quart stockpot put tripe
and pig's feet and add water to
cover. Bring to a boil, pour off
water, and add broth.

Add onions, bay leaf, cracked
pepper, dried chiles, garlic,
oregano, and cumin, and bring
to a boil. Reduce heat to a
rapid simmer and continue
cooking until meats are tender
(3 to 4 hours).

When cool enough to
handle, remove pig's feet and
bone them. Return boned meat
to pot, add remaining ingredients except accompaniment,

and simmer for 20 to 30 minutes. Adjust seasoning.

Serve hot, accompanied with
a basket of hot flour tortillas.

Makes 8 to 10 cups, 8 hearty servings

Cheese and Chile Soup
Mexico

As you ladle up this savory
sizzling soup with its garnish of
stringy cheese, you'll be re-
minded of the texture of a
classic French onion soup.

4 cups rich beef broth
10 cloves garlic, peeled
4 large tomatoes, chopped
3 medium onions, quartered
1/2 teaspoon mixed dried
    herbs (see page 13)
1 scant teaspoon sugar
1/4 teaspoon ground cumin
1 medium onion, cut into rings
1 long fresh mild green chile,
    cut into thin rings
1 red bell pepper, seeded and
    cut into thin rings
1 cup each grated sharp
    Cheddar cheese and grated
    mozzarella cheese
1 cup mild or hot chunky
    salsa, commercial or home-
    made (see Salsa Son-of-a-
    Gun, page 157)
1 teaspoon minced cilantro, for
    garnish

In a large saucepan bring
broth, garlic, tomatoes, quartered onions, herbs, sugar, and
cumin to a gentle boil. Reduce
heat to simmer and continue
cooking for 30 minutes. Purée
in a blender and return to pan.

Add onion rings, chile, and
bell pepper to soup and simmer until vegetables are tender
(about 15 minutes).

Toss together cheeses. Ladle
soup into a heated serving
dish. Add cheese and salsa and
stir gently. Sprinkle with
cilantro and serve immediately.

Makes 5 to 6 cups, 4 to 6
servings

California Gazpacho
Family recipe

Who said soups have to be hot?
A cold soup on a hot day can
be as refreshing as a hot soup
is comforting on a cold day,
and to me, gazpacho is the
king of cold soups. And when I
say gazpacho I don't mean just
cold tomato soup or a puréed
mass, or something all watery
with an oil slick floating on it,
I mean GAZPACHO.

If you want an impressive
presentation, try the following.

Continued

California Gazpacho, cont.

Start with a 50-pound block of ice. Set a stainless steel mixing bowl on top of ice and fill with hot water. When ice has melted enough to form an indentation, remove bowl, scoop out melted water from ice, throw out water in bowl, and replace with bowl filled with more hot water. Repeat process until you have formed a bowl in top of block of ice. Set entire block on a tray that will catch the water as block gradually melts. Use indentation in ice as a serving bowl. It makes a spectacular display and keeps gazpacho cold as well.

1 can (46 oz) tomato juice
1 cup rich beef broth
1 cup cream sherry
1/2 red onion, cut into thin rings
2 stalks celery, diced
1/2 each green and red bell
    pepper, seeded and cut into
    thin strips
1 long fresh mild green or
    yellow chile, seeded and cut
    into thin rings
1/2 large cucumber, peeled and
    diced
1 large tomato, diced
2 avocados, diced
1/2 cup sliced mushrooms
1 can (2 1/2 oz) sliced black
    olives, drained

1 can (4 oz) diced peeled green
    chiles
4 green onions, including tops,
    minced
1/4 cup minced fresh parsley
1 tablespoon minced cilantro
1/8 teaspoon ground cumin
Freshly ground black pepper,
    to taste
1 cup hot chunky salsa, com-
    mercial or homemade (see
    Salsa Son-of-a-Gun, page 157)
1/4 cup olive oil
1 cucumber, for garnish
3 to 4 lemon slices, for garnish
Salsa, Tobasco sauce, and
    lemon wedges, for accompa-
    niment

In a large serving bowl, combine all ingredients except salsa, olive oil, garnishes, and accompaniment; chill thoroughly. Stir salsa and oil into gazpacho. Using a fork with sharp tines, firmly drag it down sides of cucumber to score skin. Cut into rings. The edge of each slice will be jagged. Float cucumber rings and lemon slices on top of gazpacho and serve ice-cold. Accompany with salsa, Tabasco sauce, and lemon wedges.

Makes 12-14 cups, 8 servings as
    a meal or 16 or more servings
    as a party side dish

Sopa de Aguacate
Mexico

The conquistadors came to Mexico in search of gold. Had I been one of those first adventurers, I would have achieved my quest when I tasted my first avocado. Here, it's the base of a rich, chilled soup.

4 cups rich chicken broth
1 onion, chopped
2 small fresh hot chiles
4 cloves garlic, chopped
1/2 cup cream sherry
3 large, very ripe avocados
Salt and freshly ground black
    pepper, to taste
Cayenne pepper, to taste
    (optional)
1 cup (1/2 pt) whipping cream
1/2 teaspoon minced cilantro,
    for garnish
1 small avocado, thinly sliced,
    for garnish

In a 2-quart saucepan bring broth, onion, chiles, and garlic to a boil. Reduce heat and simmer for 15 to 20 minutes. Cool, then purée in a blender. Return mixture to saucepan.

Purée sherry and large avocados in blender until smooth. Whisk into soup. Season to taste with salt, pepper, and cayenne (if desired) to taste. Chill until ready to serve.

Ladle soup into a chilled serving bowl. Whip cream and gently fold into chilled soup. Sprinkle top with cilantro, and carefully lay slices of avocado on top of soup. Serve immediately.

Makes 4 to 6 cups, 4 to 6 servings

In the film titled *Becket*, Thomas à Becket is credited with introducing the fork to England in the twelfth century. He didn't. The fork actually didn't come into common use until the seventeenth century. Even at the court of Elizabeth I, using a fork was still considered rather foppish and pretentious. One of her favorite courtiers, Robert Dudley, the Earl of Leicester, once said, "A good Englishman hath no need to make hay with his food, pitching it into his mouth with tiny forks."

Cradle-of-the-Deep Summer Soup
Family Recipe

This dish was originally a hot soup of Celtic origin. My mother added the salsa and put it on ice to serve during hot California summers.

6 cups defatted chicken broth
1 pound soft-fleshed white fish fillets, such as butterfish or sole
6 cloves garlic, crushed
1 onion, quartered
3/4 teaspoon fresh dill or 1/2 teaspoon dried dill
Juice of 1 lemon
1/2 teaspoon sugar
1/2 pound salmon fillets, poached and chilled
1/2 pound firm-fleshed white fish, such as swordfish or monkfish, poached, boned, and chilled
1/2 pound cooked shelled shrimp
1 crab, cooked and shelled (see page 12)
1 cup mild or hot chunky salsa, commercially prepared or homemade (see Salsa Son-of-a-Gun, page 157)
Lemon slices and dill sprigs, for garnish
Baguette, for accompaniment

In a 2 1/2- or 3-quart saucepan, bring broth, soft-fleshed fish, garlic, onion, dill, lemon juice, and sugar to a boil. Reduce heat and simmer for 20 minutes. When somewhat cool, purée in a blender. Chill.

Cut salmon and firm-fleshed fish into smaller than bite-sized chunks. Pour soup into a chilled serving bowl. Add fish, shellfish, and salsa. Stir gently. Garnish with lemon slices and dill sprigs. Serve chilled with a baguette.

Makes 7 to 8 cups, 8 servings

SALADS

When I speak of salads, I mean salads, not grudging bits of fodder with smatterings of oil and vinegar. For me, a salad has to include a variety of ingredients, not just lettuce, although I never slight lettuce. I usually use a selection of greens: iceberg, romaine, curly endive, perhaps some fresh crisp spinach, a few nasturtium leaves, or a little fresh basil. What else? Well, a world of thrilling vegetables is out there, just waiting to hop into your salad bowl and have a party.

Hot foods are excellent in a salad bowl. Chiles, of course—mild or mighty, sweet, fresh, pickled, crushed, sliced, diced. What's a salad without garlic, unless it's a fruit salad, and then you can invite ginger—grated fresh, or crystallized, or preserved red ginger. Horseradish or mustard should be on the ingredients list as well. A salad just wouldn't be the same without them.

When I was growing up, a meal was incomplete without a salad, and often the meal was only a salad. In those

days there weren't handy-dandy sprouters, so we sprinkled alfalfa seeds on wet paper, rolled up the paper, and waited for the seeds to sprout. In place of a yogurt maker, a sleeping bag kept yogurt the right temperature. Do you have any idea how hard it was in 1946 to try to talk a classmate into trading a bologna sandwich for a jar of homemade yogurt? I was the first kid on the block whose family had a wok. (I was also the only kid in fourth grade with sandals—did you ever try to play kickball with sandals? Well, I managed to survive my parents' avant-garde lifestyle, through the 1940s and, with more difficulty, through the 1950s— and, of course, in the 1960s that meant I was already where everyone else was trying to get.) But back to salads, which is where it's always really been at as far as my family's eating habits were concerned. We still feel that you can't sit down to dinner without a huge bowl of salad.

Tabbouleh
North Africa

I like to pile this salad onto a platter lined with curly endive or escarole, surround it with sliced tomatoes, cucumber, and red onion rings, and scatter black olives over the whole.

1/2 cup fine bulgur or commercial tabbouleh mix (see Note)
2 ripe but firm tomatoes, minced
1 red onion, minced
6 to 8 green onions, including tops, minced
2 stalks celery, minced
1 each green and red bell pepper, seeded and minced
2 small fresh hot chiles, minced
1 cup minced fresh parsley
1 tablespoon minced cilantro
2 tablespoons minced fresh mint (omit if using tabbouleh mix)
6 to 8 cloves garlic, finely minced
1/3 cup freshly squeezed lemon juice
1 teaspoon sugar, or more to taste
1/3 cup each olive oil and light-flavored vegetable oil
Salt, coarsely ground black pepper, and crushed dried hot chiles, to taste

In a large bowl pour enough boiling water over bulgur to cover completely. Let soak until all moisture has been absorbed (about 20 minutes). If using tabbouleh mix, follow instructions on package.

Toss bulgar lightly with tomatoes, onions, celery, bell peppers, fresh chiles, parsley, cilantro, mint, garlic, lemon juice, and sugar. Mix together oils and stir gradually into bulgur. Add salt, pepper, and dried chiles to taste; chill.

Serves 4 to 6

NOTE—Boxes of bulgur or tabbouleh mix can be found in the supermarket in the section with couscous and pilaf or in the bulk foods department.

Guacamole Salad
California-Mexican Cuisine

The king of dips makes as superb a salad as it does a party nibble.

Several small inner leaves from head of romaine
1/3 cup One-Step-Beyond Guacamole (see page 16)
3 or 4 slices each tomato and avocado
3 or 4 slices seeded fresh mild-to-hot chile, preferably yellow
1 pickled jalapeño chile
Tortilla chips, for accompaniment

Arrange lettuce leaves on a salad plate. If they are large, snap off some of white end, sliver it with a sharp knife, and pile in middle of plate. Spoon guacamole in center of plate. Arrange tomato, avocado, and fresh chile attractively around edge. Add pickled chile.

Serve chilled, with tortilla chips.

Makes 1 serving

Gobba Ghanouj Salad
Middle East

Full of chunks and gobs of
many delightful things, this
Middle Eastern eggplant dip
makes an outstanding salad.

*Leaves of curly endive or
    escarole*
*1/3 cup Gobba Ghanouj (see
    page 17)*
*3 to 4 slices each ripe tomato,
    cucumber, and seeded fresh
    mild-to-hot chile*
6 Greek olives
1 lemon slice
French bread, for accompaniment

Arrange greens on a salad
plate. Mound Gobba Ghanouj in
center. Alternate slices of
tomato, cucumber, and chile
along one side. Intersperse
olives and top with lemon
slices. Chill before serving.
Accompany with French bread.

Makes 1 serving

Capsicum Salad
Family Recipe

Green, red, and yellow peppers
make this piquant salad a
delight for the eye. This zesty
dish is a family favorite served
chilled with fresh sourdough
baguettes. I always include a
pepper mill, and shakers of
Parmesan cheese and hot-
pepper flakes on my table, for
extra flavoring.

*1 each large green, red, and
    yellow bell pepper, seeded
    and sliced into thin strips*
*2 long fresh mild chiles, seeded
    and cut into rings*
*3 small fresh hot chiles, seeded
    and cut into thin rings*
1 red onion, cut into thin rings
*1 can (4 oz) diced peeled green
    chiles*
*1/2 cup julienned cooked lean
    ham*
*1/2 cup julienned Gruyère or
    Swiss cheese*
*Capsicum Salad Vinaigrette
    (recipe follows)*

In a large bowl toss together all
salad ingredients except dressing. Chill while you prepare
Capsicum Salad Vinaigrette.

Pour dressing over salad and
lightly toss. Serve chilled.

Serves 4 to 6

Capsicum Salad Vinaigrette

4 cloves garlic, crushed
*1 small fresh hot chile
    (optional)*
1/3 cup vegetable oil
1/4 cup cider vinegar
1/8 to 1/4 teaspoon sugar
*1/4 teaspoon mixed dried
    herbs (see page 13)*
*3/4 teaspoon fresh dill or 1/4
    teaspoon dried dill*
*1/2 teaspoon Dijon mustard
    (with mustard seed)*

Purée all ingredients in a
blender until creamy.

Potato-Capsicum Salad
Family Recipe

Potato salad was always my mother's way of feeding a cast of thousands. This creamy, zesty version was among her many recipes.

6 large boiled potatoes, peeled
   and cut into bite-sized slices
1 red onion, cut into thin rings
1 green bell pepper, seeded and
   cut into thin strips
1 red bell pepper, seeded and
   cut into thin rings
2 small fresh hot chiles, cut
   into thin rings
2 long fresh mild chiles, seeded
   and cut into thin rings
1 teaspoon capers, drained
1/3 cup minced fresh parsley
2 stalks celery, trimmed and
   thinly sliced
Mayonnaise-Salsa Dressing
   (recipe follows)
Freshly ground pepper and
   crushed dried hot chiles, for
   accompaniment.

In a large bowl combine all salad ingredients except dressing and accompaniment. Make Mayonnaise-Salsa Dressing.

Pour dressing over salad and lightly toss. Chill before serving. Accompany with ground pepper and crushed dried hot chiles.

Serves 8

Mayonnaise-Salsa Dressing

1/3 cup mayonnaise, commercial
   or homemade (see Basic One-
   Egg Mayonnaise, page 152)
4 cloves garlic, crushed
1/3 cup mild or hot chunky
   salsa, commercial or homemade (see Salsa Son-of-a-
   Gun, page 157)
1 tablespoon sweet pickle
   relish

In a blender purée mayonnaise and garlic until garlic is incorporated. Stir in salsa and pickle relish.

Rajma-Chana Salat
India

This Indian chick-pea and bean salad looks inviting piled onto a platter lined with escarole or curly endive. Note that the dressing must chill at least two hours before serving.

1 cup each canned or cooked
   chick-peas, small white
   beans, black beans, small red
   beans, and lentils, drained
   and well rinsed
1 cup raw, thawed frozen, or
   cooked fresh peas
1 cup yellow wax beans,
   canned, freshly cooked, or
   frozen and thawed
4 to 6 green onions, including
   tops, cut into 2-inch-long
   slivers
1 medium red onion, sliced into
   rings and the rings halved
1/2 cup minced fresh parsley
1 tablespoon minced fresh
   coriander
2 small fresh hot chiles, seeded
   and cut into thin rings
1 small lemon, sliced into thin
   rings, seeded, and the rings
   quartered
Salt and coarsely ground black
   pepper, to taste
Rajma-Chana Dressing (recipe
   follows)

In a large bowl toss together all ingredients except salt, pepper, and dressing. Chill salad while you make Rajma-Chana Dressing.

Season salad with salt and pepper to taste and pour over dressing. Toss lightly and serve chilled.

Serves 8 to 10

Rajma-Chana Dressing

1/4 cup light-flavored vegetable oil
1 tablespoon olive oil
2 tablespoons cider vinegar
1/2 teaspoon sugar
6 cloves garlic, finely minced
1/2 teaspoon minced fresh ginger
1/4 teaspoon each crushed dried hot chiles, ground cumin and dry mustard
1/8 teaspoon each ground fenugreek and anise seed

In a jar with a tight-fitting lid, shake all ingredients vigorously. Set aside for at least 2 hours, shaking occasionally.

Ceylonese Curried Rice Salad
Sri Lanka

Comfits, Middle Eastern spices, and fresh herbs combine to make a dish with an unusual flavor. Do not expect it to taste like Grandma's Thanksgiving Day fruit salad. Chapati, a type of Indian bread, makes an appropriate accompaniment. If it is unavailable, flour tortillas are an excellent substitute.

3 cups steamed long-grain white rice
1 large red onion, diced
4 stalks celery, diced
8 green onions, including tops, finely chopped
1/2 cup chopped fresh mint leaves
1/4 cup each minced candied orange peel and minced crystallized ginger
1/4 cup slivered blanched almonds
1 tablespoon sesame seed
1/2 teaspoon anise seed
1 teaspoon minced fresh coriander
2 seedless oranges, separated into segments and cut into smaller than bite-sized pieces
1/2 teaspoon crushed dried hot chiles
Orange Ginger Dressing (recipe follows)
Egg Lace (recipe follows)
1 head curly endive, trimmed, washed, and drained
2 oranges, peeled and cut into rings
1 papaya, seeded and thinly sliced
1/2 cantaloupe or other small melon, seeded and cut into thin wedges
1 small red onion, cut into rings, for garnish
Mint sprigs, for garnish
Chapatis or flour tortillas, for accompaniment

In a large bowl mix together rice, diced red onion, celery, green onions, mint, orange peel, ginger, almonds, sesame seed, anise seed, coriander, orange segments, and dried chiles. Chill salad while you prepare Orange Ginger Dressing and Egg Lace.

To assemble, line a serving platter with endive. Pour dressing into rice mixture and gently toss. Pile salad into center of endive-lined platter. Surround with cut fruit, sprinkle Egg Lace over top, and garnish with onion rings and mint sprigs. Serve with chapatis.

**Serves 8 as an appetizer,
6 as a meal**

Orange-Ginger Dressing

1/3 cup frozen orange juice concentrate
1/2 cup plain yogurt
1 teaspoon finely grated fresh ginger
1 teaspoon curry powder
1/8 teaspoon each cayenne pepper, ground coriander, and ground cinnamon

In a blender purée all ingredients until creamy. Refrigerate until ready to use.

Egg Lace

Oil, for deep-frying
2 eggs
1/8 teaspoon each ground turmeric and ground cinnamon
1 teaspoon sugar

In a wok or other heavy pan, heat about 2 inches of oil. In a bowl beat together remaining ingredients. When oil reaches deep-frying temperature (375° F), use your fingers to drizzle egg mixture into hot oil in 2 or 3 batches. As soon as egg has solidified, but before it begins to brown, remove from pan with a slotted spoon and drain on paper towels. Let cool. Fried egg should resemble lace.

Abalone Salad
Japan

The unique flavor of miso (soybean paste) gives this dish its distinctive quality. Preparing the green onions is tricky. If the end result is a messy little package, you're on the right track.

1 can abalone (see Note)
1 can smoked oysters (see Note)
1 can (6 1/2 oz) minced or chopped clams
1 1/2 quarts water
1 bunch green onions, including tops, roots trimmed
2 cucumbers, cut into thin rings
1 small red onion, cut into thin rings
Miso Dressing (recipe follows)

Drain abalone and cut into julienne strips. Drain oysters, reserving oil for Miso Dressing; drain clams, reserving liquid for Miso Dressing.

Bring the water to a rapid boil and plunge green onions into water. Leave only until the water returns to a boil. Drain immediately and put into cold running water until thoroughly cold. Drain.

Next, wrap green onions one at a time. Begin about 2 inches from root end, where white starts to turn green. Bend green leaves and wrap around white part. Continue wrapping but leave enough green to tuck end under wrapping to secure. Set aside.

To assemble salad place two or three overlapping rows of cucumber rings down center of an oval or oblong serving platter. Lay a row of red onion rings along each side of cucumber slices. Place green onions in a row down center of cucumbers. Add abalone spears in a crisscross pattern over

whole. Scatter smoked oysters and minced clams over all. Refrigerate until ready to serve. Make Miso Dressing.

Drizzle dressing over salad. Serve chilled.

Serves 4 to 6

NOTE—Abalone comes in soup-size cans that vary in ounces depending on the producer and the size of the abalones. The amount isn't critical for this recipe. Canned abalone is usually found only in Asian markets. Canned smoked oysters, available in most markets, frequently are packed in the same size of tin, which can also vary in weight.

Miso Dressing

1 tablespoon miso
1/4 cup sake
1 scant teaspoon sugar
1/4 teaspoon cayenne pepper, or to taste
4 cloves garlic, finely minced
1/2 teaspoon finely grated fresh ginger
1/2 teaspoon sesame seed
Reserved oyster oil and clam liquid from Abalone Salad

In a bowl mix all ingredients thoroughly until miso is dissolved. Taste and add more cayenne if you wish.

Ensalada de Nopalitos
Mexico

Nopalitos are the young leaves of the nopal (prickly-pear) cactus, a plant that is indigenous to the high deserts of Mexico. They became an integral part of early California cuisine when Franciscan padres planted them in mission gardens. They are now found in Latin groceries and many supermarkets.

1 large jar (16 to 20 oz) or two cans (10 oz each) nopalitos, drained and rinsed thoroughly under cold running water
3 large tomatoes, diced
1 cucumber, peeled and diced
1 red bell pepper, seeded and cut into thin strips
4 to 6 green onions, including tops, minced
1/2 red onion, cut into rings
1 1/2 teaspoons minced cilantro
2 stalks celery, trimmed and chopped
2 small fresh hot chiles, seeded and sliced into thin rings
Ensalada de Nopalitos Dressing (recipe follows)

In a large bowl toss together all ingredients except dressing. Refrigerate while you make Ensalada de Nopalitos Dressing. Pour dressing over salad and toss. Serve chilled.

Serves 6 to 8

Ensalada de Nopalitos Dressing

1/4 cup light-flavored vegetable oil
1/4 cup mild or hot chunky salsa, commercial or homemade (see Salsa Son-of-a-Gun, page 157)
1/4 teaspoon coarsely ground black pepper
1/8 teaspoon ground cumin and dried oregano
4 cloves garlic, finely minced
Crushed dried hot chiles, to taste (optional)
Salt, to taste

In a jar with a tight-fitting lid, vigorously shake all ingredients except chiles and salt. For a hotter dressing, add crushed chiles to taste. Season with salt as desired.

Bean Curd and Peanut Salad
Thailand

Kimchee (hot pickled Chinese cabbage; see page 161) and daikon (Japanese radish) give this salad its sparkle.

2 eggs
1/4 teaspoon cayenne pepper
1 1/2 teaspoons finely minced fresh parsley
Oil, for coating skillet
1 cup bean curd (tofu) cubes (1/2 in.)
1 cup coarsely chopped kimchee, commercial or homemade (see page 161)
1 cup fresh bean sprouts
1/2 cup thinly sliced daikon
1/4 pound snow peas, trimmed and slivered lengthwise
1/2 small red onion, sliced into thin rings
1/3 cup chopped roasted peanuts
Bean Curd and Peanut Salad Vinaigrette (recipe follows)

Beat together eggs, cayenne, and parsley. In a lightly oiled skillet, make 4 thinly rolled omelets. Cool omelets and cut into thin strips. Set aside.

In a shallow bowl toss together bean curd, kimchee, bean sprouts, and daikon.

Continued

Sprinkle snow peas over top, then scatter with onion rings and egg strips. Sprinkle peanuts over all.

Make Bean Curd and Peanut Salad Vinaigrette and drizzle over salad. Serve chilled.

Serves 4 to 6

Bean Curd and Peanut Salad Vinaigrette

1/4 cup light-flavored vegetable oil
1/4 cup white vinegar
1/4 cup minced fresh hot chiles
1/2 teaspoon grated fresh ginger
4 cloves garlic, finely minced
3 tablespoons vinegar
Salt and coarsely ground black pepper, to taste
Cayenne pepper, to taste (optional)

In a blender purée all ingredients.

Lomi-Lomi Salmon
Hawaii

The Hawaiian word *lomi* means to knead or massage. Be sure to incorporate the seasonings into the flesh of the fish gently, mixing thoroughly without turning it into mush. Make this salad with the best fresh salmon you can find, and serve it very cold. I often put the bowl in the freezer until it is extremely cold but not yet frozen. In Hawaii the bowl is frequently served sitting in a tray of chipped ice.

1 pound raw salmon
6 to 8 green onions, including tops, chopped
1 large red onion, diced
1/3 cup minced seeded fresh hot chiles
1 tablespoon kaakuie nut (see Note)
Salt, coarsely ground black pepper, and crushed dried hot chiles, to taste
2 large ripe tomatoes, diced

Remove bones and skin from salmon and dice fish. Rinse thoroughly under cold running water. Drain. Combine fish with onions, chiles, kaakuie nut, and salt, pepper, and dried chiles to taste. Lomi, or incorporate seasonings into fish. Add tomatoes to bowl and gently toss. Serve very cold.

Serves 4 to 6

NOTE—Don't panic if you have never heard of kaakuie nut or can't find it in the store. As a substitute shell some walnuts and toast slowly in the oven. Grind with a mortar and pestle. The result is almost identical.

FISH

When I bite into an oyster, I taste all that the sea has to offer. I see pirates and pearls, schooners and sea monsters, great crashing waves engulfing a jetty and long, lonely stretches of sand where the sea oozes landward and then—with a sigh and a gentle hiss—rolls back to its bed. The sea, the beginning of life itself, gives us winter walks on wind-swept sands, quiet together times on sunny beaches, clamming and musseling, sails on a bay, fishermen, clambakes, cioppino, cracked crab, sashimi.

It amazes me that some people do not like fish. I suspect that the only way they have ever eaten it is as a hunk of dried-out fried fillet covered with store-bought tartar sauce. If that were the only fish I had ever eaten, I probably wouldn't like it much either. This chapter provides recipes to convert any fish hater, and to delight those who love fish. I find the treasures of the deep among the most varied and versatile of all this earth's harvest—a feeling shared by the peoples of many cultures.

Clams with Rice
Galvanized Gullet Contribution

A transatlantic pilot who loves hot food gave me this recipe and joined the Galvanized Gullet during a flight 30,000 feet in the air.

4 dozen small clams in season, well scrubbed (see page 11)
4 cans (6 1/2 oz each) chopped clams
2 tablespoons olive oil
1 large onion, minced
4 cloves garlic, minced
2 cups long-grain white rice
4 small fresh hot chiles, cut into thin rings
3 medium tomatoes, chopped
1 medium bell pepper, seeded and minced
3/4 teaspoon minced fresh dill or 1/4 teaspoon dried dill
1 tablespoon crushed dried chiles
1 tablespoon sugar
2 1/2 cups light chicken broth
1/2 cup dry white wine
1/2 cup minced fresh parsley
2 tablespoons minced cilantro
Salt and coarsely ground black pepper, to taste

Wash clams and set aside. Drain canned clams, reserve juice, and set aside. Preheat oven to 350° F.

In a 5- to 6-quart casserole over moderately high heat, heat oil and sauté onions and garlic until onions are translucent but not browned. Add rice and cook, stirring frequently, for about 5 minutes. Stir fresh chiles, tomatoes, bell pepper, dill, dried chiles, and sugar into rice, and cook, stirring often, for another 3 to 4 minutes.

Add broth, wine, and reserved clam juice, and bring to a boil. Arrange whole clams on top of rice, cover with a tight-fitting lid, and bake until clams are open, liquid is mostly absorbed, and rice is tender (30 to 45 minutes). Remove from oven, and stir in canned clams, parsley, and cilantro. Season to taste with salt and pepper, cover, and let sit for 5 minutes before serving.

Serves 4

Oysters Jean Laffite
Cajun Cuisine

Like many folk heroes, Jean Laffite was actually a scalawag, but to a downtrodden people, which the Cajuns were, he represented liberty, rebellion, and freedom of spirit. This may explain why this lusty creation of baked oysters with piquant sauce, the product of Cajun culinary artistry, was named in his honor. If any of the prebaked oyster mixture is left over, it is delicious spread on French bread and toasted.

1 cup butter
1/2 cup cooked and drained fresh or frozen spinach
1/4 cup each minced watercress leaves, minced fresh basil, minced fresh parsley, and minced celery
1/2 cup minced green onion tops
1/2 cup minced onion
4 cloves garlic, minced
1 small fresh hot chile, minced
1/4 teaspoon cayenne pepper, or to taste
Salt and freshly ground black pepper, to taste
3 dozen oysters in the shell, in season (see page 11)
1/2 cup grated Swiss cheese
3 or 4 lean bacon strips
French bread, for accompaniment

In a large saucepan melt butter. Add spinach, watercress, basil, parsley, celery, onions, garlic, chile, cayenne, and salt and pepper to taste. Simmer until greens are wilted and onions are soft. Purée in a blender until smooth.

Scrub oyster shells and open. Cut oysters free from shells but return each to deepest half of shell. Pour any liquid from oysters into blender. Purée ingredients in blender again and put a generous dollop of mixture on top of each oyster.

Preheat oven to 375° F. Cut bacon crosswise into very narrow strips. Sprinkle each oyster with cheese and a few bits of bacon.

Bake oysters until mixture begins to brown and bubble (about 10 minutes), testing after about 5 minutes.

Serve piping hot with French bread.

Serves 6

ON BAKING OYSTERS

An easy way to bake oysters in the half shell is to pour rock salt into a flat baking pan and then sit the oysters on it. The salt keeps the oysters from toppling over. Be sure to test oysters for doneness as they bake, since cooking time depends on size. Overdone oysters have an unappealing texture. What kind of oysters should you use? The kind you happen to like. I prefer the large Pacific oysters for any dish that is cooked, whereas I like to eat the tiny Gulf or East Coast oysters raw.

Budín de Pescado y Marisco
Mexico

With a soufflé, the elements are out to get you. It will probably fall in the time it takes to carry it from the oven to the table. Don't panic. It will still taste good. Tell your guests that flat is a characteristic of the soufflés of Tehuantepec.

1 large cooked crab
1 pound cooked tiny shrimp, or 1/2 pound cooked tiny shrimp and 1/2 pound cooked scallops
3 tablespoons vegetable oil
1/2 cup minced onion
3 cloves garlic, minced
1 small fresh hot chile, seeded and minced
2 cups milk
1 cup grated Swiss cheese
1/2 cup ricotta
1/4 teaspoon each freshly ground black pepper and dried oregano
1/8 teaspoon ground cumin
1/2 teaspoon sugar
4 eggs, separated
3 green onions, including tops, finely minced
1/3 cup mild or hot chunky salsa, commercial or home-made (see Salsa Son-of-a-Gun, page 157)
1 teaspoon minced cilantro
Salt, to taste
Cayenne pepper, to taste (optional)
Oil, for preparing soufflé dish
1 tablespoon minced fresh parsley
1 tablespoon grated Parmesan cheese
1 teaspoon paprika

Crack and clean crab (see page 12) and remove meat. Finely mince all shellfish and refrigerate. In a heavy pan heat oil and gently sauté onion, garlic, and chile until soft but not browned (1 to 2 minutes). Remove from heat.

Preheat oven to 350° F. In a blender purée milk, Swiss cheese, and ricotta. Add onion mixture, black pepper, oregano, cumin, sugar, and egg yolks; purée again. Pour into a large bowl. Add green onions, salsa, cilantro, and shellfish. Stir well and season to taste with salt. If you want the dish to be hotter, very gradually add cayenne to taste. Beat egg whites until stiff but not dry and gently fold into milk-seafood mixture. Pour into an oiled 2-quart soufflé dish.

Toss together parsley, Parmesan, and paprika and sprinkle over top. Bake until high, fluffy, and golden brown (30 minutes). Test for doneness with a bamboo skewer. Serve immediately.

Serves 6

End-of-the-Catch Pie
Cajun Cuisine

This shellfish pie is superb when served hot and is also delicious eaten cold on a hot day with mustard, pickles, and good beer.

2 large cooked crabs in season
1 pound prawns
2 dozen mussels in season
(see page 11)
1 pint oysters, drained
1 pound scallops
2 tablespoons freshly squeezed
lemon juice
1/2 teaspoon coarsely ground
black pepper
3/4 teaspoon minced fresh dill
or 1/4 teaspoon dried dill
2 small fresh hot chiles,
chopped
1/4 cup minced fresh parsley
1/2 cup chopped fresh or
canned okra
Catch Pie Sauce (recipe
follows)
1 recipe Basic Pastry (see
page 149)
1 egg white

Prepare shellfish. Crack and clean crabs (see page 12). Remove meat from body, break off small legs, and put in a bowl. Reserve large legs and claws. Peel prawns but leave on tails. In a large pan of boiling water, cook mussels until they begin to open. Remove to cold water and, when cool enough to handle, shuck and add to other seafood in bowl. Save 6 shells that are still hooked together. Add oysters and scallops to other shellfish. Sprinkle with lemon juice, pepper, dill, chiles, and parsley. Stir and refrigerate until needed.

If using fresh okra, wash well in cold water, drain, and slice into rings. Blanch for 3 to 4 minutes and set aside. If using canned okra, rinse well in a strainer and set aside.

Make Catch Pie Sauce and prepare Basic Pastry. Preheat oven to 500° F.

To assemble, roll out pastry and line a 9-inch pie pan. Add all shellfish except large claws and legs of crabs and all but 6 or 8 prawns to sauce and stir gently. Add okra. Pour cooled Catch Pie Sauce into pie shell. Cover with top crust and crimp down. Lightly beat egg white and coat surface of pastry. With a small sharp knife, make a slit

in pastry for each of the remaining prawns. Insert a prawn into each slit, pushing it into pie ingredients but letting tail and about 1/2 to 1 inch of body remain exposed. Repeat for crab claws and legs and for the 6 reserved mussel shells.

Bake at 500° F for 2 minutes. Reduce heat to 350° F and continue baking until crust is golden brown and flaky (about 30 minutes).

Serves 6 to 8

Catch Pie Sauce

2 tablespoons lard or bacon
drippings
2 tablespoons flour
1 tablespoon vegetable oil
1 large onion, chopped
8 cloves garlic, minced
4 large tomatoes, diced
4 green onions, including tops,
finely chopped
2 stalks celery, diced
1 medium bell pepper, seeded
and diced
1/2 teaspoon mixed dried
herbs (see page 13)
1/4 teaspoon ground nutmeg
1 teaspoon sugar
Salt, to taste
Crushed dried hot chiles, to
taste (optional)

Make a roux with lard and flour (see On Roux, below). Scrape into a small bowl and set aside.

In a heavy skillet over moderate heat, heat oil and add onion and garlic. Sauté until onion is translucent but not browned (2 to 3 minutes). Add tomatoes and stir for about 1 minute. Then add green onions, celery, and bell pepper, and stir well. Add herbs, nutmeg, and sugar. Stir well and continue cooking for another 2 to 3 minutes. Season to taste with salt. Gradually add dried chiles (if desired), 1/8 teaspoon at a time. Stir and continue cooking for 1 minute. Taste and repeat if more hotness is desired.

Scrape roux into sauce, stir well, and simmer until thick (about 10 minutes). Remove from heat and cool.

ON ROUX

"First you make the roux," is a phrase often heard in a Cajun kitchen. Since the roux is elemental in Cajun and Creole cookery, you may want to make more than needed for End-of-the-Catch Pie (see page 50) and store it in the refrigerator for future use. It keeps indefinitely. Follow the same recipe no matter how much you are making: Put fat (lard or drippings) in a heavy pan over high heat, add an equal amount of flour, and stir rapidly until mixture begins to bubble. Immediately reduce heat to lowest setting and continue cooking, stirring constantly, until mixture is nut brown. The entire process takes ages (about 15 to 20 minutes for 2 tablespoons each of lard and flour) but there is no substitute.

Escabeche
Philippines

Zesty spices and sharp cider vinegar blend together to give zip to this tasty dish of spiced pickled fish from the Philippines.

1 firm-fleshed white fish (2 1/2 to 3 lb), such as swordfish, shark, or monkfish, with head, tail, and fins
2 tablespoons butter
2 tablespoons vegetable oil
6 cloves garlic, cut into thin slivers
1 tablespoon grated fresh ginger
4 small fresh hot chiles, cut into thin rings
1/2 teaspoon mixed pickling spices
1 large onion, cut into 1/8-inch-thick slices
1 each red and green bell pepper, seeded and cut into rings
1/2 cup cider vinegar
1/3 cup dark brown sugar
Salt, coarsely ground black pepper, and cayenne pepper, to taste
1 1/2 teaspoons cornstarch dissolved in 1/2 cup water
Watercress or parsley sprigs, for garnish (optional)

Ask fishmonger to clean and scale fish but leave on head, tail, and fins. Wash fish thoroughly inside and out and pat dry. With a sharp knife cut off head and tail, and cut remaining body into 1-inch-thick steaks. Reassemble fish on a heatproof platter to look as if it were still whole. Place platter in a bamboo steamer inside a wok and steam over high heat until done (about 20 minutes). Keep warm.

In a heavy skillet over moderate heat, heat butter and oil and add garlic, ginger, chiles, and pickling spices. Sauté gently, stirring constantly, until garlic and chiles are soft but not browned. Add onion, bell peppers, vinegar, and sugar, and cook, stirring gently without mashing vegetables, until vegetables are soft (no more than 5 minutes). Season

Continued

to taste with salt, pepper, and cayenne. Add cornstarch and water mixture to skillet. Continue cooking, stirring gently, until sauce is thickened, translucent, and glossy.

Remove vegetables with a slotted spoon and slip them between slices of fish. Pour sauce over fish and, garnish with watercress (if desired). Serve hot.

Serves 4

Gan Shao Xia Ren
China

Freshness is the essence of this stir-fried fish with peppers. Stir-fry, one of finest of the culinary arts, ensures that it does not arrive at the table overcooked.

*2 pounds scallops or firm-
  fleshed white fish fillets,
  such as swordfish, shark, or
  monkfish*
2 tablespoons peanut oil
*2 tablespoons each soy sauce
  and rice wine or dry sherry*
*1 tablespoon grated fresh
  ginger*
6 cloves garlic, finely minced

*1/2 teaspoon crushed dried hot
  chiles*
1 tablespoon tomato paste
1 teaspoon sugar
*6 small fresh hot chiles, seeded
  and cut into thin rings*
*1 small red bell pepper, seeded
  and cut into thin rings*
*4 green onions, including tops,
  cut into 2-inch lengths*
*1 stalk celery, cut on diagonal
  into 1/2-inch chunks*
*1 tablespoon cornstarch dis-
  solved in 1/4 cup chicken
  broth*
Steamed rice, for accompaniment

Cut fish into bite-sized chunks. In a large wok or skillet over high heat, heat oil until it is very hot. Fry fish chunks in hot oil, a few at a time. Gently toss for about 2 minutes, being careful not to break them apart. Remove fish from pan with a slotted spoon and drain on paper towels or a wire rack.

To oil in pan add soy sauce and wine. Stir. Add ginger, garlic, dried chiles, tomato paste, and sugar, and toss for about 2 minutes. Add fresh chiles, bell pepper, green onions, and celery, and stir-fry until vegetables are heated through but not wilted. Pour in cornstarch mixture and continue cooking, tossing gently,

until sauce is thickened and glossy (about 3 minutes). Return the fish to wok and toss gently to coat evenly. Cook, tossing gently without breaking fish apart, for another 2 minutes.

Serve on a bed of steamed rice.

Serves 6

Caruru
Brazil

The origins of this dish combining shrimp and fish can be traced to Africa—the clue is its use of peanuts and okra, two ingredients indigenous to that continent.

2 tablespoons butter
2 tablespoons vegetable oil
*2 pounds shelled prawns, tails
  left on*
*2 pounds firm-fleshed white
  fish, such as swordfish,
  shark, or monkfish, cut into
  bite-sized pieces*
1 medium onion, chopped
6 cloves garlic, minced
*1 medium bell pepper, seeded
  and chopped*
2 large tomatoes, diced
3 small fresh hot chiles, minced

1 1/2 cups commercial coconut milk or homemade coconut milk using 1 coconut plus 1 cup boiling water (see page 12)
1/2 cup roasted peanuts, coarsely ground
1 tablespoon finely minced cilantro
1 cup sliced blanched fresh or thawed frozen okra
Salt and coarsely ground black pepper, to taste
4 cups hot steamed rice, for accompaniment
1 recipe Môlho de Pimenta e Limão (see page 156), for accompaniment

In a heavy skillet or wok over high heat, heat butter and oil. Fry prawns, a few at a time, tossing them until pink (2 to 3 minutes). Repeat for fish, being careful not to break it apart. Set aside to drain.

In the same skillet sauté onion, garlic, and bell pepper until onion is translucent but not browned. Stir in tomatoes, chiles, and coconut milk. Reduce heat to medium and continue cooking until tomatoes and coconut milk have reduced to produce a sauce (about 30 minutes). Stir in peanuts, cilantro, and okra, and cook for another 5 minutes. Return shrimp and fish to skillet and stir gently just until heated through. Season to taste with salt and pepper.

Mound rice onto a heated serving dish and pour Caruru over. Serve hot with Môlho de Pimenta e Limão

Serves 6

Poached Shark Steaks with Piquant Mayonnaise
Family Recipe

This recipe could almost be a salad and is certainly a refreshing and delightful dish to serve when the temperature soars.

1 tablespoon vegetable oil
1/4 cup distilled vinegar
1 bay leaf
6 shark steaks (1 in. thick)
Piquant Mayonnaise (recipe follows)
6 to 12 leaves of bibb lettuce or 1 bunch watercress
Dijon mustard, to taste
Lemon and tomato slices, for garnish
Tomato slices, for garnish
3 hard-cooked eggs, sliced, for garnish
Pitted black olives, for garnish

In a large skillet bring 1 inch of water, oil, vinegar, and bay leaf to a boil. Gently slide in shark steaks. Let water return to a boil, reduce heat to maintain a simmer, and cover with a tight-fitting lid. Poach fish until steaks are done but not falling apart (8 to 10 minutes). Test doneness by slicing into one with the tip of a sharp knife; it should be white all the way through.

Remove fish from water, rinse under cold running water, and let drain. Refrigerate. Make Piquant Mayonnaise and chill.

To assemble, put 1 or 2 leaves of bibb lettuce on each of 6 salad plates. Place a poached shark steak on lettuce. Spread a dollop of Piquant Mayonnaise over surface of steak. Put a dollop of Dijon mustard on each steak. Arrange slices of lemon, tomato, and egg to form an attractive pattern, and finish with 1 or 2 olives. Chill before serving.

Serves 6

Piquant Mayonnaise

*1 cup mayonnaise, commercial
or homemade (see Basic
One-Egg Mayonnaise, page
152)*
*1/2 cup hot chunky salsa,
commercial or homemade
(see Salsa Son-of-a-Gun, page
157)*
4 cloves garlic, finely minced
*2 green onions, including tops,
minced*
1/2 teaspoon minced cilantro
*1 1/2 teaspoons minced fresh
dill or 1/2 teaspoon dried
dill*
*2 tablespoons minced fresh
parsley*

In a bowl mix all ingredients well using a fork. Do not use a blender or food processor; the mixture should not be homogeneous. Chill.

Pakki Hui Machli
India

When you have a good part of a day to spend in the kitchen, you might try making this whole stuffed fish with coriander sauce. It's a show-stopper.

*1 firm-fleshed white fish (4 lb),
such as sole, flounder, or
turbot, with head, tail, and
fins*
*Pakki Hui Machli Stuffing
(recipe follows)*
*Coriander Sauce (recipe
follows)*
Oil, for coating pan
1 egg, lightly beaten
2 hard-cooked eggs
1 bunch watercress
1 medium tomato, thinly sliced
1 lemon, thinly sliced
*1 tablespoon minced fresh
coriander*

Ask fishmonger to clean and scale fish but leave on head, tail, and fins. Wash fish well inside and out; pat dry.

Preheat oven to 350° F. Prepare Pakki Hui Machli Stuffing, pack firmly into fish, and truss shut. Place in a baking dish with a tight-fitting lid.

Make Coriander Sauce, pour over fish, cover, and bake for 30 to 45 minutes. Occasionally remove fish from oven and baste with sauce from bottom of dish. Remove fish from oven, transfer to a heatproof serving dish, and place under broiler for 1 or 2 minutes.

In a lightly oiled omelet pan over moderate heat, pour beaten egg and cook. When egg has formed a skin on bottom but is not dry, roll into a long omelet. Remove to a flat cutting surface and let cool. When egg is cool, thinly slice.

Remove whites from hard-cooked eggs and finely chop. Put yolks through a sieve using the back of a spoon to produce a pile of yellow fluffy powder; reserve.

To assemble, surround fish on serving platter with watercress. Arrange tomato and lemon slices alternately among watercress. Sprinkle sliced omelet down center of fish and surround with egg whites. Sprinkle entire fish with coriander.

Place baking dish with remaining Coriander Sauce on top of stove over a moderate heat. Add reserved powdered egg yolks and bring to a simmer, stirring constantly. Scrape into a small bowl and serve as an accompaniment to fish.

Serves 6 to 8

Pakki Hui Machli Stuffing

2 cups cooked long-grain white
  rice
1 large onion, diced
6 cloves garlic, minced
1 teaspoon minced fresh ginger
2 small fresh hot chiles, minced
1/2 cup minced fresh parsley
1 1/2 teaspoons minced fresh
  coriander
1/2 teaspoon sugar
3 eggs
Salt and pepper, to taste

In a large bowl mix together all
ingredients and set aside.

Coriander Sauce

2 tablespoons vegetable oil
2 tablespoons butter
8 cloves garlic, minced
2 small fresh hot chiles, minced
1 tablespoon minced fresh
  ginger
1/2 teaspoon each ground
  coriander, ground turmeric,
  dry mustard, ground
  fenugreek, and ground
  cinnamon
1/4 teaspoon each ground
  cumin and ground cardamom
1/8 teaspoon ground cloves
1 large onion, minced
4 large tomatoes, diced
1 cup minced green onions,
  including tops

2 tablespoons minced fresh
  coriander
1/3 cup freshly squeezed lemon
  juice
1/4 cup vegetable oil
1 tablespoon sugar
Salt, freshly ground black
  pepper, and cayenne pepper,
  to taste

In a medium saucepan over
moderate heat, heat the 2
tablespoons oil and butter. Add
garlic, chiles, ginger, and
spices, and cook, stirring
constantly, for 5 minutes. Add
onion, tomatoes, green onions,
coriander, lemon juice, the 1/4
cup oil, and sugar. Season to
taste with salt, black pepper,
and cayenne. Cook, stirring
frequently, for 10 minutes. Cool
slightly and purée in a blender
until smooth.

Jambalaya
Cajun

In bayou country this rice and
seafood one-dish dinner is very
hot, and those who consume it
are true candidates for admis-
sion into the Galvanized Gullet.
However, if you haven't spent
your days wrestling alligators,
you may prefer this somewhat
tamer version. If you want it

several degrees hotter, pile on
the crushed dried hot chiles
and cayenne pepper.

2 large cooked crabs
1 bay leaf (optional)
Chicken broth, as needed for
  cooking liquid
1/4 cup vegetable oil
1 large onion, chopped
6 green onions, including tops,
  chopped
3 stalks celery, chopped
1 large bell pepper, seeded and
  chopped
8 cloves garlic, minced
1/2 teaspoon crushed dried hot
  chiles, or to taste
1/4 teaspoon coarsely ground
  black pepper
1/2 teaspoon sugar
3/4 teaspoon fresh dill or 1/4
  teaspoon dried dill
1/2 teaspoon mixed dried
  herbs (see page 13)
1 cup long-grain white rice
2 pounds cooked, peeled, and
  deveined medium-sized
  shrimp
2 pounds small clams in season
  (see page 11)
1/2 cup minced fresh parsley
1 teaspoon minced cilantro
Salt and coarsely ground black
  pepper, to taste
Cayenne, to taste (optional)

Continued

Crack and shell crabs according to directions on page 12. Reserve meat. Pound shells and place with liquid and crab butter in a large saucepan with a tight-fitting lid. Add enough water to cover shells and add bay leaf (if desired). Bring to a rapid boil. Reduce heat to simmer, cover, and continue to simmer for 1 hour. Strain through soft muslin and save liquid. Measure and, if necessary, add enough chicken broth to make 4 cups of liquid.

In a large heavy pan or casserole with a tight-fitting lid, heat oil and add vegetables, garlic, chiles, pepper, sugar, and herbs. Sauté until vegetables are soft but not browned (about 3 minutes). Taste and add more chiles if desired. Add rice and stir to coat evenly with oil and vegetable mixture.

Pour crab liquid over vegetables. Bring to a boil, reduce heat to simmer, cover, and cook until rice is almost tender but still al dente (about 30 minutes).

When rice is ready, stir in reserved crab meat, shrimp, clams, parsley, and cilantro. Season to taste with salt, blackpepper, and cayenne (if desired). Cover and continue to simmer just until clams have opened and rice is tender. Mixture will still be a little soupy.

Serve from casserole or mound into a large deep serving dish that has been heated.

Serves 8

Teesryo
India

Not a bottle from your spice rack, but rather ginger, coriander, turmeric, cinnamon, cardamom, and cayenne are used to create the curry for this exceptional dish of steamed clams.

2 tablespoons butter
2 tablespoons vegetable oil
2 large onions, cut into very thin rings
2 small fresh hot chiles, cut into thin rings
1 tablespoon grated fresh ginger
1/2 teaspoon each ground coriander and ground turmeric
1/8 teaspoon each ground cinnamon and ground cardamom
1/4 teaspoon cayenne pepper
1/3 cup shredded fresh coconut (see page 12)
1/4 cup freshly squeezed lemon juice
1/2 teaspoon minced fresh coriander
1/2 teaspoon sugar
Salt, to taste
6 dozen small clams in season, well scrubbed (see page 11)
Fresh coriander sprigs and lemon slices, for garnish

In a large heavy pan or wok with a tight-fitting lid over high heat, heat butter and oil. Sauté onions and chiles until onions are translucent but not browned (2 to 3 minutes). Add ginger, spices, coconut, lemon juice, and fresh coriander, and toss with onions and chiles for about 2 minutes. Reduce heat to simmer. Add sugar and season to taste with salt. Add clams, cover, and steam until clams open (8 to 10 minutes).

With a slotted spoon remove clams to a deep serving dish. Turn up heat and cook juices in pan, stirring briskly, for about 1 minute. Pour over clams. Garnish with coriander sprigs and lemon slices and serve immediately.

Serves 6

Baked Cheese with Seafood Stuffing
Family Recipe

Essentially a fondue, this dish is best served bubbling hot, with a basket of French-bread cubes to be speared on fondue forks and dunked.

1 round (4 lb) Edam cheese
1/2 pound cooked tiny shrimp
1/2 pound cooked crabmeat
*   (see page 12)*
1 tablespoon butter
1 tablespoon vegetable oil
1 large onion, minced
1/2 cup minced mushrooms
1/4 cup minced fresh parsley
1/4 cup cream sherry
1/4 teaspoon cayenne pepper
1/4 teaspoon coarsely ground
*   black pepper*
2 tablespoons cornstarch
Salt and cayenne pepper, to
*   taste*
Oil, for coating pan
Cubes of French bread, for
*   accompaniment*

Cut a slice about 1 inch thick from top of cheese. With a spoon scoop out inside of cheese, leaving a shell about 1/2 inch thick all around. Do the same with top. Set aside.

On large holes of a grater, grate enough of the removed cheese to make 2 cups and reserve. Mince shrimp and crabmeat and set aside.

Preheat oven to 350° F. In a heavy skillet over moderate heat, heat butter and oil. Add onion and sauté until translucent but not browned. Add mushrooms, parsley, sherry, cayenne, and pepper. Sauté gently until vegetables are soft but not browned (2 to 3 minutes).

In a large bowl toss grated cheese with cornstarch and add shrimp, crab, and vegetable mixture. Season to taste with salt and cayenne and transfer mixture to the cheese shell. Put on lid, set in an oiled heatproof serving dish, and bake until rind begins to sag (15 to 20 minutes). Serve immediately, with bread cubes.

Serves 12 to 15 as an appetizer,
6 as an entrée

Seviche
Mexico

Seviche requires no cooking (the lime juice performs a similar function), making it easy on the cook when the temperature soars and tempting to heat-frayed appetites. In some regions of Mexico, clams and cooked shrimp are added to the raw fish—this is a dish that can cost as much or as little as you wish.

2 pounds firm-fleshed boneless fish or shellfish, such as butterfish, sole, salmon, scallops, shrimp, or a combination
2/3 cup freshly squeezed lime juice, or more, if necessary
1 red onion
1 large or 2 small tomatoes, diced
4 green onions, including tops, finely chopped
1 small bell pepper, seeded and cut into thin strips
1 small fresh hot chile, or more to taste, minced
4 cloves garlic, minced
1 teaspoon minced cilantro
1/8 teaspoon ground cumin
1/2 teaspoon sugar
1/4 teaspoon coarsely ground black pepper
Salt, to taste

Dice fish into smaller than bite-sized pieces. If scallops are large, cut in half. Shell shrimp. If large, cut into pieces the same size as the fish. Combine seafood in a large bowl and cover with lime juice (add more juice if necessary; seafood must be covered). Mix thoroughly and refrigerate at least 2 hours.

Dice one half of the red onion; slice the other half into thin rings. Add red onion, tomato, green onions, bell pepper, chile, garlic, cilantro, cumin, sugar, and pepper to fish. Season to taste with salt, and refrigerate for at least 1 hour. Taste and add more fresh chiles if desired. Serve chilled.

Serves 12 as an appetizer, 6 as an entrée

Ruth's New-World Paella
Family Recipe

Although a quarter century my senior, my late mother-in-law, Ruth, always struck me as my contemporary. She never stopped learning and never stopped teaching. Her education took her from rural America to the theaters of London, New York, and San Francisco; the galleries of Paris; the kibbutzim of Israel; the sacred burial grounds of India; and along the Great Wall of China. From the pyramids along the Nile to the pyramids of the Yucatan, Ruth was busy feeding her insatiable thirst for knowledge.

A superb cook, Ruth made it a part of her travel experiences and education to learn about the cuisines of the people and places she visited and to share this knowledge with people at home. From one of her adventures Ruth brought back this zesty New World form of paella, a Spanish seafood, chicken, and rice dish. I remember her when I share this marvelous dish and good Mexican beer with my good friends. Chorizo sausages are available in many supermarkets and Latino specialty shops.

1/4 cup olive oil
6 chorizo sausages, commercial
   or homemade (see Chorizo,
   page 95)
1 cup diced cooked lean ham
12 chicken drumsticks
1 large onion, chopped
10 cloves garlic, minced
4 small fresh hot chiles, minced
1 large tomato, diced
1 each large green and red bell
   pepper, seeded and cut into
   thin strips
1/4 teaspoon ground cumin
1/2 teaspoon coarsely ground
   black pepper
Crushed dried hot chiles, to
   taste (optional)
1/2 teaspoon (1/4 gram)
   saffron
2 cups long-grain white rice
1 pound cooked tiny shrimp
1/2 cup minced fresh parsley
1 tablespoon minced cilantro
6 cups (approximately) light
   chicken broth
1 large crab, cooked and
   cleaned (see page 12)
12 prawns
12 each clams and mussels in
   season (see page 11)
1/2 cup fresh or frozen peas
2 lemons, cut into wedges

In a large paella pan, heavy skillet, or wok with a tight-fitting lid over medium heat, heat olive oil. Sauté chorizo until browned on all sides (3 or 4 minutes). Brown ham, then chicken drumsticks. Set aside. Sauté onion, garlic, and fresh chiles until onions are translucent but not browned. Add tomato and stir mixture until it begins to form a sauce (3 to 4 minutes). Add bell peppers, cumin, black pepper, and dried chiles (if desired). Continue cooking over moderate heat for about 5 minutes. Add saffron and stir.

Turn up heat to high and add rice, stirring to coat evenly with tomato-chile mixture. Add shrimp, parsley, and cilantro and toss gently. Add enough broth to reach about 1 inch above surface of rice. Continue cooking over high heat until stock has been reduced to level of surface of rice.

While stock is boiling, break off crab legs and separate body into chunks; arrange on top of rice. Cut chorizo in half and push each chunk down into rice. Push drumsticks, prawns, clams, and mussels into rice. Scatter peas and diced ham over the top and arrange the lemon wedges.

As soon as level of broth has just barely evaporated to level of rice, cover with a tight-fitting lid, reduce heat to lowest setting, and cook until rice is tender (30 to 45 minutes). Fluff rice with a fork and serve immediately from pan.

Serves 10

The Visigoths demanded a ransom of three thousand pounds of pepper to stop the siege of Rome.

CHAPTER SIX

BEEF AND LAMB

It has taken me a long time to come to terms with the fact that by eating meat I am depriving a fellow animal inhabitant of this planet of its life, just to make mine a little more enjoyable. For, of course, people do not need nearly as much meat, in particular red meat, in their diet as those of us living in Western cultures consume. However, I've come to believe that we weren't intended to totally do without it either. So my choice now is to regard beef and lamb as a treat rather than as a staple.

In this chapter then, from a born-again carnivore, are some of the delights of fellow meat eaters around the world—meat eaters who like it hot!

Wok Meat
Family Recipe

This is not specifically an Asian dish. My sons invented it some years ago. Since then it has gone through numerous refinements, to become one of our favorite family recipes—something we serve when there's a movie on TV that keeps us away from the dining table. (We are addicted Bogey and Hepburn fans. We'll even give up chocolate mousse for *Casablanca*.) Sometimes my sons serve Wok Meat with a pile of hot, steamy flour tortillas so that everyone can make burritos. At other times they accompany it with pita bread or French bread to make sandwiches. Any way you serve Wok Meat, it's great, and it's not much work.

1 1/2 to 2 pounds lean tender beef
1/4 cup light-flavored vegetable oil
1 each medium red and green bell pepper, seeded and sliced into thin rings
10 cloves garlic, minced
2 large onions, sliced into thin rings
2 small fresh hot chiles, or more to taste, sliced into thin rings

2 cups sliced mushrooms
1/2 cup catsup
1/2 cup soy sauce
1/3 to 1/2 cup dark brown sugar, or to taste
1 teaspoon mixed dried herbs (see page 13)
1/2 teaspoon coarsely ground black pepper
Salt, to taste
Baguettes, for accompaniment

Partially freeze beef, which will enable you to slice it exceedingly thin. With a sharp knife, slice beef across grain as thin as possible. Then cut slices into strips about 1/2 inch long.

In a wok or large frying pan over high heat, heat oil to almost smoking. Add strips of beef, a few at a time, and toss until just seared (1 to 2 minutes for each handful). As each batch is done, remove with a slotted spoon and set aside.

Add bell peppers to wok and toss until hot throughout. Remove with a slotted spoon and set aside. Sauté garlic for 1 minute, then add onions and chiles and sauté until limp. Add mushrooms and toss. Add catsup, soy sauce, sugar, herbs, and pepper.

Return meat to wok and reduce heat to a high simmer. Cook, uncovered, until a thick sauce results (about 10 minutes). Return bell peppers to wok during last 2 to 3 minutes of cooking time. They should be cooked but not limp. Season to taste with salt. Serve with baguettes.

Serves 6

Sik Sik Wat
Ethiopia

Traditionally, *wat*, beef and pepper stew, is served in a tightly woven basket lined with overlapping pieces of *injera*, a kind of millet bread with the texture of a tortilla. Sitting around the basket, diners tear off pieces of injera and wrap them around a bit of meat. It is also traditional to include cloves as an ingredient, but I always leave cloves out because I detest them. Intensely hot and complex in flavor, this dish makes a magnificent meal when complemented by chilled fresh fruit.

20 small dried hot chiles
2 1/2 to 3 pounds boneless beef
1/4 cup peanut oil
10 to 12 cloves garlic, minced
2 large onions, cut in thin rings
4 small fresh hot chiles, cut in thin rings

1 teaspoon crushed dried hot
  chiles
1 tablespoon grated fresh
  ginger
1/4 teaspoon ground fenugreek
1/8 teaspoon ground cloves
  (optional)
1/2 teaspoon ground cinnamon
1/4 teaspoon each ground
  nutmeg, ground cardamom,
  and ground coriander
2 tablespoons paprika
1/4 cup Berberé sauce (see
  page 157)
2 large ripe tomatoes
1/2 cup dry full-bodied red
  wine
1/3 to 1/2 cup sugar
1 teaspoon coarsely ground
  black pepper
Salt, to taste
1 tablespoon minced fresh
  cilantro, for garnish
2 lemons, cut into wedges, for
  garnish
1 recipe Injera (see page 148)
  or 8 to 10 large flour tortillas, for accompaniment

Put dried chiles into a medium
bowl and cover with boiling
water. Leave for 1 hour, drain,
and repeat. Soak until you are
ready to use them, then drain.

Trim beef of excess fat and
cut into paper-thin strips about
1 inch wide and 2 inches long.
In a large heavy pan or casserole over moderate heat, warm

oil. Add meat and toss just until
pieces are seared. Remove and
set aside. Add garlic, onions,
and fresh chiles, and sauté until
soft but not browned (2 to 3
minutes).

Add dried chiles, fresh
ginger, spices, and Berberé, and
cook, stirring constantly, for 2
minutes. Add tomatoes, wine,
sugar, pepper, and salt to taste.
Stir and reduce heat to rapid
simmer. Cook until beef is very
tender (1 to 1 1/2 hours). Stir
occasionally to prevent sticking.
Taste for salt and other seasonings about halfway through
cooking and adjust to taste.

To serve, line a shallow
basket or serving platter with
overlapping injera. Pour in
stew, sprinkle with cilantro,
and garnish with lemon
wedges. Set basket in middle of
table so guests can serve
themselves.

Serves 8

Piononos
Puerto Rico

Plantains are rarely ripe enough
when you buy them at the
store. Put them in a paper bag
and leave in a cool, dry place
until the skins turn almost
completely black. Only then

will they taste as sweet as they
should. For this dish, plantain
strips are browned, shaped into
rings, filled with a savory meat
mixture, and deep-fried. Be
sure to use plantains; bananas
cannot be substituted.

4 large plantains
2 tablespoons butter
4 tablespoons light-flavored
  vegetable oil
1 large onion, chopped
4 cloves garlic, minced
1 medium red bell pepper,
  seeded and chopped
2 small fresh hot chiles, or
  more to taste, minced
1 1/2 pounds lean ground beef
2 tablespoons flour
1 teaspoon ground turmeric
1 teaspoon mixed dried herbs
  (see page 13)
1/2 teaspoon paprika
1/2 cup minced fresh parsley
2 large tomatoes, chopped
1/2 teaspoon coarsely ground
  black pepper, or more to
  taste
2 tablespoons dark brown
  sugar
2 tablespoons distilled vinegar
1 cup finely diced cooked lean
  ham
Oil, for deep-frying
4 eggs, beaten

Continued

Peel plantains and cut length-wise into 4 strips. In a heavy skillet over medium heat, melt butter with 2 tablespoons of the vegetable oil. When butter is melted and incorporated with oil but not browned, add plantains, a few at a time. Using large chopsticks, a slotted spoon, or tongs, turn plantains until they are golden brown (about 3 minutes). Drain on paper towels and set aside.

In the same skillet over medium heat, add the remaining vegetable oil. Sauté onion, garlic, bell pepper, and chiles until onions are translucent but not browned (2 to 3 minutes). Add beef and stir briskly to break apart. Meat should be cooked only until no pink shows (3 to 4 minutes). Stir in flour until thoroughly incorporated. Add turmeric, herbs, paprika, parsley, tomatoes, pepper, sugar, vinegar, and ham. Stir, reduce heat to rapid simmer, and continue to cook, stirring, until mixture thickens enough to hold its shape when pressed together. Remove from heat and allow to cool enough to handle.

Shape each strip of fried plantain into a ring, overlapping ends slightly and securing with a wooden toothpick. Spoon beef mixture into center of each plantain ring and pack firmly with your hands.

Into a wok or other deep pan, pour enough oil to deep-fry; heat to 375° F. Using a slotted spoon, dip each *pionono* into beaten eggs to coat evenly, then slide carefully into hot oil. Brown until done (2 to 3 minutes). If they brown too quickly, reduce heat slightly.

Serves 6

Gomen Sega
Ethiopia

This Ethiopian dish is not unlike its Asian cousin, Stir-Fried Ginger Beef and Mustard Greens (see page 69), but the seasoning is more complex and reminiscent of a curry.

2 tablespoons lard
3 pounds boneless chuck
2 large onions, sliced into thin rings
6 cloves garlic, minced
1 each medium green and red bell pepper, seeded and cut into thin strips
1/2 teaspoon minced fresh ginger
1/4 teaspoon ground turmeric
1/8 teaspoon each ground cardamom, ground cinnamon, and ground nutmeg
1 whole clove
1/4 teaspoon coarsely ground black pepper
1 cup beef broth
8 to 10 small fresh hot chiles
2 medium leeks, including 4 inches of greens, washed well and cut into 2-inch lengths
2 pounds mustard greens, including blossoms, coarsely chopped
1 recipe Injera, (see page 148) or 8 to 10 hot flour tortillas
Salt, to taste

In a large skillet or wok over medium-high heat, melt lard. Cut meat into 1/4-inch-thick slices. Cut each slice into strips approximately 1/2 inch wide by 2 to 3 inches long. Sauté in lard only until just browned. Remove and set aside. Sauté onion rings, garlic, and bell peppers until soft (about 2 minutes). Remove and set aside.

Add ginger, spices, and pepper to lard in pan. Cook over high heat, stirring constantly, for about 1 minute. Pour in broth and bring to a boil. Reduce heat to rapid simmer, add chiles, and return meat to skillet. Cover and cook for 5 minutes. Add the leeks and cook for another 5 minutes. Return onions, garlic, and bell peppers to skillet and simmer until just tender (2 to 3 minutes). Lay mustard greens on top of other ingredients, cover, and steam until greens are tender (approximately 15 minutes).

Line a basket or deep serving platter with injera and place wilted mustard greens on top. Season meat and vegetable mixture with salt to taste, spoon over greens, and serve at once.

Serves 6 to 8

Empanadas
Mexico

Almost every culture that uses ovens puts yummy things inside a nice flaky crust and bakes the little pastry package. There have been small pies filled with meat, cheese, or vegetables as far back as people have had ovens to cook them in. Like Cornish pasties, empanadas are tasty, handy, portable, and an excellent way to use up leftover bits of food. So don't let me dictate your choices. Be creative: Fill them with anything you want. Pork, chorizo, chicken, tuna, cheese, and mushrooms are all fine. Try adding minced black olives or hard-cooked eggs. Hot or cold, they are a delight, so double or triple the recipe and stash a batch in the freezer.

1 tablespoon lard
1 large onion, chopped
6 to 8 cloves garlic, minced
1 pound ground beef
1 medium bell pepper, seeded and chopped
2 large tomatoes, chopped
1/2 cup minced fresh parsley
1/2 teaspoon crushed dried hot chiles, or more to taste
1/2 teaspoon dried oregano
1/4 teaspoon ground cumin
1 teaspoon sugar
1/8 teaspoon coarsely ground black pepper, or more to taste
1 teaspoon minced cilantro
Salt, to taste
2 recipes Basic Pastry (see page 149)
1 egg white
Oil, for coating baking sheets

In a heavy skillet over medium heat, melt lard. Sauté onion and garlic until onion is translucent but not browned. Add beef and sauté, stirring to break into small pieces, until done but not dry. Add bell pepper, tomatoes, parsley, chiles, oregano, cumin, sugar, pepper, cilantro, and salt to taste. Reduce heat to rapid simmer and cook, stirring occasionally, until thick (3 to 4 minutes). Cool.

Preheat oven to 350° F. Prepare Basic Pastry and roll out to 1/8 inch thick. Cut into 4- or 5-inch rounds (see Note). Place 1 heaping tablespoon of meat mixture on each pastry round. Fold pastry in half. Moisten edges lightly and press edges together with tines of a fork to seal.

Lightly beat egg white. Paint surface of each empanada with egg white, place on lightly oiled baking sheets, and bake until golden brown (15 to 20 minutes). Remember that filling is already done. All you are cooking is pastry.

Makes about 15 Empanadas

VARIATION
An alternate cooking method is to fry empanadas in about an inch of hot lard or vegetable oil until golden brown, then drain on paper towels.

NOTE—An empty, 2-pound coffee can makes an ideal cutter. With a pair of pliers, carefully pull off blunt lip to produce a sharp edge. If you want, you can use tin snips or an electric saw with a metal-cutting blade to cut the can down to about 3 inches tall.

Grillades and Grits
Creole Cuisine

Sent to the table accompanied by rich New Orleans coffee with chicory, these grits topped with braised beef fillets in a piquant sauce make a perfect beginning to a lazy spring morning—in New Orleans or anywhere else.

4 small beef fillets or veal
*   steaks*
1/4 cup unbleached all-purpose
*   flour*
1 teaspoon salt
1/2 teaspoon sugar
1/2 teaspoon freshly ground
*   black pepper*
1/2 teaspoon mixed dried
*   herbs (see page 13)*
1 teaspoon paprika
1/8 teaspoon cayenne pepper
2 tablespoons lard
Piquant Sauce (recipe follows)
4 cups water
1 cup quick-cooking hominy
*   grits*

Trim meat of all excess fat. Put flour, 1/2 teaspoon of the salt, sugar, pepper, herbs, paprika, and cayenne into a small paper or plastic bag and shake well. Drop in fillets one at a time and shake. Shake off excess flour and lay fillets on a flat surface. With a kitchen mallet or the dull edge of a large butcher knife, lightly pound both sides of meat to incorporate flour and seasonings.

In a heavy skillet over medium-high heat melt lard and sauté fillets until browned on both sides (no more than 5 minutes). Set aside and keep warm until ready to use.

Make Piquant Sauce. Add meat to sauce, reduce to the lowest-possible heat, and cover with a tight-fitting lid. Keep warm until ready to assemble.

In a medium saucepan bring the water to a boil. Add the remaining salt and slowly stir in grits. Cook, stirring until thick (about 5 minutes).

To serve, mound grits on a heated serving platter and lay fillets around it. Pour Piquant Sauce over all and serve hot.

Serves 4

Piquant Sauce

2 large onions, chopped
6 cloves garlic, minced
Lard, as needed for sautéing
1 large bell pepper, seeded and
*   chopped*
1 stalk celery
2 small fresh hot chiles
2 large tomatoes, chopped
2 cups rich beef broth
1/4 teaspoon each dried thyme,
*   dried oregano, and dried*
*   sage*
1 teaspoon sugar
1 bay leaf
1/2 cup chopped fresh parsley
1/2 tablespoon minced cilantro
Salt, coarsely ground black
*   pepper, and crushed dried*
*   hot chiles, to taste*

In same pan used to cook meat, over medium heat sauté onions and garlic, adding a bit more lard if necessary. Sauté until soft but not browned (3 to 4 minutes). Add bell pepper, celery, and fresh chiles, and sauté, stirring, for 1 to 2 minutes. Add tomatoes, and cook over high heat, stirring constantly, until juices from tomatoes have been extracted and mixture becomes quite liquid (10 to 15 minutes). Add broth, herbs, sugar, and bay leaf. Bring to a boil, reduce heat to a rapid simmer, and continue to cook, stirring frequently, until mixture reaches the consistency of tomato sauce (20 to 30 minutes). Stir in parsley and cilantro, and season to taste with salt, black pepper, and dried chiles. Continue to simmer, stirring for about 2 minutes.

Bobotie
South Africa

In Africa, where hunting has long been popular, this meat and egg casserole was originally made with a variety of small wild game and wild birds' eggs. With the enforcement of stricter game laws, the same pie is now prepared, with great success, from the meat of commercially raised animals. This version uses beef and chicken. Bobotie is traditionally served with steamed rice.

4 eggs
1 cup milk
2 slices French bread
2 tablespoons butter
1 tablespoon corn or other light-flavored oil
2 tablespoons Madras-style curry powder
1 large onion, diced
4 cloves garlic, minced
2 pounds coarsely ground beef
1 pound lean boneless beef, diced into bite-sized pieces
3 chicken breasts, boned and cut into bite-sized pieces
2 tart cooking apples, peeled, cored, and diced
1/2 teaspoon mixed dried herbs (see page 13)
1 scant teaspoon ground cinnamon
1 tablespoon grated fresh ginger
1/2 teaspoon cayenne pepper, or more to taste
1/2 teaspoon coarsely ground black pepper
3 tablespoons dark brown sugar
1/3 cup freshly squeezed lemon juice
1/2 teaspoon grated lemon rind
1/2 cup seedless raisins
1/2 cup slivered blanched almonds
Salt, to taste
6 hard-cooked eggs
Blanched almond halves, to taste
Steamed rice, for accompaniment

Beat together eggs and milk. Crumble bread into mixture and stir well. Set aside.

In a medium saucepan over medium-high heat, melt butter with oil. Lightly singe curry powder, stirring rapidly, for about 2 minutes. Add onion and garlic and sauté until onion is translucent but not browned.

Add ground beef and sauté until just done, stirring well to break apart any chunks. Add diced beef and sear on all sides. Toss chicken with other ingredients in pan to coat evenly and gently sauté. Stir in apples, herbs, cinnamon, ginger, cayenne to taste, black pepper, sugar, lemon juice, rind, raisins, slivered almonds, and salt to taste. Simmer for 5 minutes. If mixture seems too dry, add water, 1 tablespoon at a time, to produce a little gravy but not to make mixture syrupy.

Preheat oven to 350° F. Cut eggs in half lengthwise. Transfer meat mixture to a 3- or 4-quart casserole. Press eggs halves into meat, cut side down, and smooth surface with the back of a large spoon.

Stir egg-milk-bread mixture again and pour over top of meat. Scatter almond halves on top and bake casserole until top is golden brown and custard is set (about 30 minutes). Serve hot from baking dish, with steamed rice.

Serves 6 to 8

Kaeng Kari Nua
Thailand

Thai cookery, with its unusual combinations of tastes and textures, appears to be a sensual blend of Indian, Chinese, and Polynesian cuisines. In another context, coconut, shrimp paste, chile, cinnamon, and lemon juice might be quite awful. Give them to a Thai chef, however, and the result is pure culinary art. These curried beef strips are hot.

2 pounds boneless lean chuck
    roast
3/4 cup plus 1 tablespoon
    peanut oil
6 small fresh hot chiles, minced
1 medium onion, diced
4 cloves garlic, minced
1 teaspoon paprika
1/8 teaspoon each caraway
    and coriander seed
1/2 teaspoon grated lemon rind
1 teaspoon grated fresh ginger
1/2 teaspoon ground cinnamon
2 teaspoons ground turmeric
3 star anise points
1 bay leaf
1 tablespoon dark brown sugar
1/2 teaspoon shrimp paste or
    1/4 teaspoon anchovy paste
    (see Note)
3 cups coconut milk, commercial or homemade using 1
    large coconut plus 3 cups
    boiling water (see page 12)

Salt, to taste
1/4 pound snow peas, trimmed
    and blanched
2 medium onions, each cut into
    8 wedges and blanched
2 medium carrots, scraped, cut
    into 2-inch-long julienne
    strips, and blanched
1/2 pound Chinese long beans,
    trimmed, cut into 2-inch-long
    strips, and blanched
2 eggs, well beaten
4 cups steamed long-grain
    white rice

Cut chuck roast into paper-thin strips 1 inch wide and 3 inches long. In a large wok over medium heat, heat 1/4 cup of the peanut oil. Add strips of beef, a handful at a time, and stir-fry until just cooked, not done. Remove from oil and drain.

Reduce heat slightly and add chiles, diced onion, and garlic. Stir-fry until vegetables are soft but not browned. Add paprika, caraway and coriander seed, lemon rind, ginger, cinnamon, turmeric, anise, bay leaf, sugar and, shrimp paste. Cook, stirring constantly, for about 2 minutes. Pour in coconut milk. Bring to a boil, lower heat to simmer, and cook, uncovered, until liquid is reduced by half (30 to 40 minutes). Add beef and continue cooking, stirring frequently, for another 15 minutes. Season to taste with salt.

While meat mixture is cooking, in another wok or large skillet, heat the 1 tablespoon of the peanut oil and stir-fry snow peas for about 1 minute. Set aside to drain, and repeat stir-frying and draining process for onion wedges, carrot strips, and long beans.

In a small pan or wok, heat the remaining 1/2 cup peanut oil deep-frying temperature 375° F. With a whisk or your finger, drizzle beaten egg into hot oil, 1 teaspoon at a time. Cook until egg has solidified but before it begins to brown (about 30 seconds). Lift out egg lace with a slotted spoon; drain on paper towels. Continue until all egg has been cooked.

To serve, pile rice on a deep serving platter. Make a well in center and pour in beef and coconut milk mixture. Place vegetables around edge. Sprinkle egg lace over top of meat and serve immediately.

Serves 6

NOTE—Shrimp paste is usually available only in Asian specialty markets or large supermarkets. Although not identical, anchovy paste may be substituted.

Stir-Fried Ginger Beef and Mustard Greens
China

A cousin of Ethiopian Gomen Sega (see page 64), this dish uses classic Chinese seasonings including five-spice powder, soy sauce, and fresh ginger.

2 tablespoons peanut oil
2 pounds tender lean beef, cut into paper-thin slices, then into 1/2-by-2-inch strips
6 cloves garlic, minced
1 tablespoon slivered fresh ginger
1 large onion, cut into bite-sized wedges
10 to 12 very small thin fresh hot chiles, blanched
2 tablespoons soy sauce
2 tablespoons beef broth
1/4 teaspoon each five-spice powder and coarsely ground black pepper
1/2 teaspoon sugar
1 tablespoon dry sherry
1 pound mustard greens, washed and shredded
1 teaspoon cornstarch dissolved in 1 tablespoon beef broth
Steamed long-grain white rice, for accompaniment

In a large wok or skillet over high heat, heat the oil. Add beef and stir-fry until browned on all sides. Remove from heat and set aside. Add garlic and ginger and stir-fry for about 1 minute. Add onion and blanched chiles and stir-fry until onion is heated through. Add soy sauce, broth, five-spice powder, pepper, sugar, and sherry, and toss together.

Return beef to pan and add mustard greens. Stir-fry until greens are wilted. Pour in cornstarch mixture and continue stirring gently until resulting sauce is glossy and somewhat thickened.

Serve at once, accompanied with steamed rice.

Serves 6

Ceylonese Lamb Curry
Sri Lanka

The curries of Sri Lanka are to me far more appealing than those of India. The liberal use of succulent fruits give Sri Lankan dishes, no matter how hot, a softer edge than their mainland counterparts. Serve this dish with chapatis, a type of Indian bread, or flour tortillas if chapatis are unavailable. For an attractive presentation, place stem end of pineapple with fronds in the center of a serving platter and ladle curry around it. You may want to set out a selection of cool accompaniments such as Minted Yogurt (see page 165), Orange Ginger Freeze (see page 167), and chilled fresh fruit.

1 breast of lamb (4 to 5 lb)
1 tablespoon each olive oil and vegetable oil
1 teaspoon crushed dried hot chiles, or more to taste
2 tablespoons Madras-style curry powder
1/2 teaspoon anise seed
1 scant teaspoon ground cinnamon
3/4 teaspoon fresh dill or 1/2 teaspoon dried dill
8 cloves garlic, finely minced
2 tablespoons grated fresh ginger
1 large onion, chopped
2 cups light beef broth
1/2 cup brown sugar, or more to taste
1/4 cup distilled vinegar, or more to taste
2 medium onions, cut into bite-sized pieces
1 large bell pepper, seeded and cut into strips

Continued

2 medium cooking apples,
peeled, cored, and cut into
bite-sized pieces
2 medium seedless oranges,
with peel, cut into thin slices
1/2 ripe pineapple, cored and
cut into bite-sized pieces
12 (approximately) preserved
kumquats (optional)
1 tablespoon cornstarch dis-
solved in 1/3 cup water or
beef broth
Salt and freshly ground black
pepper, to taste
1/2 tablespoon minced fresh
coriander
1 generous tablespoon minced
fresh mint leaves
4 green onions, including tops,
minced
Pineapple spears and mint
sprigs, for garnish
(optional)
Steamed white or saffron rice,
for accompaniment
Hot steamed chapatis or flour
tortillas, for accompaniment

Ask butcher to cut each section
of breast across bone into 1-
inch strips. Cut strips of meat
apart between ribs. Put meat in
a large pot, cover with cold
water, and bring to a boil. Boil
for 5 minutes and drain.

In a large skillet over high
heat, heat oils until they are
hot. If they begin to smoke,
reduce heat slightly. Add chiles,
herbs and spices, garlic, ginger,
and chopped onion. Cook,
stirring rapidly, until a paste is
formed (about 2 minutes). Add
meat and stir to coat evenly.

Pour in broth, reduce to a
rapid simmer, and cook, stirring
occasionally, until meat is very
tender (about 1 hour). Add
sugar and vinegar and taste. If
you want a more distinctly
sweet-and-sour taste or more
heat, add more sugar, vinegar,
and dried chiles.

Add onion pieces, bell
pepper, and fruit, and continue
simmering until apples are
tender but not falling apart
(about 5 minutes). Stir in
cornstarch mixture and continue to simmer, stirring gently,
until sauce is thickened and
glossy (no more than 10 minutes). Season to taste with salt
and pepper. Add coriander,
mint, and green onions, and
stir lightly.

Pour curry onto a heated
serving platter. Garnish with
pineapple spears and mint
sprigs (if desired). Serve with
rice and chapatis.

Serves 6 to 8

Badami Gosht
India

Coconut milk, almonds, yogurt,
and exotic spices blend to give
this dish its rich, complex
flavor. Note: the lamb needs to
marinate overnight in the masala.

Almond Masala (recipe follows)
2 1/2 pounds lean boneless lamb,
cut into bite-sized cubes
2 tablespoons peanut oil
2 tablespoons butter
2 large onions, minced
6 cloves garlic, minced
Hot steamed rice, for accompa-
niment

Make Almond Masala, add lamb,
and marinate in refrigerator
overnight.

In a large wok or heavy skillet,
over medium heat warm together
oil and butter. Sauté onions and
garlic until soft but not browned
(2 to 3 minutes). Remove lamb
from marinade with a slotted
spoon and brown in wok on all
sides. Pour in remaining marinade and let it cook rapidly,
stirring constantly, for 1 minute.
Reduce heat to low and continue
to simmer, stirring occasionally,
until meat is very tender (15 to
20 minutes). Remove meat to a
heatproof dish and set aside.

Raise heat to high and cook
remaining masala, stirring to

prevent sticking, until somewhat reduced and thickened (5 to 6 minutes). Just before serving, put meat under high heat of broiler and leave until edges just begin to get crisp. Remove from broiler and pour reduced masala over it. Serve at once with rice.

Serves 6

A note on terminology: In this country *lamb* means an animal 6 to 12 months old. If it is over a year old, it cannot legally be called *lamb,* but it may be labeled as *yearling lamb.* This older animal will have a stronger flavor. The term *spring lamb* used to be applied to an animal born in the fall and slaughtered at 6 months, in the spring. Today, however, sheep give birth all year, so there is no longer such a thing as spring lamb. In other countries, young sheep from 6 months to 18 months are sold under the name *mutton; lamb* is reserved for animals under 6 months old, which may be prepared for special occasions such as weddings and Easter. No matter what it's called, however, lamb is very tasty indeed.

Almond Masala

1 teaspoon (1/2 gram) saffron
2 tablespoons hot water
1/2 cup unsalted blanched almonds
3 cups coconut milk, commercial or homemade using 1 large coconut and 3 cups boiling water (see page 12)
1 teaspoon caraway seed
1/8 teaspoon anise seed
1/2 teaspoon ground cinnamon
1/4 teaspoon ground cardamom
2 teaspoons grated fresh ginger
1/2 teaspoon cayenne pepper, or more to taste
1/8 teaspoon ground cloves
1 tablespoon sugar
1 cup (8 oz) plain yogurt
Salt, to taste

Soak saffron in the hot water for 10 minutes. In a blender purée saffron and the water, almonds, 1 cup of the coconut milk, caraway and anise seed, cinnamon, cardamom, ginger, cayenne, cloves, and sugar until smooth. Pour into a bowl and stir in the remaining coconut milk, yogurt, and salt to taste.

Lancashire Hot Pot
England

It's not capsicum but black pepper and yellow mustard that make this dish—from the heart of Beatles country—rock and roll. Serve this lamb and oyster stew right from the casserole, and accompany it with good English beer, horseradish, and hot brown mustard (see page 6).

1/4 cup unbleached all-purpose flour
1 1/4 teaspoon salt, or more to taste
2 teaspoons coarsely ground black pepper, or more to taste
1 teaspoon dry mustard
3 tablespoons paprika
2 pounds lean lamb, cut into bite-sized pieces
6 to 8 lamb kidneys, each cut in half lengthwise
3 tablespoons lard
1 large onion, chopped
2 cups beef broth
1 scant teaspoon sugar
1/4 teaspoon dried thyme
4 large potatoes, peeled and thinly sliced
2 pints oysters, drained
12 small boiling onions, peeled
1 pound small mushrooms, quartered
1/2 cup grated sharp Cheddar cheese
1/4 cup fine bread crumbs
1/2 cup minced fresh parsley

Continued

Put flour, 1 teaspoon of the salt, 1 1/2 teaspoons of the pepper, mustard, and paprika into a small paper bag and shake. Drop in lamb and kidneys and shake to coat each piece. Shake off excess flour.

In a heavy skillet over high heat, heat lard until it is hot but do not let it smoke. Brown lamb and kidneys on all sides, remove with a slotted spoon, and set aside. Sauté chopped onion in lard remaining in skillet and pour in broth, sugar, thyme, the remaining salt, and the remaining pepper. Reduce heat to medium and cook, stirring, for about 2 minutes. Taste and adjust seasonings. It should be very peppery. Remove from heat.

Preheat oven to 350° F. Place half the potato slices on the bottom of a 5-quart casserole with a tight-fitting lid. Arrange lamb, kidneys, oysters, boiling onions, and mushrooms in layers over potatoes. Top with the remaining potatoes. Pour in broth.

In a bowl toss together cheese, bread crumbs, and parsley, and sprinkle over potatoes. Cover casserole and bake until meat is very tender when pierced with the tip of a sharp knife and liquid is almost all absorbed (about 1 1/2 hours). Remove lid during last 15 minutes to allow cheese to brown.

Serves 6 to 8

Whole Stuffed Leg of Lamb
Greece

Sent to the table garnished with orange slices and crisp watercress, this leg of lamb is elegant fare for any occasion. The lamb needs to marinate overnight. When the butcher bones the lamb, remember to bring the bone home for future use.

Leg of Lamb Stuffing (recipe follows)
1 large leg of lamb (7 to 8 lb), boned
Dill Weed and Mustard Marinade (recipe follows)
1/2 cup beef broth
Lettuce leaves, tomato wedges, and lemon slices, for garnish (optional)

Make Leg of Lamb Stuffing and pack firmly into leg of lamb. Truss shut with bamboo or metal skewers.

Make Dill Weed and Mustard Marinade. Put stuffed leg of lamb in a deep dish, pour marinade over, and rub it into meat on all sides. Refrigerate overnight, turning and rubbing several times.

Preheat oven to 350° F. Place lamb in a roasting pan with a tight-fitting lid. Mix broth with remaining marinade and pour over leg of lamb. Cover and bake until meat is very tender (about 1 1/2 hours). Remove lid during last 20 minutes and raise heat to 400° F to brown.

To serve, set on a heated platter and surround with lettuce leaves, tomato wedges, and lemon slices (if desired). Using a sharp slicing knife, cut straight through lamb, making 1-inch-thick slices.

Serves 6 to 8

"Upon what meat doth this our Caesar feed, that he is grown so great?" *Julius Caesar,* Act I, Scene II

Leg of Lamb Stuffing

2 cups al dente cooked bulgur
6 cloves garlic, minced
1 large onion, chopped
2 stalks celery, chopped
1 large bell pepper, seeded and
  chopped
6 small fresh hot chiles, seeded
  and minced
Seeds from fresh hot chiles, to
  taste (optional)
1/3 cup minced fresh parsley
1 tablespoon minced fresh dill
  or 1 teaspoon dried dill
1/2 teaspoon ground cumin
Juice of 2 lemons
1 teaspoon grated lemon peel
1 bay leaf
1/3 cup each pine nuts and
  dried currants
2 eggs, lightly beaten
1 teaspoon sugar
Salt and coarsely ground black
  pepper, to taste

In a large bowl combine all
ingredients.

My great-grandfather, like all
cattlemen of the American
frontier, saw sheep only as a
plague grazing their way across
the pastures of the San Joaquin
valley in California, rendering
them useless to cattlemen.

Dill Weed and Mustard Marinade

1 cup freshly squeezed lemon
  juice
1/4 cup sugar
1/4 cup olive oil
1 tablespoon minced fresh dill
  or 1 teaspoon dried dill
4 cloves garlic, finely minced
1/4 teaspoon cayenne pepper
1 bay leaf
1 teaspoon dry mustard
1/2 teaspoon mixed dried
  herbs (see page 13)
1 1/2 teaspoons paprika
Salt and freshly ground black
  pepper, to taste

In a large bowl thoroughly
combine all ingredients.

Pumpkin Brede
South Africa

Pumpkin, originally a New
World plant, soon found itself
at home in the accommodating
South African climate. This tasty
lamb and pumpkin stew makes
excellent use of the transplant.

3 tablespoons lard
2 to 2 1/2 pounds boneless lean
  lamb, cut into bite-sized
  pieces
2 large onions, cut into 1/4-
  inch-thick slices

4 cloves garlic, finely minced
3 or 4 small fresh hot chiles,
  chopped
1 teaspoon grated fresh ginger
1/2 teaspoon ground cinnamon
1/4 teaspoon each ground
  cumin and ground allspice
1/8 teaspoon ground cloves
2 pounds pumpkin, seeded,
  peeled, and cut into bite-
  sized cubes (about 5 cups)
1 cup beef broth
3 tablespoons dark brown
  sugar
Salt and freshly ground black
  pepper, to taste

Preheat oven to 350° F. In a
heavy casserole with a tight-
fitting lid, over moderate heat
warm lard. Add lamb and
brown on all sides. Add onions
and cook, stirring gently, until
tender but not browned (2 to 3
minutes). Add garlic, chiles,
ginger, and spices, and, cook
over moderate heat, stirring, for
about 2 minutes. Add pumpkin
and toss until evenly coated
with spices. Pour in broth. Add
sugar and salt and pepper to
taste. Bring to a boil and
immediately remove from heat.
Cover and bake until lamb is
tender (about 45 minutes).
Serve hot.

Serves 6

Leyla's Lamb Shank, Garlic, and Pepper Casserole
Turkey

My friend Leyla, of Tartar ancestry, was born in Japan and lived there until she moved to Turkey at the age of 17; now she is a Californian. For those of you who may not know who Tartars are, they are the last of the Golden Horde, the descendants of Batu Khan. She taught me that eggplant does not have to be a blotchy gray steamed mush. She makes the very best piroshki I have ever eaten. And her recipes for Gobba Ghanouj (see page 17), kabobs, and lots of dishes with yogurt in them are in this book. Leyla taught me that garlic is a staple vegetable, not a creature of dubious character to be used penuriously on occasion, as is illustrated by this Turkish recipe. It calls for 30 to 40 cloves of garlic, or "a double handful," as Leyla says. You may question the use of 30 cloves of garlic as well as the absence of cooking liquid. Remember that when garlic is cooked for a long time over low heat, the harsh acid is dissipated and what remains is a wonderful sweet flavor. The long, slow cooking also draws the liquid from the meat and vegetables, which therefore baste themselves. Cabbage leaves and a double thickness of paper bag act as a steam-lock on top.

You will need an ovenproof container with a tight-fitting lid, large enough to accommodate all of the ingredients. A dutch oven is ideal. You can also use a slow cooker if it will hold all the ingredients. To make this casserole a complete meal, accompany with French bread and a crisp green salad with dill vinaigrette.

6 meaty lamb shanks, each sawed into 2 or 3 sections
10 boiling onions or 3 large onions cut into quarters
2 large bell peppers, seeded and cut into quarters
3 large potatoes, peeled and cut into quarters
8 small fresh hot chiles
2 long slim fresh mild chiles
2 large carrots, cut into 2-inch pieces
1 cup large fresh or thawed frozen lima beans
30 to 40 cloves garlic
6 tomatoes, each no more than 2 inches in diameter
2 florets fresh dill or 1/2 teaspoon dried dill
1/2 teaspoon mixed dried herbs (see page 13)
Salt and coarsely ground black pepper, to taste
Cabbage or grape leaves, for covering casserole
Vegetable oil, for coating paper bag

In a dutch oven or other large ovenproof container, place lamb shanks. Then layer over onions, bell pepper, potatoes, chiles, carrots, lima beans, garlic, and tomatoes. Sprinkle on herbs and season to taste with salt and pepper.

Use enough cabbage leaves to make a tight blanket over top of meat and vegetables. Cut a double thickness of brown paper bag that is about 1 inch larger than lid of container. Coat on both sides with oil until paper is saturated. Lay it on top of cooking vessel and cover. Put casserole in a cold oven, turn temperature setting to 300° F, and cook until meat falls off bone (5 to 6 hours).

To serve, arrange ingredients on a heated platter. Strain pan juices, heat but do not thicken, and serve in a gravy boat to pour over each serving.

Serves 6

PORK

One of the greatest dietetic tragedies for the poor and working classes of northern Europe was the passage of laws forbidding the keeping of pigs near houses.

Previously every cottager was able to raise a pig, which was the basis for the family's diet the year around. From the traditional September slaughter throughout autumn, the family could enjoy fresh meat and black pudding (blood sausage). Throughout winter there were salted joints and pickled brawns (a traditional preparation midway between head-cheese and pâté.) Come Christmas, there were the traditional boar's head and mince pies. The rest of the pig provided salt meat, pies, boiled pork, ham, bacon, and lard for the remainder of the winter.

The removal of the cottager's pig had rather disastrous effects. The health of poor country families declined rapidly as a result of the pig acts. During World War II many European countries repealed these laws and offered incentives to encourage families to start raising their own pigs again.

ON CHICHARRÓNES

My introduction to true *chicharrónes* was in Mazatlán. Mazatlán sits on the rim of a long, gently curving, crescent-shaped bay. The north end contains the kind of hotels designed to isolate travelers from the country they are visiting. The south end of the bay is the real Mexico.

Here, open-air cantinas, perched on ancient pilings, cantilever over the bay. Children play in the tide and search the sands for sunbathers' lost treasures. When the sun goes down, you learn the meaning of the word *promenade*. Young people and old people, lovers and children, families pushing prams and dragging toddlers by the arm—all fill the streets for an evening's entertainment. Smells pungent and seductive drift from burro-drawn carts, and the sound of mariachis spreads across the water from one of the teetering establishments on the edge of the bay.

I once wandered into a small cantina that looked promising and, mustering my vocabulary of two dozen Spanish words, asked what was cooking. A handsome young man behind the counter of the open-air kitchen managed with an equally spare English vocabulary to inform me that food would not be ready for about an hour and offered me a beer.

I seated myself at a table by the arched opening draped with bougainvillea. He returned with two beers and, plopping down across the table from me, sat there grinning. We drank our brews and looked at each other with the embarrassment that comes from being unable to communicate. We managed to exchange names—his was Ramón—and we were soon rescued by the entrance of a friend of his, who possessed a considerably larger English vocabulary. The friend hailed us, went to the bar, returned with three beers, and in exceedingly broken but rather extensive English launched into a dissertation on his philosophy of life. He had gotten as far as his feelings on the space program when a tall gentleman entered the cantina, hailed them with bravado, went to the bar, and returned with four beers. Snagging a chair from a neighboring table, he joined us. They all raised their bottles and said, "*Sí* Geraldine, *Sí* California, *Sí* cervesa. Good.", and we drained our bottles. So I figured it was about time for my round. I rose to go to the bar and was forcibly thrust back into my seat. Ramón made the next run.

After several more rounds went down our throats, a small man with a huge gunnysack on his back came in. My friends hailed him. He trotted to our table, unshouldered his sack, and took out the biggest chicharrónes I have ever seen. He produced a paper plate, broke the giant pig skins into manageable pieces, and sprinkled them with hot sauce. I eagerly reached for a chunk.

I could see the smug smiles begin to creep across the faces of my friends. "Just wait 'til she tastes that," each was thinking to himself. Well, I popped down several of those drenched with the most fire and their jaws dropped. They had to reclaim their status in my eyes and their own. Snatching up another bottle of sauce from the counter, they drenched the chicharrónes and started munching. Much to their amazement, I kept up. This of course called for several more rounds of the fine local brew. When the small—and not very good—mariachi band arrived, we were in a quite jocular mood.

Actually, the band was far worse than not very good. My friends took the instruments away from the band. My friends played, and we sang and drank more beer. An American couple who had ventured out of the protective cocoon of the north end of town sent more beer to our table.

Sometime after three in the morning, our arms cradling the numerous bottles of beer we had convinced the cantina to sell us before closing, we sang our way up the back streets until we came to Ramón's house, where, much to the distress of a sleepy green parrot, we continued our revelry until the sun came up.

Chicharrónes con Salsa
Mexico

Big gnarly chunks of pig skin, deep-fried in large pieces, are served with this chile sauce. Not to be confused with the wimpy little pork skins sold in small packages. The big chicharrónes that are sold in Latino markets and in supermarkets in areas with a large Latino population are wonderfully chewy and salty.

1 package (5 oz) large chicharrónes
4 large tomatoes, chopped
1 large onion, chopped
6 cloves garlic, minced
4 small fresh hot chiles, minced
1 medium onion, cut into thin rings
1 each red and green bell pepper, seeded and cut into thin rings
2 stalks celery, chopped
1/2 teaspoon sugar
1/4 teaspoon dried oregano
1/8 teaspoon ground cumin
1/4 teaspoon coarsely ground black pepper
1 can (4 oz) diced and peeled green chiles
6 to 8 green onions, including tops trimmed and chopped
1/2 cup minced fresh parsley
1/2 tablespoon minced cilantro
2 tablespoons olive oil
Salt and coarsely ground black pepper, to taste

Break the chicharrónes into bite-sized pieces and place in a heatproof bowl. Add enough boiling water to cover and leave until soft (about 15 minutes).

In a blender purée tomatoes, chopped onion, garlic, and fresh chiles. Pour into a large saucepan and bring to a boil. Reduce heat to rapid simmer and cook, stirring occasionally, for about 10 minutes. Add onion rings, bell peppers, celery, sugar, oregano, cumin, and pepper, and continue simmering for another 10 minutes.

Drain the chicharrónes and put into a serving bowl. Cover with sauce, add canned chiles, green onions, parsley, and cilantro, and toss. Drizzle with olive oil and toss lightly. Season to taste with salt and pepper. Serve hot or cold.

Serves 6

I have a large sheet of Formica that I use for a work surface. It is much easier to keep clean than is wood. You can usually buy the material inexpensively from a contractor who remodels kitchens. What you want is the piece that has been removed from a countertop to accomodate a sink. It's sort of like buying a doughnut hole.

Stuffed Pork Chops
Family Recipe

It may take a bit of effort to stuff these pork chops and seal them with bamboo skewers, but the results are well worth the effort. They are delicious served with steamed rice and spicy applesauce.

6 large boneless pork chops, at least 1 inch thick
1 tablespoon butter
1 tablespoon corn or other light-flavored vegetable oil
1 medium onion, minced
2 tart apples, peeled, cored, and finely chopped
3 cloves garlic, minced
2 small fresh hot chiles, minced
1/4 cup dried currants
3/4 teaspoon minced fresh dill or 1/4 teaspoon dried dill
1/4 teaspoon each ground cinnamon, dried savory and grated fresh ginger
1 teaspoon brown sugar
1/2 cup bread crumbs
1 egg, lightly beaten
Milk, as needed for moistening
Salt and freshly ground pepper, to taste
Steamed rice and spicy applesauce, for accompaniment

With a sharp knife make deep incision in side of each chop, forming a pocket. Set aside.

In a heavy skillet over medium heat melt butter with oil. Lightly sauté onion, apples, garlic, and chiles. Add currants, herbs and spices, ginger, and sugar, and continue cooking, stirring gently, until ingredients are blended and apples are soft (no more than 10 minutes). Remove from heat and let cool.

Add bread crumbs and egg. If mixture is not moist enough to hold together when pressed into a ball in your hand, add milk, a few drops at a time, until it is the right consistency. Season to taste with salt and pepper. Firmly pack stuffing into pockets in pork chops and truss shut with a bamboo skewer. Grill to desired doneness on a charcoal grill or under a broiler.

Serves 6

West Oakland Barbecue
Black American Cuisine

Flint's Barbecue in Oakland is one of the stops on my California tour for overseas guests. It's right up there at the top of the list with the ultimate wine country picnic in Sonoma, The Sequoias, Point Lobos, and, of course, Yosemite.

I have consumed my share of barbecued pork of various cuisines around the world, but none, in my estimation, can compare with the barbecue I've found in West Oakland, California.

Barbecue Sauce (recipe follows)
10 pounds spareribs

Prepare Barbecue Sauce and coat ribs liberally. Cook to desired doneness over charcoal, under a broiler, or in the oven. Baste frequently with sauce throughout cooking.

Serves 8 to 12

Barbecue Sauce

1 bottle (14 oz) catsup
2 large onions, chopped
2 large bell peppers, seeded and chopped
12 cloves garlic, minced
6 small fresh hot chiles, minced
1 tablespoon crushed dried hot chiles
1 cup brown sugar
1/2 cup distilled vinegar
1 tablespoon mixed dried herbs (see page 13)
1/2 teaspoon smoke flavoring (see Note)

In a blender purée all ingredients. Put into a saucepan and bring to a boil. Reduce heat to simmer, and cook, stirring frequently, until a thick glossy sauce results (20 to 30 minutes). Sauce may be stored for several weeks in the refrigerator, in a jar with a tight-fitting lid.

NOTE—Smoke flavoring is available in the sauce or spice section of most markets.

Carbonada
Argentina

This meat, vegetable, and fruit stew is made all the more festive when it is served in the pumpkin shell surrounded by lighted candles. If the pumpkin does not have a flat base, wring out a tea towel in hot water, roll it up lengthwise, then twist it to form a ring. Set towel on a serving plate to form a base for the pumpkin. Disguise the towel with parsley, watercress, curly endive, or even small-leafed ivy and a few flowers such as marigolds.

1 pumpkin (12 to 15 lb)
1/2 cup butter, at room temperature
1 teaspoon each ground cinnamon and chili powder
1 cup plus 1 tablespoon brown sugar
2 tablespoons olive oil
3 pounds boneless pork loin, trimmed and cut into 1-inch cubes
1 medium onion, chopped
6 cloves garlic, minced
1 medium bell pepper, seeded and chopped
2 large tomatoes, chopped
4 cups beef broth
1/2 teaspoon crushed dried hot chiles, or more to taste
1/2 teaspoon dried oregano
1 teaspoon minced cilantro
1/4 teaspoon freshly ground black pepper
2 pounds yams, peeled and cut into 1/2-inch chunks
6 to 8 small fresh mild chiles
10 to 12 small boiling onions, parboiled
2 small zucchini, cut into 1/2-inch pieces
2 ears of corn, shucked and cut into 1/2-inch slices
4 to 6 peaches, peeled and cut in half
2 small seedless oranges, with peel, cut into thin slices
Salt, to taste

Preheat oven to 350° F. With a large knife cut off top of pumpkin to make a lid. Scoop out seeds and pulp. Rub inside with butter. Mix cinnamon and chili powder with 1 cup of the brown sugar, and sprinkle inside pumpkin. Tilt pumpkin from side to side to coat evenly. Set pumpkin in a shallow baking pan and bake until inside is tender but shell is firm enough to hold its shape (30 to 45 minutes).

In a large, heavy saucepan over medium heat, heat olive oil and sauté pork until browned on all sides. Remove with a slotted spoon and set aside. Add onion, garlic, bell pepper, and tomatoes, and continue cooking, stirring occasionally, until vegetables are soft (about 5 minutes). Pour in broth. Add crushed chiles, the 1 tablespoon brown sugar, oregano, cilantro, and black pepper, and bring to a boil. Add browned meat, boil for about 2 minutes, then reduce heat to simmer and continue cooking, stirring occasionally, for 15 minutes. Add yams, mild chiles, and boiling onions, and simmer until meat is very tender (about 15 minutes). Add zucchini, corn, peaches, and

Continued

oranges, and continue to simmer until zucchini is just done (about 5 minutes). Season to taste with salt.

To serve, place pumpkin on a serving platter and pour in stew. Top with lid and serve immediately. Scoop a bit of flesh from pumpkin for each serving of stew.

Serves 6 to 8

Sweet-and-Sour Pork à la Dr. Yen
Family Recipe

My first father-in-law was Chinese-Hawaiian and a skilled surgeon. Like many old-fashioned men, he considered regular kitchen work beneath his dignity, but he did on occasion, and with great aptitude, engage in the culinary arts. When he made sweet-and-sour pork, he always started with a whole leg of pork. The way he boned that joint was magical. He inserted a long, thin, exceedingly sharp knife into the leg next to the bone, at the large end. Holding the knife still, he grabbed the knuckle of bone that protruded from the small end and rotated the leg around the blade of the knife. Then he effortlessly pulled the bone out of the leg, leaving a solid chunk of meat on the kitchen counter. I have been trying to perfect his technique for over 25 years without success. If you master it, please let me know.

2 1/2 to 3 pounds boneless pork loin
1 tablespoon soy sauce
1 tablespoon dry mustard
1/2 teaspoon each ground ginger, cayenne pepper and salt
1 teaspoon sugar
1/4 cup peanut oil
6 cloves garlic, minced
1 1/2 teaspoons grated fresh ginger
1 1/2 teaspoons tomato paste
1/4 cup soy sauce
1/4 cup chicken broth
4 small fresh hot chiles, cut into thin rings
1 bell pepper, preferably red, seeded and cut into thin strips
1 large onion, cut into bite-sized wedges
6 green onions, including 4 inches of green tops, trimmed and cut into 2-inch lengths
1/8 teaspoon five-spice powder
1 tablespoon sugar, or more to taste
2 tablespoons rice vinegar or distilled vinegar, or more to taste
1 teaspoon cornstarch dissolved in 1 tablespoon chicken broth
Salt and freshly ground black pepper, to taste
Crushed dried hot chiles, to taste (optional)
Steamed white rice, for accompaniment

Cut pork into 1/4- by 1/2- by 2-inch strips. Mix together the 1 tablespoon soy sauce, mustard, ginger, cayenne, salt, and 1 teaspoon sugar, and massage into pork.

In a large wok over medium-high heat, heat peanut oil until it is almost hot. Sauté pork until browned on all sides. Remove from wok and set aside. Add garlic and ginger and stir-fry until heated through but not browned. Add tomato paste, the 1/4 cup soy sauce, and broth, and stir together until well blended. Add fresh chiles, bell pepper, and onion, and stir-fry until vegetables are heated through (no more than 2 minutes). Return meat to pan and toss. Add green onions and toss again. Add five-spice powder, the 1 tablespoon sugar, and vinegar, and continue to stir-fry 1 to 2 minutes. Pour in the cornstarch mixture and stir-fry until sauce is somewhat thickened and glossy (about 2 minutes). Season to taste with salt and pepper.

If you want a more distinct sweet-and-sour flavor, add more sugar and vinegar to taste. For a hotter dish, gradually add dried chiles, a bit at a time, to taste. Serve pork immediately with steamed white rice.

Serves 6 to 8

Mu Shu Rou
China

This stir-fry of pork and peppers with eggs calls for Asian sesame oil, which is available in Asian specialty shops and some supermarkets. It also calls for soy sauce. When cooking with soy sauce, I seldom use additional salt.

*2 pounds boneless pork butt or
    loin*
1/4 cup peanut oil
*1 tablespoon each soy sauce,
    cream sherry, and beef broth*
*6 small fresh hot chiles, seeded
    and cut into thin rings*
*1 large red bell pepper, seeded
    and cut into thin strips*
1 cup thinly sliced mushrooms

*4 or 5 green onions, including
    tops, cut lengthwise into thin
    2-inch-long strips*
Oil, for coating pan
5 eggs, lightly beaten
1/4 cup soy sauce
1/4 cup beef broth
2 tablespoons cream sherry
1 teaspoon Asian sesame oil
4 cloves garlic, minced
*1/2 teaspoon each grated fresh
    ginger and crushed dried
    hot chiles*
*1/4 teaspoon each coarsely
    ground black pepper and
    dry mustard*
*1 scant teaspoon sugar, or
    more to taste*
*1 teaspoon cornstarch disolved
    in 1 tablespoon beef stock*
Salt, to taste

Cut pork into paper-thin slices. Then cut each slice into strips 1/4 inch wide and 2 to 3 inches long. In a large wok or skillet over high heat, heat oil. Add pork, a handful at a time, and stir-fry until it is lightly browned on all sides. Add the 1 tablespoon soy sauce, the 1 tablespoon sherry, and the 1 tablespoon broth, and heat until boiling. Add fresh chiles, bell pepper, and mushrooms, and stir-fry for 3 to 4 minutes. Add green onions and stir-fry for 1 minute. Scoop ingredients from wok with a slotted spoon

and arrange on a heated serving plate. Keep warm.

With an oiled brush or paper towel, lightly oil an omelet pan and heat. Pour in half the beaten eggs. Tilt pan to distribute egg mixture evenly. As soon as a skin forms on bottom of egg, pull it to one side of pan and tilt pan again to let uncooked portion of egg run to bottom of pan. Continue this gentle tilting of pan and scooping aside of cooked egg until egg is set but not dry. Remove to a plate and repeat with the remaining egg. Break apart egg curds and toss with vegetables and pork on serving plate.

Heat wok again and add remaining ingredients except salt. Bring to a boil, stirring constantly. Reduce heat and simmer, stirring, until sauce is somewhat thickened, translucent, and glossy. Season to taste with additional sugar and salt. Pour over pork and eggs, and serve immediately.

Serves 6

Hong Shao Di Bang
China

In the Chinese culture, the color red symbolizes good luck and fertility. That is why red-cooked meats like this pork dish are popular.

6 to 8 dried Chinese cloud ear mushrooms or shiitake mushrooms
1 pork loin or shoulder (5 to 6 lb)
1/2 cup soy sauce
1 tablespoon tomato paste
3 tablespoons sugar
2 whole star anise (16 points)
1/4 cup rice wine or dry sherry
2 cups chicken broth
1 teaspoon crushed dried hot chiles
1 tablespoon slivered fresh ginger
8 cloves garlic, minced
1 teaspoon dry mustard
1 cup water
4 cups steamed long-grain white rice, for accompaniment

Soak mushrooms in warm water to cover for 1 hour; drain and set aside.

Put pork in a large pot, cover with water, and bring to a boil. Boil for 15 minutes. Drain. Return pork to pot. Combine remaining ingredients except rice and add to pot with pork. Bring to a boil, reduce heat to simmer, cover, and continue cooking, turning meat occasionally, until pork is tender (about 3 hours).

Remove pork to a cutting board and allow to cool slightly. Remove star anise from remaining liquid and, turning up heat, reduce to a thick sauce. When pork is cool enough to handle, cut into thin strips, and return to thickened sauce in pan. Toss gently over high heat to coat evenly.

Pile steamed rice onto a serving platter and arrange pork on top of it. Drain mushrooms and cut into quarters. Toss in sauce and, when heated through, arrange on top of pork. Spoon remaining sauce over all and serve immediately.

Serves 6 to 8

Shi Zi Dou
China

The translation of this dish is "Lions' Heads." It got its name because the meatballs with cabbage around them looked like lions with manes.

Lions' Heads Meatballs (recipe follows)
1 head napa cabbage
1/2 cup light beef broth
3 tablespoons soy sauce
3 tablespoons cream sherry
1 tablespoon peanut oil
3 cloves garlic, minced
1/4 teaspoon grated fresh ginger
1/4 teaspoon crushed dried hot chiles, or more to taste
Salt and freshly ground black pepper, to taste
1 teaspoon cornstarch dissolved in 1 tablespoon beef broth

Prepare Lions' Heads Meatballs.

Cut head of cabbage cross-wise to make leaves at least 5 or 6 inches long. (Reserve stem end to use in another dish with stir-fried vegetables.) Separate leaves of head end and wash well under running water. Use only larger outer leaves. (Save small inner leaves for future use with stem end.) Drain leaves.

In a large wok over high heat, bring broth, soy sauce, sherry, oil, garlic, ginger, hot chiles, and salt and pepper to a boil. Add cabbage leaves and toss gently to coat evenly with sauce. Cover with a tight-fitting lid and reduce heat to low. Steam leaves until wilted (about 10 minutes). Add cornstarch mixture and stir gently until sauce is thickened. Add meatballs and heat through.

To assemble, lay cabbage leaves on a heated serving plate and place a meatball on each leaf of cabbage. Tuck extra cabbage among meatballs. Pour extra sauce over dish and serve immediately.

Serves 6

Lions' Heads Meatballs

2 pounds ground pork
3 tablespoons soy sauce
2 green onions, including tops, minced
6 cloves garlic, minced
1 1/2 teaspoons minced fresh ginger
2 small fresh hot chiles, minced
1 medium onion, minced
1/2 teaspoon five-spice powder
6 canned water chestnuts, drained and finely minced
2 tablespoons cornstarch
1/2 teaspoon sugar
2 eggs, lightly beaten
1/4 teaspoon coarsely ground black pepper
2 tablespoons peanut oil

In a large bowl mix together all ingredients except oil. Form into 12 meatballs. In a large heavy skillet over high heat, heat oil. Reduce heat to moderate and fry meatballs, three or four at a time, turning them occasionally to brown well on all sides. Set aside.

Makes 1 dozen Meatballs

Roast Pork Calypso
Jamaica

When the pork is roasted, the alcohol cooks out of the chile-rum sauce, leaving only the essential flavor.

1 pork loin (6 to 8 lb)
2 cups chicken broth
1 cup dark brown sugar
8 to 10 cloves garlic, minced
1/2 tablespoon grated fresh ginger
1/8 teaspoon ground cloves
1 medium onion, minced
Juice of 2 oranges
1 teaspoon grated orange rind
1 teaspoon crushed dried hot chiles
1/4 teaspoon coarsely ground black pepper
1/4 cup freshly squeezed lime juice
1/2 cup crushed canned pineapple
Salt, to taste
1/3 cup dark Jamaican rum
Watercress sprigs and orange slices, for garnish (optional)

Preheat oven to 350° F. With a sharp knife score pork on fat or skin side to make diagonal cuts about 1/4 inch deep at 1-inch intervals. Place pork, scored side up, in a roasting pan and add broth. Cover and bake for 1 to 1 1/2 hours.

In a blender purée remaining ingredients except rum and garnish. Remove pork from oven and allow to cool. Remove pan juices and reserve. Rub purée from blender into flesh of pork and pour remainder over top. Return to oven, uncovered, and bake for another 45 minutes to 1 hour, basting occasionally with liquid in pan.

Degrease reserved pan juices. In a medium saucepan over high heat, reduce juices to about 2/3 cup, stirring frequently. When pork is done, remove from oven and place on a heated serving platter; set pork aside and keep it warm. Skim fat from roasting pan and scrape remaining juices and marinade into reduced stock. Stir together over high heat. Add rum and continue cooking, stirring constantly, for about 3 minutes. Strain and pour over pork on platter. Garnish with watercress sprigs and orange slices. Serve hot.

Serves 6 to 8

Shadowpoint Tamale Pie
Family Recipe

My parents' home, wherever it was at any given time, was always headquarters for the local artists and intelligentsia. Although my parents never found themselves in opulent circumstances, they entertained often and lavishly, particularly when they lived in their "Other Eden" at Lake Elsinore, California. Shadowpoint, that home, was truly a paradise, particularly if you were five years old and didn't have to take care of it. The 6 acres of chickens, apricots, walnuts, and overgrown lawn rambled down a gentle slope to the lake itself: a warm, still, green lake that beckoned on summer nights when the moon cast its path across the surface.

My father, a powerful swimmer, would put me on his back on those silver nights and together we would swim the shimmering moon path. We never quite reached the moon but it never occurred to me that we wouldn't, sooner or later. Tonight just wasn't the right night. Anyway, it would be time to swim back to the ramada, where a party might be in full sway. There could be 200 Young Democrats, or Friends of Wallace (that's Henry, not George), or perhaps the local Folk Dance Society. The ramada was built over the water, furnished with a bar, Victorian rattan furniture, and potted palms. The strains of concertina and balalaika would drift out over the lake, and brilliant people, sure of their ability to save the world, laughed and danced and splashed in the lake and ate. Everyone always brought plenty of food, and my mother fixed more, and you can bet your F.D.R. button that one of the things on the groaning board would be this tamale pie.

Since this was an economy dish that my mother made for entertaining large numbers of people when the cupboard was bare, you may wonder about the liberal use of expensive olives. My father cured his own. We used olives as most people use salt. They were in everything, on everything, and with everything. You can also make this dish in an economical way. Use inexpensive ground beef or chili meat, leftover meat or poultry, or cut down the amount of meat and add more onions and other vegetables. I have even taken a turkey carcass from the freezer, boiled it, picked off the meat, and used it in this pie.

2 tablespoons lard
3 large onions, chopped
10 cloves garlic, finely minced
3 small fresh hot chiles, finely minced
2 large bell peppers, seeded and chopped
2 stalks celery, chopped
2 pounds ground pork
2 tablespoons chili powder
1 tablespoon brown sugar
1/2 teaspoon ground cumin
1 tablespoon minced cilantro
1/2 cup minced fresh parsley
1/2 teaspoon coarsely ground black pepper
1 tablespoon tomato paste
1 cup beef broth
Salt and crushed dried hot chiles, to taste
3 cups water plus 1 teaspoon water
1/2 teaspoon salt
1 cup yellow cornmeal
1 can (6 oz) pitted black olives, drained
2 or 3 medium tomatoes, sliced
1 small onion, sliced into thin rings
1 small bell pepper, seeded and sliced into thin rings
1/3 cup each grated sharp Cheddar cheese and grated Swiss cheese
2 green onions, including tops, minced

In a large, heavy skillet over high heat, melt lard but do not let it smoke. Sauté onions and garlic until translucent but not browned (2 to 3 minutes). Add fresh chiles, chopped bell peppers, and celery, and sauté until vegetables are heated through and beginning to soften but are not browned. Add pork and stir-fry to break into small bits. If pork is browning too rapidly, reduce heat to moderate. Sauté meat until all signs of pink are gone but it is not brown and hard.

Add chili powder, sugar, cumin, cilantro, parsley, pepper, and tomato paste, and stir well. Pour in the broth, stir, and bring to a boil. Reduce heat to simmer. Season to taste with salt and dried chiles, and continue simmering until most of liquid has evaporated and a thick saucy mixture results (about 30 minutes).

Meanwhile, in a medium saucepan bring the 3 cups water to a boil. Add the 1/2 teaspoon salt. Slowly stir in cornmeal. Reduce heat and stir until thick (about 5 minutes). Let cornmeal sit until cool enough to handle. When cool, use your hands to press cornmeal onto bottom and sides of a 3- or 4-quart casserole. This cornmeal "crust" should be about 1/2 inch thick.

Preheat oven to 350° F. To assemble pie, stir black olives into meat mixture, reserving a few for garnish. Spoon meat into cornmeal-lined casserole. Arrange tomato slices slightly overlapping in a ring around sides of dish. Arrange onion rings in a circle inside of the tomatoes. Place bell pepper rings overlapping each other in center. Toss together cheeses and green onions and sprinkle over surface of pie. Scatter reserved black olives on top and bake until cheese is melted and beginning to brown (about 30 minutes).

Serves 12

Chancho Adobado
Peru

Old World pork and New World yams are combined in a zesty orange and lemon sauce to produce a satisfying dish.

Orange and Lemon Sauce
  (recipe follows)
2 1/2 to 3 pounds boneless
  pork, cut into 1-inch cubes
2 large yams
2 tablespoons lard
1/2 cup water
Minced cilantro, for garnish
  (optional)
12 hot small flour tortillas, for
  accompaniment

Make Orange and Lemon Sauce. Add pork and refrigerate overnight.

Boil yams until tender, peel, and cut into 1/2-inch-thick slices. Set aside.

In a heavy skillet over high heat, heat lard until it is hot but do not let it smoke. Sauté pork until well browned on all sides (no more than 5 minutes). Reduce heat to simmer and pour in sauce. Add the water and simmer, covered, stirring occasionally, until meat is very tender (45 minutes to 1 hour). Spoon meat onto a heated serving platter. Add slices of yam to sauce and simmer until heated through.

To serve, place yams in a ring around meat on heated serving platter. Pour over sauce and sprinkle with cilantro (if desired). Accompany with hot steamed flour tortillas.

Serves 6

Orange and Lemon Sauce

1 can (6 oz) frozen orange
    juice
1/2 cup freshly squeezed lemon
    juice
4 cloves garlic, finely minced
1 teaspoon ground cumin
1 tablespoon minced cilantro
1/2 teaspoon crushed dried hot
    chiles
1/4 teaspoon coarsely ground
    black pepper
2 tablespoons olive oil
1/4 teaspoon dried oregano
Salt, to taste

In a medium bowl mix together
all ingredients.

Laulau
Hawaii

This pork and fish recipe
traditonally uses two kinds of
tropical leaves, one edible, the
other not. Edible taro leaves are
very difficult to find; spinach is
a reasonable substitute. Ti
leaves, available from florists,
are not eaten; however, used as
a wrapping, they impart a
subtle aroma to food. If you
cannot find ti leaves, substitute
squares of aluminum foil.

1 pound boneless lean pork
1 pound salmon fillets
1 pound butterfish fillets
3 cups shredded taro leaves or
    fresh or frozen spinach
Crushed dried hot chiles,
    coarsely ground black
    pepper, and salt, to taste
Kaakuie nut, if available, or
    toasted walnut, to taste
    (optional; see Note on page 46)
20 ti leaves or 10 squares
    aluminum foil

Chop pork and fish into smaller
than bite-sized pieces.

If using ti leaves: For each
laulau lay one leaf on top of
another to form a cross. Place a
small mound each of pork,
salmon, butterfish, and taro
onto large end of one leaf.
Sprinkle to taste with dried
chiles, pepper, salt and kaakuie
nut. Roll up until you come to
end of leaf. Place rolled leaf
crosswise on broad end of
second leaf and roll again.
Filling should not be visible. Tie
shut by splitting the fibrous
stem and using it as a string. If
using aluminum foil: Place
filling and seasonings onto each
square. Fold foil to form small,
tightly sealed packages.

Place packages in a steamer,
pour in boiling water, and steam
for 30 minutes. Serve hot.

Makes 10

CHAPTER EIGHT

SAUSAGES AND VARIETY MEATS

I find it unfortunate that these superb and versatile culinary contributions play a small role in the traditional North American diet. Until recently, most people ate sausages only at the breakfast table. Variety meats (innards and extremities), or offals *as the English call them, were limited to an often greasy sodden dish called* liver and onions. *Kidneys and chicken livers were considered feline fare in many homes.*

In many other cultures, sausages and variety meats have been elevated to far greater status. Sausages have attained a level nearly equal to that of rare wines. Production is often regionally based, and towns and villages are renowned for their local creations. The *choucroute garni of Alsace and the Berner plate of Bern, Switzerland, are two examples.*

Markets in the United States carry liver and sometimes even a choice between calf's liver and lamb's liver. Kidneys are a bit more scarce. Heart, brains, sweetbreads, tongue, tripe, chitterlings, fries, liets (lungs), and oxtail are usually found only in specialty markets.

A delightful British concoction called a "mixed grill" makes the most of these fine foods. The dish consists of a selection of variety meats and a good sausage grilled under an open flame and served with brown sauce and hot brown mustard.

MAKING SAUSAGES

To make sausages, you first need hog casings, the intestines of hogs that have been thoroughly cleaned and prepared for use. You probably won't find them at a local supermarket, but small specialty butchers often carry them. They come either prepackaged or in bulk.

To keep hog casings, do not freeze. Freezing removes the elasticity from the tissue, which will cause sausages to burst during cooking if not before. Instead pack casings in salt. Put 1 cup of salt in a bowl, add casings, and knead them with your hands. Then put the casings and all of the salt in a refrigerator dish or plastic bag in the refrigerator. They will keep indefinitely.

To use casings, soak the amount you need in fresh running water for a few minutes. Drain and cut into the lengths required. Slip one end over the water tap; holding it in place with one hand, turn on the faucet. This washes excess salt from inside of casing and also opens the casing up to make it easy to use. Hold the rinsed casing by one end and draw it between two fingers of your other hand to wipe off excess water.

To stuff the sausages, you can use a hand or electric grinder with a sausage-stuffing attachment. I find both difficult to operate because they require three hands: one to continuously pack the meat into the machine, one to operate the machine, and one to constantly keep easing the stuffed sausage along so meat won't pack unevenly into portions that will be too fat and burst. I suggest using a hand stuffer, a small metal gadget that looks a lot like a funnel with a broad nozzle. They are usually available at kitchen supply shops or small hardware stores.

Another solution is to make your own stuffer using a 2-liter plastic beverage bottle, 3 inches of 1-inch-diameter plastic tubing, and a permanent-bond adhesive. Cut off the mouth of the bottle about 3 inches from the opening, making a funnel. Force tubing over end of bottle and glue into place.

To stuff a casing, first tie a knot in one end. Gather it up and slip open end over stuffer, gathering all of the casing onto end of stuffer. Begin packing meat into stuffer. As meat begins to fill casing, a bubble of air may begin to form; prick bubble with a needle or sharp skewer. Ease meat along to distribute it evenly in casing. Be careful not to pack meat too tightly or sausages will burst in cooking. When you come to within about 3 or 4 inches of end, remove sausage from stuffer and tie off end.

For some sausages, such as Cajun Boudin (see page 96), leave sausage in 2- to 3-foot lengths. For others, such as Chorizo (see page 95), make individual 3- to 4-inch links. Twisting the casing every 3 inches is an ineffective way to make individual links because the sausages will easily untwist themselves. Nor is using string or thread desirable. Instead use hog casing itself. Cut off a 4- to 5-inch length of casing. Gather it up and run your fingers through the center of what should now look like a fat wrinkled rubber band. Hold it open with your fingers and cut into 1/4-inch lengths with a pair of sharp kitchen scissors. Stretch out lengths into 4- or 5-inch-long strings, perfect for tying off individual lengths of sausage.

For individual links, make the sausage a little thinner than usual. This allows extra room for expansion when the meat is compacted as you tie off links.

The process of making sausages is complicated, but do not be discouraged; experience is the best instructor.

VARIETY MEATS

It is unfortunate that people in the United States have shied away from variety meats. Anyone who, like me, was raised on a farm is well aware that the finest treat available—the reward for the backbreaking work of butchering day—is freshly cooked liver and kidneys. There is nothing that can compare with the liver of any animal, lightly sautéed in butter with a hint of garlic and fresh herbs, within two or three hours of butchering.

One of the joys in shopping abroad is the great abundance of variety meats. Not only are liver, kidneys, heart, tongue, fries, and tripe always available, but they are from a range of animals: pigs, lambs, cows, calves, chickens, turkeys, ducks, and geese. What are fries? Fries are a by-product of gelding the male animal of any species. The cowboys on my great-grandfather's cattle ranch knew them as Rocky Mountain Oysters.

Variety meats make for some fine eating, but as with many foods, it's all in the cooking. The traditional scrambled eggs and brains is an abominable dish in my estimation, but poached brains in a zesty vinaigrette is tasty indeed. I have known many people who vowed they hated liver and would never touch it again, and who at my table were unaware they were eating it. Liver prepared with gentle artistry is virtually unrecognizable from the petrified offering usually served. I find *tripe à la mode de Caen* or a fine pâté preferable to a fried steak any day.

Mixed Offal Shish Kabob
Greece

These shish kabobs are the most-prized part of the Greek Easter celebration. They are traditionally made from the variety meats of the lambs or kids roasted whole for the holiday feast.

Wine and Garlic Marinade
(recipe follows)
1/2 pound tripe
1 pound lambs liver
1 pound lambs heart
1 pound lambs kidneys
12 to 15 small fresh medium-hot chiles
2 small zucchini, cut into 1/2 inch slices
1 small eggplant, cut into 1-inch cubes
2 medium onions, cut into bite-sized pieces
1 large red bell pepper, seeded and cut into bite-sized pieces
1 pound small mushrooms
Pilaf or steamed rice, for accompaniment

Make Wine and Garlic Marinade.

Cut tripe into 1/4-inch-wide strips as long as you can make them. Put strips in a large saucepan, cover with water, and bring to a boil. Drain,

Continued

cover with water again, and boil until very tender. Drain and pat dry.

Cut remaining meats into bite-sized chunks. Leave fat on kidneys. Place meats and remaining ingredients in a bowl and pour over marinade; turning to cover. Leave unrefrigerated for at least 2 hours.

To assemble, pick a piece of tripe from marinade and pierce one end of strip with a skewer, leaving the other end hanging free. Fill skewer with a selection of the other ingredients, threading alternately. When skewer is almost full, pick up loose end of tripe and wrap it in a spiral up skewer, securing it at tip when you reach end. Continue until you have used all ingredients.

To cook place kabobs on a grill 4 inches above a bed of coals. Cook to desired doneness, turning occasionally. Baste with extra marinade during cooking. Serve at once with pilaf.

Serves 6 to 8

Wine and Garlic Marinade

1/2 cup olive oil
1/2 cup dry red wine
1 tablespoon sugar
10 cloves garlic, minced
1 teaspoon crushed dried hot chiles
1 teaspoon dry mustard
1/2 teaspoon dried oregano
1 sprig rosemary, or 1 teaspoon dried rosemary
2 bay leaves, bruised
1 tablespoon chopped cilantro
1 tablespoon chopped fresh basil
1/2 teaspoon coarsely ground black pepper
Salt, to taste

In a glass jar with a tight-fitting lid, combine all ingredients and shake vigorously.

Pig's Feet with Black Bean Sauce
China

Pig's feet have remained pedestrian fare in the culinary hierarchy of the United States. About the only way we see pigs' feet is pickled in a big jar. Fortunately, many other cultures have treated trotters with far greater respect, as this delicious Chinese creation shows. Black bean sauce is a paste made of fermented black beans and is available in Asian markets and some supermarkets.

3 pounds pig's feet
2 tablespoons peanut oil
3 tablespoons black bean sauce
6 cloves garlic, minced
1 tablespoon grated fresh ginger
1 teaspoon crushed dried hot chiles
1 teaspoon dry mustard
1/4 cup soy sauce
1/4 cup cream sherry
2 cups chicken or pork broth, or more as needed
1/3 cup minced fresh parsley, for garnish
Steamed rice, for accompaniment

Ask the butcher to split pig's feet and cut them crosswise as well. Put them in a large saucepan, cover with cold water, and bring to a boil. Drain, cover again, and boil for 30 minutes.

In a large, heavy pan heat oil over medium heat and add bean sauce, garlic, ginger, and chiles. Sauté for 1 minute, then add mustard, soy sauce, and sherry. Stir over medium heat to form a paste, then add pig's feet and toss to coat evenly with bean sauce. Continue cooking until they brown slightly (about 2 or 3 minutes). Pour in broth, bring to a boil, reduce heat to rapid simmer, cover, and continue cooking until feet are very tender (about 1 hour). Check occasionally to see if more broth is needed.

Place feet on a serving dish, spoon over sauce from pan, and garnish with parsley. Serve with steamed rice.

Serves 4

Liang Ban Yao Pian
China

Used often in European cookery, kidneys are not a frequent guest at the Chinese table. This marinated kidney dish, however, artfully elevates them to an Asian delicacy.

*Soy and Ginger Marinade
   (recipe follows)
6 pork kidneys
1 medium leek
1/2 cup thinly sliced mushrooms
1 red bell pepper, seeded and
   cut into thin rings
Watercress, for lining bowl
1 teaspoon sesame seed, for
   garnish*

Make Soy and Ginger Marinade.

Cut kidneys into paper-thin slices and remove large pieces of fat. Put kidneys in a strainer and set strainer in a bowl. Set another large bowl under tap, fill it with cold water, and leave tap running. Pour boiling water over the kidneys. Lift kidneys out of hot water and set in cold running water; leave until cold. Empty bowl of hot water. Place kidneys in strainer in empty bowl and pour hot water over them. Again plunge kidneys in cold running water.

Repeat process a third time. Drain thoroughly and put kidneys in a large shallow refrigerator dish.

Cut leek on the diagonal into thin slices, including 4 inches of green tops. Wash leeks thoroughly and blanch in the same manner as kidneys, but use only one hot-water bath. Drain thoroughly and add to kidneys in refrigerator dish. Repeat with mushrooms. Place bell pepper rings over all. Shake marinade vigorously and pour over kidneys and vegetables. Stir gently to cover all ingredients with marinade and refrigerate for at least 4 hours, turning occasionally to ensure that kidneys and marinade are covered with marinade.

To serve, place on a bed of watercress and sprinkle with sesame seed. Serve chilled.

Serves 4 to 6

Soy and Ginger Marinade

1/4 cup peanut oil
1/4 cup rice vinegar
2 tablespoons soy sauce
1 teaspoon Asian sesame oil
*1 tablespoon finely grated fresh
    ginger*
6 cloves garlic, minced
*2 small hot chiles, finely
    minced*
*1/2 teaspoon crushed dried hot
    chiles*
1/2 tablespoon sugar
1/4 cup minced fresh parsley
Salt, to taste

In a jar with a tight-fitting lid, combine all ingredients and shake vigorously.

Son-of-a-Bitch Stew
Family recipe

This stew of chitterlings and chiles with dumplings is armed and dangerous.

Buffalo still roamed the shortgrass prairie when my great-grandfather crossed this continent to California and built Packwood Ranch. They were so plentiful that it was not yet an evilness to bring one down to provide the wagon train with fresh meat for the next week. The choicest tidbits—the tongue and the brains—went to the family of the man who fired the shot that brought the beast down. But the next best thing, shared by all who participated in the hunt and the dressing out, were the intestines, well cleaned and made into Son-of-a-Bitch Stew.

This zesty stew, originally made on the prarie with buffalo, became a specialty of the table at the Packwood Ranch. There weren't any buffalo in the San Joaquin valley of California, but there were bear, boar, deer, and soon the cattle of the ranch itself, and Son-of-a-Bitch Stew was just too good to forego because of a little thing like not having a heard of buffalo in the back-

yard. At Packwood, the concoction took on a definitely Latin flavor, the influence of the Mexican women who assisted the Chinese cook, but it was always served with that uniquely American phenomenon, feather-light dumplings (see On Dumplings, page 94). I have used chitterlings (the large intestines of pigs) for this version, but I've chosen to spare your own insides by not following the original recipe in my great-grandmother's journals. It called for 1 pound of chopped dried hot chiles to make the stew in a large enough quantity to feed the entire ranch. My mother remembered, however, that it was pure fire as it was served at Packwood. This is a recipe that can be as hot as you can take it, but make sure you have lots of beer and a dish of Put-Out-the-Fire Salsa Cruda (see page 166).

2 pounds chitterlings
1/2 cup distilled vinegar
2 tablespoons lard
2 large onions, chopped
20 cloves garlic
12 whole small fresh hot chiles
*6 small fresh hot chiles, cut
    into thin rings*
*1/2 tablespoon crushed dried
    hot chiles, or more to taste*

*1 teaspoon mixed dried herbs
    (see page 13)*
1 tablespoon chili powder
1 tablespoon minced cilantro
3 stalks celery, chopped
1 large bell pepper, chopped
*3 large tomatoes, coarsely
    chopped*
12 small boiling onions, peeled
1 can (14 oz) hominy, drained
2 tablespoons sugar
1/2 cup blackstrap molasses
*1 scant teaspoon coarsely
    ground black pepper*
1 bay leaf
1/2 cup minced fresh parsley
3 cups beef broth
Salt, to taste
*1 tablespoon flour mixed with
    1/4 cup water or broth*
*Country Dumplings (recipe
    follows)*

Wash chitterlings thoroughly
and cut into 2- to 3-inch-long
chunks. Put them into a large
pot with a lid and add vinegar.
Add enough water to cover
completely. Bring to a boil over
high heat and boil rapidly for
15 minutes. Drain and cover
with fresh water. Bring to a
boil and reduce heat to rapid
simmer. Cover and continue to
simmer until chitterlings are
very tender (about 3 hours).
Add more water during cooking
if necessary. Drain and pat dry
with paper towels.

In a dutch oven or heavy
casserole, heat lard. Do not let
it smoke. Sauté chitterlings, a
few at a time, until browned
on all sides. Remove with a
slotted spoon and set aside.
Add onions and sauté until
translucent (2 to 3 minutes).
Return chitterlings to pan. Add
remaining ingredients except
flour-water mixture and dumplings. Bring to a boil. Reduce
heat and simmer for 1 hour.
Stir occasionally to prevent
sticking.

Add flour-water mixture and
stir to distribute evenly. Cook
over moderate heat until stew
is lightly thickened and gravy is
glossy. Make Country Dumplings and add to stew.

Serves 6

The original recipe calls for a
leaf of California bay laurel,
which you should use if you
can obtain it. It also calls for "a
fistful of dried digger weed," an
ingredient that appears in
several of the original recipes
in my great-grandmother's
journals. I have consulted with
the research departments of
several excellent libraries in
California, and no one has ever
heard of it. However, it is
everyone's educated guess that
it must have been something
used by the Indians who were
called Diggers, particularly
since my great-grandfather was
Governor of the Diggers and
they had a camp by Packwood
Creek on his (at one time
their) property. Whatever the
ingredient was, today it should
have a different name; *Digger*
was a rather derogatory and
uneducated term the white man
gave to all California Indians.
Indians today—and I count
myself, being part Paiute,
among them—find it offensive.

Country Dumplings

1 cup unbleached all-purpose
   flour
1/2 tablespoon baking powder
1/2 teaspoon sugar
Pinch salt
2 tablespoons butter or lard
2/3 cup water mixed with 1
   tablespoon distilled vinegar

In a large bowl mix together dry ingredients and cut in butter with a pastry blender. Make a well in center of dry ingredients and, using a fork, stir in water and vinegar mixture. Stir vigorously until batter is well mixed and comes away from sides of bowl, somewhat losing its sticky texture.

To cook dumplings, stew should be bubbling over moderate heat but not boiling rapidly or it might stick and burn. Drop dough, 1 tablespoon at a time, onto top of stew. Maintain heat at a level that allows stew to continue to bubble lightly. Immediately put a tight-fitting lid on stew and cook untouched for 20 to 25 minutes, depending on size of dumplings (see On Dumplings, following).

ON DUMPLINGS

Every cuisine has dumplings in one form or another, but in my experience only in the United States are they feather-light, moist clouds of delicate flavor that might float out of the pot if you raise the lid without caution. In other cultures dumplings are baked, boiled, and steamed, and contain liver, cheese, eggs, fish, potatoes, and sour cherries. All of these preparations, including Chinese Hot Potstickers (see page 136) and Havasaupi Cornmeal Dumplings (see page 114), are delicious but they are not American country-style dumplings.

Most people who can make traditional American dumplings probably learned from their mothers. In nine encyclopedic tomes by various culinary experts, I could not find one recipe that even approached the way my mother taught me to make dumplings. In these books the batter always contains eggs and a lot of butter or lard. The cooking methods vary from putting the batter or dough on top of water and overboiling the dumplings to putting the dumplings on top of a stew, boiling them uncovered for 5 minutes, then covering for 5 minutes and considering them done. One recipe requires turning the dumplings every 2 minutes to cook them on both sides.

In the word of Nero Wolfe, "Phooey." These ingredients and methods are all too likely to produce soggy, heavy lumps of lead. Eggs make dumplings heavy, as do fat and even milk. Dumplings must have their privacy, 20 to 25 minutes of it. Removed too early, they will be underdone and collapse; removed too late, they will have begun to absorb too much moisture. For best results, spoon dough on top of stew, put on a tight-fitting lid, and leave dumplings alone for 20 to 25 minutes. It's tempting to lift the lid and take a look, but don't. If you are afraid that the lid is allowing steam to escape as the dumplings cook, you can try the old country trick of kneading up a paste of plain flour and water and using it to seal the lid.

Dumplings must be served immediately. Not "just as soon as 'Spiderman' is over" or "right after the next inning." When the dumplings are done, you either eat them or you feed them to the dog.

SAUSAGES

Evidence indicates that early humans, before they learned the skill of pottery, cooked food not only by roasting it in or over a fire but also by pit cookery. In this method, foods were cooked by filling pits with water, adding food, then filling the pits with stones that had been heated in a fire. The food was boiled or steamed, which rendered hard roots and grains more appealing than when they were cooked directly over flames. For nomadic peoples the obvious drawback to pit cookery was that the food had to be brought to the container and heat source.

Before the development of pottery, however, another cooking vessel was available to the early cook. It was waterproof, reasonably heatproof, and ultimately portable: the stomach of the animal itself. Animals hunted in the autumn had been eating ripened grains; when the entire stomachs of the animals were cooked in embers or hung over a fire, the result was palatable and nourishing.

People then discovered that adding other soft meats—liver, kidneys, heart, and some of the fat—to the grains in the stomach created an excellent delicacy.

Pudding originally consisted of meat and grain stuffed into the stomach or intestine and boiled or steamed. Over the centuries, newly available seasonings and eventually dried fruits were added to the ingredients. The Christmas plum pudding we hear so much of now did not originally contain plums; but it was plumb full of goodness.

Chorizo
Mexico

This is real Chorizo, hot, spicy pork sausage resembling those found in Latino markets. It can be fried, broiled, steamed, or barbecued, then put on a bun or wrapped in a tortilla. The sausages may be stored in plastic bags in the refrigerator for up to two weeks or in the freezer indefinitely.

3 pounds ground pork
1 cup cornmeal
3 large onions, minced
20 cloves garlic, minced
4 small fresh hot chiles, minced
1/2 cup minced cilantro
1 teaspoon dried oregano
1 scant teaspoon ground cumin
3 tablespoons chili powder
1 scant teaspoon freshly ground black pepper
1 teaspoon crushed dried hot chiles
1 tablespoon sugar
1/4 cup distilled vinegar
Salt, to taste
3 yards hog casings

In a large bowl mix together well all ingredients except casings. Test for seasoning by frying a small patty. Adjust seasonings. Cut casings into 1-yard lengths and proceed according to instructions for Making Sausages (see page 88). Tie off into individual 4-inch links, but leave each yard in a continuous string.

Hang over a wooden dowel to allow skins to dry thoroughly (about 1 hour in hot weather). Then, fry or steam. Prick skins to prevent bursting. Sausages are always best when cooked slowly.

Makes about 3 dozen 4-inch sausages

Cajun Boudin
Cajun Cuisine

This beef, pork, and rice sausage is my favorite recipe in this book and the finest sausage I have ever eaten. The recipe here is considerably toned down from the classic Cajun version because you may not yet be a dedicated member of the Galvanized Gullet. However, if you prefer, add more chiles, Tabasco sauce, and cayenne. Cajun Boudin is good to eat at room temperature as a snack like salami, or steamed and served hot as the main course of a meal. If you make boudin, don't tell anyone. Your life will never be the same. You will be considered a boudin machine only.

2 pounds ground beef
2 pounds ground pork
4 cups al dente steamed rice
4 large onions
20 cloves garlic, or more to taste
6 small fresh hot chiles, or more to taste
2 stalks celery
1 each large red and green bell pepper
2 medium leeks, including 4 inches of green tops
6 green onions, including tops
1 cup minced fresh parsley
1/3 cup minced cilantro
1 teaspoon crushed dried chiles, or more to taste
1 teaspoon coarsely ground black pepper
2 tablespoons sugar
1 teaspoon mixed dried herbs (see page 13)
Salt, to taste
Oil, for frying
4 yards hog casings

Put meats and rice into a large bowl. Using a very sharp knife, very finely mince onions, garlic, chiles, celery, bell peppers, leeks, and green onions.

Add finely minced vegetables to meat and rice. Sprinkle remaining ingredients except oil and hog casings over meat and vegetables, and mix thoroughly with your hands. To test for seasoning, make a small patty and fry in a bit of oil. Adjust seasonings.

Mix thoroughly after adding more seasonings. Cut hog casing into 1-yard lengths. Stuff casings according to instructions for Making Sausages (see page 88). Pack firmly but not tightly, or sausages will burst when cooked. Tie off. Pierce boudin all over with a skewer to keep sausages from bursting.

Using a heavy pan—roasting pan, casserole, wok, or dutch oven—with a tight-fitting lid, coil boudin around themselves so that they lie in flat layers in the container. Pour in enough water to reach top of the boudin. Cover and simmer over low heat for about 1 1/2 hours.

Leave sausage in cooking liquid until cool. Carefully lift lengths of boudin from cooking vessel and place in a colander. Rinse under running hot water to remove grease that has adhered during cooking. Pat dry.

Makes about 4 yards

Chaurice
Cajun Cuisine

This is another wonderful culinary contribution from Cajun country. You may not be able to understand patois, but everyone understands good eating—and this hot pork sausage is it.

4 pounds coarsely ground pork
1 pound coarsely ground pork fat
4 large onions, chopped
1 cup minced fresh parsley
1/4 cup minced cilantro
30 cloves garlic, finely minced
6 small fresh hot chiles, minced
1 teaspoon crushed dried hot chiles
2 teaspoons freshly ground black pepper
2 teaspoons ground thyme
1/2 teaspoon ground nutmeg
1/2 teaspoon ground cinnamon
1/2 teaspoon fennel seed
2 tablespoons sugar
Salt, to taste
3 yards hog casings

In a large bowl mix well all ingredients except casings, using your hands. Cut casings into 1-yard lengths and proceed according to directions for Making Sausages (see page 88).

Sausages may be cooked fresh. If you have a home smoker, they are excellent smoked. They also may be simmered, steamed, fried, or barbecued to desired doneness. No matter what method you use, remember to prick skin before cooking.

Makes about three 1-yard sausages

Hot Italian Sausages
Lombardy

These sausages are good cooked when fresh for any meal or snack. They are also delicious smoked, and make excellent gifts.

4 pounds coarsely ground pork
1 pound coarsely ground pork fat
4 onions, minced
20 cloves garlic, minced
1 tablespoon crushed dried hot chiles
1/2 cup minced fresh cilantro
1 tablespoon mixed dried herbs (see page 13)
1 teaspoon freshly ground black pepper
1 teaspoon fennel seed
1 tablespoon sugar
Salt, to taste
3 yards hog casings

In a large bowl mix together well all ingredients except hog casings. Fry a patty to test for seasoning. Adjust seasonings to taste.

Cut casings into 1-yard lengths and proceed according to directions for Making Sausages (see page 88). Tie off into 4-inch links and leave each yard of links intact.

Sausages may be simmered, steamed, fried, or barbecued. Cook to desired doneness. Remember to prick skin before cooking.

Makes about 3 dozen 4-inch links

CHICKEN, TURKEY, AND RABBIT

Throughout the ages, poultry has been such an important part of the human diet that it might be considered the ultimate culinary staple. People in virtually all cultures raise poultry as a major part of their diets. Poultry is tasty, nutritious, and versatile. It is also an economical source of animal protein.

A meal of chicken and dumplings or a chicken stir-fry served with rice is an excellent and inexpensive way to feed a family. Yet poultry can also be elegant. Stuffed and sautéed chicken breast is fit for a king, and a beautifully roasted turkey makes any table festive.

There are no recipes for duck, goose, or game hen in this book. In my opinion their flavors just don't lend themselves well to hot and spicy seasonings. There is one recipe, however, for rabbit as its taste and texture is more like chicken than any other meat.

CHICKEN

Jean Anthelme Brillat-Savarin wrote in *The Physiology of Taste,* "Poultry is for the cook what canvas is for a painter . . . ; it is served to us boiled, roasted, fried, hot or cold, whole or cut up, with or without sauce, boned, skinned, stuffed, and always with equal success."

Tomb paintings dating from the middle of the Old Kingdom in Egypt show slaves herding flocks of chickens to accompany the pharaoh into the next world, and numerous small figurines of both chickens and ducks have been found in tombs. Ancient Egyptians were so fond of chicken that they made sure they had a constant supply by incubating eggs in caves with oil lamps used to provide the necessary heat.

According to a Chinese legend, the first of the Three Celestial Rulers of China created chickens and pigs so that humans would always be happy. The earliest pictograph in the Chinese language representing "home" shows a pig and a chicken under a roof.

The Forme of Cury is the first cookbook written in England. It was penned by the royal chef of King Richard. Historians differ as to whether the sovereign was Richard I, the Lion Hearted, or Richard II. Since Coeur de Lion spent but nine months of his 10-year reign in England, my vote would go to Richard II. No matter whom the author of England's first cookbook served, one thing is certain: he considered "chekyn" a most noble dish to serve one's lord.

Kumquat-May Chicken
Family Recipe

The late science fiction writer Randall Garrett was an outrageous punster. Years ago, after eating this sweet and spicy baked chicken dish, he asked for the recipe. I told him that preserved kumquats might be difficult to find. He responded, "I'll find them, my lady, kumquat may . . . . " Nowadays, happily, kumquats are more widely available than they used to be.

1/4 cup light-flavored vegetable oil
1 roasting chicken, cut into serving pieces
1/2 cup orange marmalade
1/3 cup soy sauce
1/3 cup cream sherry
1 tablespoon minced fresh ginger
10 cloves garlic, minced
1/2 tablespoon crushed dried hot chiles
1 scant teaspoon dry mustard
1 scant teaspoon mixed dried herbs (see page 13)
1/2 teaspoon ground cinnamon
1/4 teaspoon ground nutmeg
1 scant teaspoon coarsely ground black pepper
1/2 cup sugar
1 large onion, cut into thin rings
1 each medium red and green bell pepper, seeded and cut into thin strips
1 small jar preserved kumquats (about 12)
Salt, to taste
Watercress sprigs, for garnish
1 seedless orange, including peel, cut into thin slices, for garnish
Steamed rice, for accompaniment

Pour oil in a heavy baking pan. Add chicken pieces and turn over in oil. Preheat oven to 350° F.

In a large bowl thoroughly mix marmalade, soy sauce, sherry, ginger, garlic, chiles, mustard, herbs, cinnamon, nutmeg, pepper, and sugar. Add onion, peppers, and kumquats, including any syrup in jar, and turn over in sauce to cover evenly. Season to taste with salt. Pour mixture onto chicken and turn chicken to coat.

Bake chicken until it is done to your liking (about 45 minutes). Turn occasionally and baste with juices from pan. When chicken is done, arrange pieces on a serving platter. Place onion, bell peppers, and kumquats over top. Surround with watercress and orange slices. Accompany with steamed rice.

Serves 4

Pollo en Mole Verde
Mexico

This chicken, swimming in green nut sauce and garnished with brilliant red tomatoes, yellow lemon wedges, and cilantro sprigs, makes a colorful dish fit for any fiesta.

1 large frying chicken, cut into serving pieces
Green Nut Sauce (recipe follows)
Tomato and lemon wedges, for garnish

In a stockpot over high heat, cover chicken with water and bring to a boil. Reduce heat to moderate and cover. Cook until tender but not falling off bone (about 30 minutes). Reserve 1 cup of broth for Green Nut Sauce. Make Green Nut Sauce. Preheat oven to 375° F.

Remove chicken from pot and place in a large, ovenproof skillet with Green Nut Sauce. Turn over to coat evenly. Bake until chicken begins to brown on edges (about 10 minutes). Remove chicken to a serving plate and pour sauce over it. Garnish with tomato and lemon wedges.

Serves 4

Green Nut Sauce

1 cup chicken broth
Powdered bouillon, to taste (optional)
1/2 cup pumpkin seed
1/2 cup blanched almonds
4 small fresh hot chiles
3 tomatoes, preferably green, chopped
1 large onion, chopped
6 cloves garlic, chopped
1/3 cup chopped cilantro
1 large bell pepper, seeded and chopped
1/2 cup chopped fresh parsley
1/2 tablespoon sugar
1/2 teaspoon freshly ground black pepper
1 tablespoon olive oil
1/4 teaspoon ground cumin

To broth or liquid from boiled chicken, add powdered bouillon (if desired) to strengthen taste.

In a blender purée broth and remaining ingredients for sauce in more than one batch if necessary. Pour purée into a heavy skillet and bring to a boil, stirring constantly. Immediately reduce heat to simmer and continue cooking for 5 minutes.

Singgang Ayam
Sumatra

Some effort is required to pound this chicken into shape, but you'll know it was worth it when you taste it, broiled in an almond and chili sauce. Note that chicken should marinate for two hours.

1 large frying chicken
Almond and Chili Sauce (recipe follows)
Steamed rice, for accompaniment

With a pair of poultry shears, cut along both sides of chicken to remove back and discard. Spread carcass open until breastbone breaks. Lay chicken on a flat surface, skin side up, and press breastbone with the palm of your hand. When the sharp breastbone pops up, discard it. Then, using the flat of a large, heavy cleaver or a mallet, pound chicken until it is flattened. Set aside; prepare Almond and Chili Sauce.

Coat chicken on both sides with sauce, roll it up tightly, and lay in a baking dish. Pour remaining sauce over chicken and marinate for at least 2 hours.

Unroll chicken, shake off excess sauce, and cook under broiler or over charcoal to desired doneness. Turn chicken occasionally and baste frequently with extra sauce. Serve hot with steamed rice.

Serves 4

Almond and Chili Sauce

2 cups coconut milk, commercial or homemade using 1 coconut and 2 cups boiling water (see page 12)
1/4 cup peanut oil
1/2 cup blanched almonds
1 medium onion, chopped
4 cloves garlic, minced
1 teaspoon grated fresh ginger
1/2 teaspoon grated lemon rind
4 to 6 small fresh hot chiles, chopped
1/2 teaspoon ground turmeric
1/2 teaspoon ground coriander
1 teaspoon chopped fresh coriander
1 teaspoon sugar
Salt, to taste

In a blender purée all ingredients. Pour into a heavy saucepan and bring to a boil. Immediately reduce heat to simmer and cook, stirring occasionally, for 10 minutes. Sometimes coconut milk curdles when it is heated. If this occurs, purée mixture in blender again.

Bastila
Morocco

Believe me, this unlikely combination of powdered sugar, cinnamon, cayenne, cilantro, saffron, and almonds works. This dish is traditionally made with pigeon. If you can find it at a local market, by all means use it, but chicken stands in quite nicely. Filo dough is what makes this pie flaky. This wheat flour dough rolled into tissue-thin sheets makes a crisp, flaky wrapper when basted liberally with butter. It is available frozen in most supermarkets and fresh in some specialty stores.

1 cup butter
1/2 cup olive oil
1 large frying chicken, including giblets, cut into serving pieces
1 large onion, minced
1 tablespoon minced cilantro
2 tablespoons minced fresh parsley
1 teaspoon grated fresh ginger
1/4 teaspoon each ground cumin and ground turmeric

3/4 teaspoon cayenne pepper
1/8 gram (1/4 teaspoon)
saffron
1 scant teaspoon ground
cinnamon
2 tablespoons sugar
1 cup light chicken broth
8 eggs, lightly beaten
Salt and freshly ground black
pepper, to taste
1 pound (approximately) filo
dough
Powdered sugar and ground
cinnamon, for dusting

In a heavy skillet over moderate to high heat, melt 1/2 cup of the butter with 1/4 cup of the olive oil. Brown chicken pieces, except giblets, on all sides, then remove with a slotted spoon and set aside.

Add giblets and onion to skillet and sauté until onion is soft but not browned (3 to 4 minutes). Stir in cilantro, parsley, ginger, spices, and sugar. Cook for about 2 minutes. Add broth and bring to a boil, stirring constantly. Return chicken to pan and turn to coat evenly. Reduce heat to simmer and cook, covered, until chicken is very tender (about 1 hour).

Set chicken and giblets aside to cool. When they are cool enough to handle, remove meat from bones and cut into very thin strips. Finely mince giblets.

Bring sauce to a boil and cook, stirring constantly to prevent burning, for 2 to 3 minutes. Reduce heat to moderate. Gently stir sauce while pouring in beaten eggs in a thin stream. Continue to stir until eggs and sauce have formed curds. Season to taste with salt and pepper.

In a small saucepan melt the remaining butter with the remaining oil.

To assemble, generously coat bottom of a heavy, 12-inch skillet with butter and oil mixture. Cover bottom of pan with a layer of overlapping sheets of filo, letting 4 inches of filo hang over side. Fold 2 sheets and place in middle of pan. Coat lightly with oil and butter mixture. Add another layer of filo in same manner and coat again. Continue until half of filo has been used. Spread half of egg mixture evenly on pastry. Add chicken and giblets. Spread with remaining egg. Gently smooth top.

Begin covering eggs with sheets of filo, following the same manner used when covering bottom of pan but do not let edges hang over sides of pan. Fold edges over to make them fit. Be sure to place 2 folded sheets in the middle of each layer of pastry and be sure to coat each layer with butter and oil mixture. When all sheets have been used, bring bottom sheets over finished pie to seal edges and coat with butter and oil mixture.

Cook pie over highest heat possible until bottom is golden brown (3 to 4 minutes). Place a large flat platter on top of skillet, hold firmly, and invert, transferring pie to platter. Coat pan liberally with oil and butter mixture, place over high heat, and slide pie back into the pan to cook other side until golden brown (3 to 4 minutes, less if it browns too rapidly).

To serve, transfer pie to serving plate, lightly sprinkle top with cinnamon and powdered sugar and, with a sharp knife or a pizza wheel, cut into wedges. Serve immediately.

Serves 6

Ceylonese Sweet-and-Sour Chicken Curry
Sri Lanka

Sweet-and-sour flavors—ginger, cayenne, and tropical fruits—combine to give this dish an unforgettable sensuality and depth of flavor. Serve with chapatis, a type of Indian bread, or tortillas.

2 small frying chickens, cut into serving pieces
Powdered bouillon, to taste (optional)
2 tablespoons each butter and olive oil
2 tablespoons Madras-style curry powder
1 teaspoon cayenne pepper, or more to taste
1 tablespoon grated fresh ginger
4 cloves garlic, minced
1 teaspoon ground cinnamon
1/4 teaspoon fennel seed
1/2 teaspoon each ground cumin and coarsely ground black pepper
1 large onion, chopped
2 cans (20 oz) pineapple chunks
1/2 cup sugar, or more to taste
1/2 cup distilled vinegar, or more to taste
Salt, to taste
2 medium onions, cut into bite-sized pieces
2 stalks celery, cut into bite-sized pieces
1 each medium red and green bell pepper, seeded and cut into 1/2-inch-wide strips
2 small seedless oranges, with peel, cut into thin rings
1 lemon, with peel, cut into thin slices
1 cup canned litchi, drained
1 cup preserved kumquats, drained
1 teaspoon minced fresh coriander
2 tablespoons cornstarch dissolved in 1/4 cup water
Steamed rice, for accompaniment
Chapatis or flour tortillas, for accompaniment

Put chicken backs, necks, and giblets in a large saucepan, cover with water, and bring to a boil. Reduce heat, cover, and simmer until meat is falling off bones. Strain and reserve broth. If it is not very flavorful, add powdered bouillon to taste.

In a large, heavy skillet or casserole over medium heat, melt butter with oil. Add curry powder and stir until slightly singed. Add spices and chopped onion, and sauté until onion is soft but not browned (2 to 3 minutes). Add chicken and brown well on all sides.

Drain pineapple chunks and reserve juice. Pour pineapple juice and reserved broth over chicken and simmer, covered, until chicken is tender (25 to 30 minutes), stirring occasionally to prevent scorching. Add sugar and vinegar and simmer for about 2 minutes. Taste. If you want a more distinct sweet-and-sour flavor, add more sugar and vinegar. For a hotter dish add more cayenne. Season to taste with salt. Add pineapple chunks and remaining ingredients except cornstarch and water mixture and accompaniment. Simmer, gently stirring, for 5 minutes. Stir in cornstarch and water, and simmer until sauce is glossy and slightly thickened.

Serve hot with rice and chapatis.

Serves 6 to 8

Kiss-the-Colonel-Goodbye Chicken
Family Recipe

On the table or in a lunch box or a picnic basket, this tasty fried chicken far surpasses the fast-food versions. When packing fried chicken, put it in a double brown paper bag, then put the paper bag into a plastic bag or container. The paper should absorb any residual grease.

1/4 cup flour
1/4 cup bread crumbs
2 tablespoons chili powder
1 teaspoon cayenne pepper
1/2 teaspoon coarsely ground black pepper
1/2 tablespoon mixed dried herbs (see page 13)
1 tablespoon paprika
1/2 tablespoon sugar
1 tablespoon finely minced cilantro
1/4 teaspoon ground cinnamon
1 scant teaspoon each ground ginger and dry mustard
1 tablespoon finely minced garlic
Salt, to taste
1 frying chicken, cut into serving pieces
Light-flavored vegetable oil, for frying

In a small paper bag, put all ingredients except chicken and oil. Shake, add chicken pieces and shake to cover evenly. Shake the excess flour off each piece.

In a large skillet over high heat, heat oil but do not let it smoke. Add chicken carefully because it may cause oil to splatter. Fry until chicken is thoroughly browned on both sides (5 or 6 minutes). Reduce heat to medium and continue to fry, turning occasionally for 12 to 15 minutes. If you want the skin crisp, fry uncovered; if you want it soft, cover during cooking. To check for doneness, cut into one of the thighs. If the meat still shows blood at the bone, let it cook a bit longer. Drain chicken on paper towels and serve at once.

Serves 4

Red Chick and Dirty Rice
Creole Cuisine

This is eatin' like eatin' is meant to be. Combine chicken with seasoned rice and a piquant sauce of chiles, garlic, and onions, and you've got creole food at its most tasty.

4 tablespoons lard
1 tablespoon flour
1 large frying chicken, cut into serving pieces
1 large onion, chopped
6 cloves garlic, minced
4 small fresh hot chiles, minced
1 medium bell pepper, seeded and chopped
6 green onions, minced
2 tablespoons paprika
1 scant teaspoon mixed dried herbs (see page 13)
1 teaspoon minced fresh dill or 1/4 teaspoon dried dill
1/4 teaspoon coarsely ground black pepper
1 scant teaspoon sugar
4 large tomatoes, chopped
2 cups rich chicken broth
1 recipe Dirty Rice, page (see page 141)

Prepare a roux with 1 tablespoon of the lard and flour (see On Roux, page 51); set aside. In a heavy skillet over moderate heat, warm the remaining lard and fry chicken until browned on both sides. Remove, drain off excess fat, and set aside.

Sauté remaining ingredients except broth and rice, stirring frequently, until a sauce begins to form. Add roux and stir to incorporate thoroughly. Pour in broth and cook for about 10 minutes, stirring occasionally to prevent scorching. Add fried chicken and cook, covered, long enough to heat chicken thoroughly (about 30 minutes).

To serve, put rice on a serving dish and place chicken pieces on top. Drizzle with any extra sauce and serve immediately.

Serves 6

Chicken Couscous
North Africa

The grain couscous is as ubiquitous in North Africa as rice is in Asia or potatoes in Ireland. It gives its name to a variety of North African dishes in which a stew tops a mound of the grain. This version, from Algiers, is moistened with one sauce and accompanied by a second one of greater vigor. Packaged couscous can be found in most supermarkets.

3 cups couscous
2 small frying chickens, cut into serving pieces
15 to 20 cloves garlic, crushed
4 large onions, quartered
1 tablespoon crushed dried hot chiles
1/2 cup chopped cilantro
1 tablespoon mixed dried herbs (see page 13)
1 bay leaf
3 cinnamon sticks
2 whole cloves
1 tablespoon sugar
1 teaspoon each dry mustard, salt and freshly ground black pepper
3 medium potatoes, peeled and quartered
12 to 15 small boiling onions
1 cup bite-sized pieces of pumpkin
5 large long fresh mild chiles
10 small fresh hot chiles, preferably red
15 dates
2 medium leeks, including 4 inches of green tops, trimmed and cut into 2-inch lengths
12 to 15 cherry tomatoes
Couscous Sauce No. 1 (recipe follows)
Couscous Sauce No. 2 (recipe follows), for accompaniment
1 cup cooked chick-peas
6 hard-cooked eggs, cut in half
1/2 cup pitted black olives, drained
1 tablespoon minced cilantro, for garnish
1 lemon, thinly sliced, for garnish

Prepare couscous according to manufacturer's directions.

Put chickens into a pot large enough to hold them both comfortably. Add garlic, quartered onions, dried chiles, chopped cilantro, herbs and spices, sugar, mustard, salt, and pepper, and cover with water. Bring to a boil and reduce heat to maintain a rapid simmer. Cook chicken until tender (about 45 minutes). Let it sit in its liquid.

Meanwhile, put potatoes and boiling onions in a large pot, cover with water, and boil until tender (20 to 30 minutes). In a vegetable steamer, steam pumpkin, fresh chiles, dates, and leeks until tender but not mushy (about 10 minutes). Add cherry tomatoes during the last few minutes of steaming. They should be hot throughout but not collapsed. Prepare Couscous Sauce No. 1 and Couscous Sauce No. 2.

To assemble, sprinkle the couscous evenly over a large serving platter. Arrange chicken, cooked vegetables, chick-peas, eggs, and olives over couscous. Cover with Couscous Sauce No. 1. Garnish with cilantro and lemon slices. Serve Couscous Sauce No. 2 in a separate bowl.

Serves 10

Couscous Sauce No. 1

4 cups chicken broth
4 tomatoes, chopped
10 cloves garlic, crushed
1/2 cup chopped fresh parsley
1/4 cup olive oil
3 large onions, chopped
1 large bell pepper, seeded and
    chopped
2 small fresh hot chiles,
    chopped
1 1/2 teaspoons sugar
Salt, to taste

Put broth in a saucepan. In a blender purée tomatoes, garlic, parsley, oil, and 2 of the chopped onions. Add to broth and bring to a boil. Reduce heat, add the remaining chopped onion and remaining ingredients. Simmer, stirring occasionally, for 45 minutes.

Reserve 1 cup for Couscous Sauce No. 2.

Couscous Sauce No. 2

1 cup Couscous Sauce No. 1
6 small fresh hot chiles
1 tablespoon grated fresh
    ginger
1 teaspoon cayenne pepper
1/2 cup sugar
1/2 cup distilled vinegar
1/2 teaspoon ground cinnamon
1/4 cup olive oil

In a blender purée all the ingredients. Put into a saucepan and simmer for 30 minutes, stirring to prevent scorching.

Sichuan Stir-Fried Chicken, Leeks, and Chiles
China

If you can find small Sichuan or Thai chiles, use them for this recipe; if not, any hot chile will do.

4 whole chicken breasts
3 tablespoons peanut oil
2 medium leeks, cut into thin
    rings and blanched
1 red bell pepper, seeded and
    cut into thin strips
6 small fresh hot chiles, cut
    into thin rings and blanched
1 teaspoon finely slivered fresh
    ginger
4 cloves garlic, thinly sliced
1 tablespoon soy sauce
1/4 cup rich chicken broth
1/4 teaspoon each five-spice
    powder and coarsely ground
    black pepper
1/2 teaspoon sugar
1 teaspoon cornstarch dissolved
    in 1 tablespoon cold chicken
    broth
Salt, to taste
Steamed rice, for accom-
    paniment

Bone chicken breasts and remove skin. Cut meat into strips 1/4 inch wide by 2 inches long. Slice skin into slivers.

In a large wok heat oil but do not let it smoke. Add chicken skin and stir-fry until crisp. Remove with a slotted spoon, drain, and set aside. Begin stir-frying chicken strips, a few pieces at a time, until heated through but not browned. Remove with a slotted spoon and set aside with skin.

Stir-fry leeks, bell pepper, and chiles in the same manner, a few at a time, for no more than 1 minute. Remove with a slotted spoon and set aside.

Add ginger, garlic, soy sauce, broth, five-spice powder, pepper and sugar to wok and cook, stirring, for about 3 minutes. Return chicken, skin, and vegetables to wok and stir-fry for 1 minute. Pour in cornstarch and broth mixture and stir gently until sauce is thickened and translucent. Season to taste with salt. Serve immediately, with steamed rice.

Serves 6 as a main course,
8 to 10 as a side dish

Kaeng Ped Cai
Thailand

Perhaps Anna and the King dined on dishes like these succulent chicken breasts swimming in coconut milk and curry spices, etcetera, etcetera, etcetera.

4 large whole chicken breasts
2 tablespoons peanut oil
1 tablespoon crushed dried hot
   chiles
6 cloves garlic, minced
1 teaspoon paprika
1/4 teaspoon grated lemon rind
1/4 teaspoon shrimp paste or
   anchovy paste (see Note,
   page 68)
1/8 teaspoon caraway seed
1/4 teaspoon ground coriander
1/2 teaspoon sugar
2 cups coconut milk, commercial or homemade using 1
   coconut and 2 cups boiling
   water (see page 12)
4 green onions, chopped
1 teaspoon chopped fresh
   coriander
1 red bell pepper, seeded and
   cut into thin strips
Salt, to taste
Steamed rice, for accompaniment

Bone chicken breasts, remove skin (reserve for stock or another future use), and cut breasts into strips 1/4 inch wide and 2 inches long.

In a large wok or skillet, heat oil until it is almost smoking. Add chiles, garlic, paprika, lemon rind, shrimp paste, caraway, ground coriander, and sugar, and stir rapidly for 1 minute. Add chicken breasts and stir-fry until evenly coated with seasonings and hot throughout (about 2 minutes).

Pour in coconut milk and bring to a boil, stirring constantly. Stir in green onions, fresh coriander, and bell pepper. Season to taste with salt. Immediately remove from heat. Serve with hot steamed rice.

Serves 6

Chicken in Peanut Sauce
West Africa

Surrounded by an array of beautiful fresh condiments, this chicken is an excellent dish for a buffet dinner. The diners may garnish their servings as they wish.

1 large frying chicken
1 teaspoon salt, plus salt to
   taste
1 tablespoon ground ginger
1/4 cup peanut oil
1 cup roasted peanuts
1 cup water
2 large onions, chopped
8 cloves garlic, minced
4 large ripe tomatoes, chopped
2 tablespoons tomato paste
1 teaspoon grated fresh ginger
1 teaspoon crushed dried hot
   chiles
1/2 teaspoon freshly ground
   black pepper
4 cups chicken broth
6 small fresh hot chiles, with
   stems
1 teaspoon sugar, or more to
   taste
12 to 15 fresh or thawed
   frozen whole okra
6 hard-cooked eggs
Minced red onion; minced green
   onion, including tops;
   chopped red, green, and
   yellow bell peppers; diced
   fresh pineapple; chopped
   salted peanuts; diced tomatoes seasoned to taste with
   dill, black pepper, and
   minced fresh chiles; diced
   avocado; diced hard-cooked
   egg; minced cilantro, for
   accompaniment

With a cleaver, chop chicken into bite-sized chunks. Combine the 1 teaspoon salt and ground ginger and rub into chicken. In a large heavy pot or casserole over moderate heat, heat oil. Brown chicken. Remove from oil with a slotted spoon and drain. Set aside.

In a blender purée peanuts and the water. Set aside.

Add onions and garlic to pot used to cook chicken. Sauté until onions are soft (2 to 3 minutes). Add tomatoes, tomato paste, fresh ginger, dried chiles, and pepper, and stir well to blend. Continue to cook, stirring frequently, until a thick sauce results (about 5 minutes). Add broth, fresh chiles, and chicken, and stir. Reduce heat to simmer and cook for 15 minutes. Stir in peanut purée and sugar. Add okra and eggs, and cook for 5 minutes longer. Season to taste with salt.

To serve, mound chicken onto a deep platter and surround with small dishes of condiments for accompaniment.

Serves 6

Brilliant Café-Inspired Red Butter Chicken
England

Southall, (pronounced in English fashion, *suthal*, not *south hall*) a suburb of London, is the heart of the city's Indian community. Small shops selling vegetables, herbs, and spices that you have never seen before line the streets. Saris drape sensuously from manikins with bright blue eyes and platinum hair. Tantalizing smells waft from stalls selling *samosas* and kabobs. The whole effect is that of a bazaar, a delightful experience that unfortunately most visitors to London never see.

Down a side street is the nondescript Brilliant Café, where I first ate red butter chicken. Once at home, my older son and I spent days trying to re-create the tastes. We are pleased with what we developed, although it is slightly different from the original. For best results, the chicken should marinate overnight.

Brilliant Café Masala (recipe follows)
2 frying chickens
1 cup butter, melted
Steamed rice, for accompaniment

Prepare Brilliant Café Masala.

Using a cleaver or poultry shears, cut chicken into bite-sized chunks. Put into a bowl large enough to hold pieces comfortably and cover with masala. Refrigerate overnight, stirring occasionally, to make sure that chicken is adequately covered.

To cook, use a large basket steamer that fits over a wok or a similar arrangement. Remove half of the chicken from marinade and place in a flat heatproof dish that fits in steamer and allows at least 1/2 inch around it. Pour boiling water into bottom of steamer. Place dish of chicken on top of the steamer and pour half of melted butter over it. Cover and steam over rapidly boiling water for 30 to 40 minutes. Test a piece for doneness. It should be just done, not dry. Add more boiling water to steamer if necessary.

When chicken is done place on a heatproof dish covered tightly with aluminum foil and put in a very low oven to keep warm while you repeat the process for remaining chicken. Pour any butter remaining from the steaming process into marinade. In a small saucepan bring butter and marinade just to a boil. Pour into a separate dish. Serve chicken with masala and steamed rice.

Serves 8

Brilliant Café Masala

3 tablespoons boiling water
1 tablespoon (1 1/2 grams)
    saffron
1/2 cup butter
1 medium onion, chopped
6 cloves garlic, chopped
4 tablespoons grated fresh
    ginger
5 small fresh hot chiles,
    chopped
4 tablespoons minced fresh
    coriander
1 tablespoon grated lemon rind
1/2 cup freshly squeezed lemon
    juice
6 tablespoons Madras-style
    curry powder
3 tablespoons ground cinnamon
1 teaspoon each ground cumin,
    ground nutmeg, ground
    cardamom, and ground
    turmeric
1 teaspoon anise seed
6 tablespoons sugar
1 cup (8 oz) plain yogurt
Salt, to taste
Red food coloring, for color

Pour the boiling water over saffron and let it sit. In a saucepan melt butter. Add remaining ingredients except yogurt, salt, and food coloring. Simmer for about 5 minutes but do not brown. Remove from heat and purée in a blender. Add yogurt, salt to taste, and enough food coloring to turn sauce the color of pomegranate juice. Purée again. Set aside.

Galinha Cafreal Zanbediana
Mozambique

The fresh, zingy flavor of this broiled chicken comes from lemon juice and coconut milk. Crisp watercress and lemon slices make an appropriate accompaniment. Note that chicken must marinate for four hours.

1 cup freshly squeezed lemon
    juice
10 cloves garlic, finely minced
2 or 3 medium-sized fresh hot
    chiles, finely minced
1 teaspoon crushed dried hot
    chiles
2 teaspoons sugar
2 tablespoons olive oil
2 small frying chickens, each
    cut in half

1 1/2 cups coconut milk,
    commercial or homemade
    using 1 coconut and 1 1/2
    cups boiling water (see
    page 12)
Salt, to taste

In a large bowl mix together lemon juice, garlic, chiles, sugar, and oil. Place chicken halves in a shallow pan and add marinade. Turn to coat evenly and marinate for at least 4 hours.

Broil chicken under moderate heat to desired doneness, turning occasionally and basting with some of the marinade.

Meanwhile, in a saucepan combine remaining marinade and coconut milk. Cook, stirring constantly, over low heat for 5 minutes. Try not to let liquid come to a boil or it may curdle. Season to taste with salt. Pour sauce into a separate dish and serve with chicken.

Serves 4

TIPS ON BUYING AND COOKING TURKEY

Let's talk turkey. I've been amazed that so many recipes for whole roasted turkey call for a small, 8- to 10-pound bird. There is a misconception that a small turkey is young and therefore more tender. All turkeys that reach the market these days are actually the same age, give or take a week or two. The difference in size is determined by breed.

However, a small turkey has many more bones per pound than a large turkey and therefore costs more per pound. In my opinion, which you may indeed choose to chuck right out the door, you should buy the largest turkey possible, which generally means about 28 pounds.

If the skin on the breast has been broken, the white meat may become dry and unpalatable when the turkey is roasted. To remedy this, take a lump of fat from the flap of skin at the body opening and lay it over the cut in the skin. This will help keep the bird from drying out during roasting.

Turkeys, by nature, tend to be dry. After all, they are land birds, unlike a goose or a duck that has to be greasy so it won't drown. Its natural body juices are lost very easily, and every time you poke a hole in a turkey, it gets a little drier. Therefore, do not pierce the breast with a fork to see if it is done. I also recommend against buying turkeys with the pop-up or retractable thermometer, which creates a hole in the breast.

For safety, roasted turkey should reach an internal temperature of 170° F. If you're not using a pop-up or retractable thermometer (which may be preset to let the bird cook to a higher temperature, by the way), then how are you to know when the turkey is done? Some cooks use the instant-read thermometer, but that, of course, will put more holes in the turkey. I prefer to "shake hands" with the bird: when the drumstick shifts easily in its socket as you gently move it back and forth, the turkey is most likely ready. At this point, if you want to be sure, you could pierce the bird with an instant-read thermometer, since there's little likelihood of further cooking being necessary.

Roast Turkey with Chorizo Stuffing
Mexican-American Cuisine

One year, my parents made a traditional Christmas dinner with a Mexican flavor. Three weeks after joining the staff of the California Juvenile Authority correctional facility at Whittier, my father was told to organize a Christmas party for the boys. My parents were thrown into something of a dither. After all, in my family, when we say "Deck the halls," we mean it, and here we were, supposed to provide a party for thirty-six teenage boys of mixed ethnic and economic backgrounds, with no budget to do it. My mother and I began baking and my dad got on the phone trying to contact the parents of the kids, many of whom were Hispanic.

Well, they came through with flying colors. A long trestle table became a cornucopia of gorgeous Latino delicacies, interspersed with fruitcake, frosted sugar cookies, date bars, spice nuts, and shortbread. The crowning glories of the feast were several huge roasted turkeys, stuffed with a hot and zesty mixture

Continued

that included chorizo, a spicy pork sausage. You can make your own (see page 95) or use a commercial brand.

1 turkey (16 to 20 lb)
Chorizo Stuffing (recipe follows)
Watercress, for garnish
Orange slices, for garnish

Preheat oven to 350° F. Remove neck and giblets from turkey and use for Chorizo Stuffing. Make stuffing.

Pack stuffing into body and neck cavity of turkey. Truss shut and put on a rack in a large roasting pan. Bake, uncovered, for 12 to 15 minutes per pound.

Remove to a large platter and garnish generously with watercress and orange slices.

Makes about 20 servings

Chorizo Stuffing

Turkey neck and giblets
3 pounds chorizo
1/3 cup yellow cornmeal
1 cup hot water
3 cups al dente cooked rice
3 large onions, chopped
4 stalks celery, chopped
1 each red and green bell pepper, chopped
20 cloves garlic, minced
4 small fresh hot chiles, minced
1 cup raisins
1 cup blanched almonds
1/2 cup chopped candied cactus, (optional; see Note)
1 teaspoon crushed dried hot chiles
1 teaspoon coarsely ground black pepper
1/2 teaspoon mixed dried herbs (see page 13)
1 teaspoon dried oregano
1/2 teaspoon ground cumin
1 tablespoon chili powder
2 tablespoons minced fresh parsley
2 tablespoons sugar
4 eggs, lightly beaten
Salt, to taste

Put neck and giblets in a saucepan and cover with water. Bring to a boil, reduce heat to maintain a simmer, and cook until very tender (about 1 1/2 hours). When cool enough to handle, pick meat from neck and chop meat. Chop giblets. Put in a large bowl. Reserve broth.

Remove casing from chorizo, break up meat into small pieces, and add to turkey. Soak cornmeal in the hot water until soft. Add cornmeal and remaining ingredients to chorizo-turkey mixture and combine thoroughly. Add just enough of the reserved broth to moisten stuffing. Fry a small amount and taste. Adjust seasonings.

NOTE—Candied cactus is available in Latino specialty markets.

Mole Poblano de Guajolote
Mexico

A variety of New World foods are combined in this delightful dish, which is usually reserved for very special occasions. In fact, mole graced Montezuma's table when he entertained the first conquistadors. You might not think to put chocolate on a turkey, but with a mole sauce it works. Unsweetened chocolate is the ingredient that gives a good mole its sensuous and unique quality. Mole may also be used for chicken or pork.

2 tablespoons melted lard
1 tablespoon salt
1 tablespoon mixed dried herbs (see page 13)
1 tablespoon minced cilantro
1 teaspoon each finely minced garlic, cayenne pepper, and ground cumin
1 tablespoon sugar
1 turkey (16 to 20 lb)
Mole Sauce (recipe follows)
1 tablespoon coarsely chopped cilantro, for garnish
2 tablespoons sesame seed, for garnish

Mix lard, salt, herbs, minced cilantro, garlic, cayenne, cumin, and sugar to form a paste; rub onto turkey, inside and out. Put turkey in a roasting pan with a tight-fitting lid. Roast in oven (don't preheat) at 325° F until tender (3 1/2 to 4 hours). Turkey will steam and remain moist. While turkey is cooking, make Mole Sauce.

When turkey is tender, remove from oven, and spoon juices out of pan (save for soup or gravy). Return turkey to oven, uncovered, and raise heat to 400° F. Roast just until turkey is browned. Pour mole over turkey and reduce heat to 350° F. Bake for 30 minutes, basting occasionally with mole.

Remove turkey to a serving platter and set aside to keep warm. Put roasting pan on top of stove. Cook mole and pan juices over high heat, stirring constantly, for 2 or 3 minutes. Pour over turkey. Sprinkle with chopped cilantro and sesame seed. Serve at once.

Makes 20 or more servings

Mole Sauce

4 cups chicken or turkey broth
1 cup blanched almonds
2 tablespoons crushed dried hot chiles
1/2 cup sesame seed
1/2 teaspoon anise seed
1/2 tablespoon ground cinnamon
1/4 teaspoon ground cloves
1/2 teaspoon each ground coriander and ground cumin
4 large tomatoes, chopped
1 cup raisins
4 small fresh hot chiles
1 large onion, chopped
1 tablespoon sugar
1/2 teaspoon or more coarsely ground black pepper
Salt, to taste
2 tablespoons lard
2 squares (2 oz) unsweetened chocolate

In a blender purée 2 cups of the broth, almonds, dried chiles, sesame and anise seed, and ground spices. You may need to purée ingredients in two batches. Pour mixture into a very large bowl. In a blender purée tomatoes, raisins, fresh chiles, onion, and sugar. Again, this may require two batches. Add to ingredients in bowl and stir. Add pepper and salt to taste.

In a heavy skillet over medium heat, melt lard. Pour in mole and simmer, stirring constantly, for 5 minutes. Add remaining broth and chocolate. Cook, stirring often, until chocolate is melted.

Rabbit Stew with Cornmeal Dumplings
Native American Cuisine

The Havasupai Indians originated this recipe. They are a small nation of Native Americans who inhabit a side valley of the Grand Canyon. In this century most of their cash income derives from leading mule pack trains to the valley floor for those of us who are either too infirm or too indolent to make it down and back up again on our own. Their valley is exquisitely beautiful, mostly free from the invasion of twentieth-century luxuries. The cornmeal dumplings of this dish will not be the high, light, and fluffy Country Dumplings served with Son-of-a-Bitch Stew (see page 92), but they are delicious.

1 large stewing rabbit (4 to 5 lb)
1/4 cup lard
15 cloves garlic
10 small boiling onions
6 small fresh hot chiles
1/2 teaspoon dried sage
1/2 tablespoon chili powder
1 teaspoon sugar
1/2 cup dried pinto beans
4 or more cups chicken broth
1 cup fresh or thawed frozen corn
1 cup canned diced nopalitos (see page 45)
Cornmeal Dumplings (recipe follows)

Cut rabbit into serving pieces. In a heavy casserole with a tight-fitting lid over medium heat, heat lard and brown rabbit on all sides. Add garlic, onions, chiles, sage, chili powder, sugar, and pinto beans. Add enough chicken broth to cover and bring to a boil, stirring to mix thoroughly. Reduce heat to rapid simmer and cook, covered, until rabbit is very tender and beans are done (1 to 1 1/2 hours). As beans absorb liquid, add more broth to maintain a moist stew.

When rabbit and beans are done, add corn and nopalitos. Stir, cover, and simmer for about 10 minutes while you prepare Cornmeal Dumplings.

Drop tablespoons of the dumpling batter onto top of stew. Cover and simmer for 25 minutes. Remove lid and serve immediately from casserole.

Serves 4

Cornmeal Dumplings

1 cup yellow cornmeal
1/2 tablespoon baking powder
1 teaspoon sugar
Pinch salt
1 tablespoon lard or shortening
1 egg
2/3 cup water

Using a pastry blender combine dry ingredients and lard until well blended. Beat together egg and water and, using a fork, vigorously mix into dry ingredients.

EGGS AND CHEESE

You might think that since I was raised on a commercial poultry ranch, I might never want to see another egg again in my life. But I adore eggs. I never feel the cupboard is bare if there are eggs. In fact, as much as I enjoy creating new dishes, experimenting, and entertaining, I could dine quite sumptuously for the rest of my life on cheese, eggs, and fruit. (Well, I would certainly hope there would be a little wine and a bottle or two of Anchor Steam Beer every now and then.)

I am not alone in my appreciation of the egg. People around the world and for thousands of years have raised poultry and enjoyed their eggs. They have become more than just a food product. The egg has come to symbolize fertility, longevity, and rejuvenation. For example, in Asia, weddings, births, and the new year are always celebrated by distributing eggs dyed a brilliant red, a color that also signifies fertility, longevity, and good luck. And on the other side of the planet, if a Navaho child finds an egg with an unbroken soft shell, it is a sure sign that he or she is favored and life will be easy.

Another of my favorite foods, cheese, has an equal—if somewhat less auspicious—reputation. Like eggs, cheese is produced around the world. But we tend to think of northern Europe, with its expanses of fertile pastures dotted with cows, as the world's most important cheese producing region. Yet nomadic peoples around the globe have made major contributions. Both sheep and goats are more efficient than cows at producing milk from far less than ideal pasturage. From them come some of the world's most prestigious and unusual cheeses.

Here, then, are some of my favorite dishes using eggs and cheese—and sometimes both!

ON OMELETS

I would love to write an entire book on nothing but omelets—although, it might be a very short book. All it really needs to say is, "Pour 2 beaten eggs into an omelet pan and put anything in the world that you like to eat, in any combination whatsoever, on top, fold in half, and serve."

But I can understand that a little more detail might be helpful. Three of my favorite omelet recipes follow. Here is how I cook an omelet: I pour the lightly beaten egg into the heated and oiled pan, let it form a light skin, and then begin putting things on top. If I'm using cheese, I always put it on first and, ever so gently, using the back of a fork, agitate the surface of the uncooked egg just until the cheese and uncooked egg begin to achieve some unity. Then I add any other ingredients. When the egg is almost set, I fold the whole thing in half, let it sit for a moment, and then slide it onto a heated plate. Now that's an omelet.

California Omelet No. 1
Family Recipe

1 teaspoon butter
1 tablespoon cream sherry
2 cloves garlic, finely minced
Oil, for coating pan
2 eggs, lightly beaten

2 tablespoons each grated sharp Cheddar cheese and grated Swiss cheese
2 tablespoons cottage cheese
1 tablespoon finely minced red bell pepper or fresh pimiento
1/2 teaspoon finely minced fresh chives and minced cilantro
1 teaspoon minced fresh mint
2 tablespoons mild or hot chunky salsa, commercial or homemade (see Salsa Son-of-a-Gun, page 157)
Salt and freshly ground black pepper, to taste
3 avocado slices, 2 tomato slices, 1 lemon slice, and sprig of cilantro, watercress, or parsley, for garnish

In a skillet over moderate heat, melt butter with sherry and sauté garlic until soft (2 to 3 minutes). Remove from heat and set aside.

Heat an 8- or 9-inch omelet pan or skillet over moderate heat, and oil lightly using a brush or paper towel. Pour in eggs and swirl pan to coat bottom evenly with eggs. When eggs have formed a thin skin on bottom, sprinkle Cheddar and Swiss cheeses on top and very gently agitate surface with the back of a fork until cheeses have begun to melt into eggs.

When eggs and cheese resemble custard but are not set and dry, add cottage cheese to one half of surface. Add remaining ingredients except garnishes. Gently fold omelet in half and cook for about 1 more minute. Reduce heat if omelet browns too rapidly.

Slide omelet onto a heated oval plate. Arrange garnishes in an attractive pattern and serve immediately.

Serves 1

California Omelet No. 2
Family Recipe

1 tablespoon butter
1 tablespoon corn or other light-flavored oil, plus oil for coating pan
1 tablespoon cream sherry
2 tablespoons chopped onion
4 cloves garlic
1 small fresh hot chile, minced
2 tablespoons each minced celery and bell pepper
4 or 5 fresh mushrooms, sliced
2 eggs, lightly beaten
4 tablespoons grated Swiss cheese
1 green onion, minced
1 tablespoon chopped pitted black olives
3/4 teaspoon minced fresh dill or 1/4 teaspoon dried dill

*Salt and freshly ground black
    pepper, to taste*
*2 tablespoons Guacamole (see
    page 16), 2 tablespoons sour
    cream, sprig of parsley, 2 or
    3 avocado slices, 2 or 3
    tomato slices, 1 or 2 pitted
    black olives, for garnish*

In a skillet over medium heat,
melt butter with the 1 tablespoon oil and the sherry. Sauté
onion, garlic, and chile until
soft but not browned (2 to 3
minutes). Add celery, bell
pepper, and mushrooms, and
sauté until soft but not browned,
(2 to 3 minutes). Set aside.

Heat an 8- or 9-inch omelet
pan or skillet over moderate
heat, and oil lightly using a
brush or paper towel. Pour in
eggs and swirl pan to coat
bottom evenly with eggs. When
eggs have formed a skin on
bottom, sprinkle cheese on top
and gently agitate surface with
the back of a fork until cheese
melts into eggs but eggs are
not cooked. Spoon cooked
vegetables over one half of
surface. Sprinkle with green
onion, olives, and dill. Season
to taste with salt and pepper
and fold omelet in half.

Slide omelet onto a heated
plate. Spoon guacamole and
sour cream over top and
garnish with parsley sprig,
avocado and tomato slices, and
black olives. Serve immediately.

Serves 1

California Omelet No. 3
Family Recipe

1 tablespoon butter
*1 tablespoon oil, plus oil for
    coating pan*
1 tablespoon cream sherry
4 cloves garlic, minced
2 tablespoons chopped onion
*2 or 3 stalks asparagus, cut on
    diagonal into 1/2-inch slices*
*1/4 red bell pepper, cut into
    thin strips*
3 or 4 mushrooms, thinly sliced
2 eggs, lightly beaten
*3 to 4 tablespoons grated
    Gruyére cheese*
*2 tablespoons mild or hot
    chunky salsa, commercial or
    homemade (see Salsa Son-of-
    a-Gun, page 157)*
*1 tablespoon canned diced
    peeled green chiles*
*1 tablespoon chopped pitted
    black olives*
*Salt and freshly ground black
    pepper, to taste*
*Sherry Butter Sauce (recipe
    follows)*
*2 tablespoons sour cream, for
    garnish*
*Coarsely ground black pepper,
    for garnish*

In a medium skillet over
moderate heat, melt butter with
the 1 tablespoon oil and sherry.
Sauté garlic and onion until soft
but not browned (2 to 3
minutes). Add asparagus, bell
pepper, and mushrooms, and
sauté until heated through and
lightly cooked (no more than 3
minutes).

Heat an 8- to 9-inch omelet
pan over moderate heat, and oil
lightly with a brush or paper
towel. Pour in eggs and swirl
to coat bottom evenly with
eggs. When eggs form a skin on
bottom, sprinkle cheese on top
and gently agitate with the
back of a fork to combine
cheese and eggs.

Spoon cooked vegetables
onto one half of surface. Add
salsa, chiles, and olives. Season
to taste with salt and pepper.
Fold omelet in half and cook
until eggs are set but not dry.
Slide onto a heated plate and
keep warm while you make
Sherry Butter Sauce.

To serve, spoon sour cream
on top of omelet, cover with
sauce, and add coarsely ground
black pepper. Serve immediately.

Serves 1

Sherry Butter Sauce

2 tablespoons butter
2 tablespoons cream sherry
1/2 tablespoon minced shallots
1/2 teaspoon minced fresh dill
    or 1/8 teaspoon dried dill
1/2 teaspoon paprika

In a saucepan over moderate heat, melt butter with sherry. Add shallots, dill, and paprika. Cook, swirling pan, until mixture is glossy and somewhat thickened (2 to 3 minutes).

Huevos Rancheros
Mexico

This is the way I prefer huevos rancheros (eggs poached in salsa), but you don't need this recipe to make the dish. If you have a favorite recipe or brand of chunky salsa you like (see page 157 for homemade Salsa Son-of-a-Gun), pour it into a pan, heat it, and add the eggs. Simple and good. Serve with hot corn tortillas and fried chorizo (see homemade Chorizo, page 95) if desired. This robust breakfast is excellent for any meal.

3 tablespoons corn or other
    light-flavored oil
2 medium onions, chopped
10 cloves garlic, minced
4 to 6 small fresh hot chiles,
    minced
1 stalk celery, chopped
1 medium bell pepper, seeded
    and chopped
4 large tomatoes, chopped
1 teaspoon mixed dried herbs
    (see page 13)
1/2 teaspoon ground cumin
2 tablespoons minced cilantro
1/2 cup minced fresh parsley
1 teaspoon sugar
2 tablespoons distilled vinegar
Salt and freshly ground black
    pepper, to taste
Crushed dried hot chiles, to taste
8 eggs

In a large, heavy skillet over medium heat, heat oil and sauté onions and garlic until soft (2 to 3 minutes). Add remaining ingredients except eggs and cook over moderate heat, stirring occasionally, until a thick sauce is formed (35 to 40 minutes).

When ready to serve, turn up heat to make sauce quite hot, stirring constantly to prevent scorching. Crack eggs on top of salsa, cover with a tight-fitting lid, reduce heat to moderate, and poach eggs to desired doneness. Gently spoon eggs onto a heated serving platter and spoon sauce around them.

Serves 4

Capsicum Quiche
Family Recipe

This quiche with cheese and three types of chiles grew out of a cooking competition that I once entered. My entries included an eggplant and pepper quiche and a smoked salmon quiche as well as this one containing various kinds of capsicum. The salmon won first place; the capsicum second. But third place escaped me: went to another competitor for a wonderful quiche with five different kinds of mushrooms.

1 recipe Basic Pastry (see
    page 149)
1 tablespoon butter
1 tablespoon cream sherry
6 cloves garlic, minced
1 medium onion, minced
1 each green and red bell
    pepper, seeded and cut into
    thin strips
1 long fresh mild chile, seeded
    and cut into thin rings
1 each red, yellow, and green
    small fresh hot chile, seeded
    and cut into thin rings
3/4 teaspoon minced fresh dill
    or 1/2 teaspoon dried dill
1 teaspoon minced fresh basil
1 tablespoon minced cilantro
1 1/2 cups milk
4 eggs, beaten
1 cup grated Swiss cheese

Salt and freshly ground black
    pepper, to taste
Sour cream, for accompaniment

Prepare pastry. Roll out and
line an 8- or 9-inch quiche pan
with removable sides. Refrigerate while you prepare filling.

In a heavy skillet over
moderate heat, melt butter with
sherry. Sauté garlic, onion, bell
peppers, and chiles until soft
but not browned (3 to 4
minutes). Remove from heat
and cool. Stir in dill, basil, and
cilantro. Preheat oven to 400° F.

Mix together milk, eggs, and
cheese. Remove quiche pan
from refrigerator and spread
vegetables evenly over bottom.
Pour over egg mixture and
smooth surface. Season to taste
with salt and pepper.

Bake quiche for 3 minutes.
Reduce heat to 350° F and
continue to bake until custard
is set (about 20 minutes).
Remove sides of quiche pan
and serve hot or at room
temperature. Accompany with
sour cream.

Serves 6

Diablo Meringue Pie
Galvanized Gullet Contribution

The first meeting of the Galvanized Gullet took place at my
house, which has a view of
Mount Diablo, a massive solitary mountain rising 3,848 feet
from an alluvial plain. This hot,
rich cheese sauce baked in a
loaf of bread and covered with
a savory meringue was created
by one of the charter members
of the Galvanized Gullet and
named not only for volcanic
intensity of the capsicum but
also for the extinct volcano in
whose shadow we dined.

Diablo Cheese Sauce
    (recipe follows)
4 egg whites
2 tablespoons freshly grated
    Parmesan cheese
3/4 teaspoon minced fresh dill
    or 1/4 teaspoon dried dill
1 large round loaf French or
    rye bread
2 tablespoons melted butter
6 cloves garlic, finely minced
Parsley, dill, or escarole, for
    garnish

Make Diablo Cheese Sauce.

Beat egg whites until they
hold peaks but are not dry.
Gently fold in Parmesan and
dill. Set aside.

Preheat oven to 375° F. Cut
top off bread and remove most
of soft interior, leaving only an
empty shell. Coat inside of
empty loaf with melted butter
and sprinkle on garlic. Bake
until bread just begins to
brown on inside (no more than
5 minutes). Remove bread and
put on an oven proof serving
dish.

Fill bread with cheese sauce.
Let extra sauce spill over sides
and onto plate. Pile on meringue. Bake until meringue
begins to brown and is set (no
more than 10 minutes). Remove
from oven, garnish, and serve
immediately.

Serves 6

In the Ukraine the child who
finds an egg still warm from
the hen and is able to bring it
to the kitchen to be cooked for
breakfast before it gets cold
will have good luck all day.

Diablo Cheese Sauce

1 tablespoon butter
3 small fresh hot chiles, chopped
1 medium onion, chopped
6 cloves garlic, chopped
2 cups milk
1 tablespoon butter
1 tablespoon flour
4 egg yolks
1/2 cup mild or hot chunky salsa, commercial or home-made (see Salsa Son-of-a-Gun, page 157)
1/2 cup each grated sharp Cheddar cheese and grated Swiss cheese
3/4 teaspoon fresh minced dill or 1/4 teaspoon dried dill
1 tablespoon minced cilantro
3 green onions, including tops, finely chopped

In a medium skillet over moderately high heat, melt butter and sauté chiles, onion, and garlic until soft but not browned (3 to 4 minutes). In a blender purée milk and sautéed vegetables.

In a saucepan over moderate heat, blend together butter and flour, stirring constantly, for 2 minutes. Slowly add in milk mixture and cook, whisking constantly, until mixture begins to thicken. Remove from heat and put 1 cup into blender.

Add egg yolks to blender and purée. Return saucepan to stove over moderate heat and very slowly pour in egg mixture, whisking constantly. Continue whisking until mixture thickens. Add salsa, cheeses, dill, cilantro, green onions, whisking constantly. When cheese is melted and thoroughly incorporated, remove from heat and set aside.

Southall Cheese Balls
Indian Cuisine

Southall, England, is the place where I first tasted these fried croquettes made with eggs and cheese and flavored with chile and curry spices. Cheese balls, along with barbecued meats, are sold from the numerous small shops and stalls that line the streets of this London suburb.

1/2 cup each grated Cheddar cheese and grated Swiss cheese
1 1/2 cups fine bread crumbs
6 cloves garlic, finely minced
1 medium onion, finely minced
3 green onions, including tops, minced
1 teaspoon finely grated fresh ginger
1/2 cup minced fresh parsley
2 tablespoons minced cilantro
1 teaspoon each cayenne pepper, ground turmeric, and dry mustard
1/2 teaspoon ground cumin
1 teaspoon sugar
2 or 3 eggs, lightly beaten
Salt and freshly ground black pepper, to taste
Light-flavored oil, for frying
2 eggs, well beaten
1 cup fine bread crumbs

Mix together thoroughly all ingredients except oil, the well-beaten eggs, and the 1 cup bread crumbs. If mixture is not moist enough to hold together when formed into a ball, add another egg and mix again. Shape into 12 round balls.

In a heavy skillet over medium-high heat, warm about 1 inch of oil; it should reach frying temperature—hot but not smoking. Dip balls into beaten eggs, shake off excess, and roll in bread crumbs. Fry, a few at a time, browning evenly (no more than 5 minutes). If balls appear to be browning too fast, lower heat. Drain on paper towels and serve hot.

Makes 1 dozen croquettes

CHAPTER ELEVEN

VEGETABLES

While much of northern Europe was populated by hunter-gatherers, Indians in the Tamaulipas Mountains of Mexico were engaged in the first struggles of the agricultural revolution, and winning. By 7000 B.C., they were engaged in the domestication of runner beans, aloe, summer squash, chiles, bottle gourds, and a form of pumpkin.

Somewhat farther south in Tehuacán, by 5000 B.C. the native population was well on the way to cultivating maize, or corn. In its wild state the ears of the indigenous maize were no more than one inch long. By the time Cortés invaded the empire of Montezuma, people of the region had succeeded in breeding a plant that produced ears almost as large and tender as those we buy today. By 5600 B.C. beans were a domestic crop in the New World, and by 3000 B.C. the potato and tomato were cultivated.

I am exceedingly glad for a New World harvest that has contributed so much to the range of vegetables available to us. Even though I am no longer a vegetarian, I still carry on my life-long love affair with vegetables.

Mixed Vegetable Curry
Thailand

A light hand is required to retain the essential fresh, crisp quality of the vegetables before they are enhanced with Red Curry Sauce. Half the sauce is served on the side for those who wish to increase the intensity of the heat. A good Thai beer makes an excellent accompaniment.

Red Curry Sauce (recipe
   follows)
12 small dried red chiles
1 cup peanut oil, plus oil for
   coating pan
1 small yam
2 eggs, lightly beaten
3 cups fresh bean sprouts
1 red bell pepper, seeded and
   chopped
4 green onions, including tops,
   minced
2 cups broccoli florets,
   blanched
4 green onions, including tops,
   cut into 2-inch lengths and
   blanched
1/4 pound long beans, trimmed,
   left whole, and blanched
1/4 pound snow peas, blanched
1 large carrot, julienned into 3-
   inch lengths and blanched
2 cups coarsely shredded bok
   choy, blanched
2 medium tomatoes, chopped

1 cup freshly grated coconut
   (see page 12)
1/2 cup chopped raw peanuts
2 or 3 fresh red mild or hot
   chiles, for garnish
1 lemon, thinly sliced, for
   garnish

Make Red Curry Sauce. Put chiles into a bowl and cover with boiling water. Soak chiles until water is cool. Drain.

Heat the 1 cup oil to frying temperature (375° F). Peel yam and cut into 1/3-inch-thick slices. Fry in oil for about 2 minutes. Drain and set aside.

Heat an omelet pan or skillet over moderate heat and oil lightly, using a brush or paper towel. Pour in half of the beaten eggs. Let eggs form a skin. When almost set, roll up and remove to a cutting board to cool while you repeat process with the remaining eggs. When each roll is cool enough to handle, cut into very thin slivers. Set aside.

In a large bowl toss together bean sprouts, bell pepper, and minced green onions. Mound into center of a serving platter.

Put prepared chiles and yams, and remaining vegetables, coconut, and peanuts in piles around base of mound. Sprinkle slivered egg over bean sprouts.

Garnish with fresh red chiles and lemon slices. Drizzle half of sauce over vegetables and serve remaining sauce in a small bowl.

Serves 6

Red Curry Sauce

2 tablespoons crushed dried
   hot chiles
10 cloves garlic, minced
2 tablespoons each grated
   fresh ginger and paprika
1 teaspoon shrimp paste (see
   Note, page 68)
1 teaspoon caraway seed
1 teaspoon grated lemon rind
2 tablespoons Madras-style
   curry powder
3 tablespoons sugar
2 tablespoons freshly squeezed
   lemon juice
2 cups light chicken broth
1/4 cup peanut oil
1/2 cup freshly grated coconut
   (see page 12)

In a blender purée all the ingredients. Pour mixture into a saucepan and bring to a boil. Reduce heat and simmer for about 15 minutes, stirring frequently to prevent scorching. Remove from heat and set aside.

Chiles and Garlic in Oil
Greece

This dish is good served as a starter with a loaf of French bread. Each diner tears off a piece of bread and smears it with some of the soft chiles, onions, and garlic. The Greeks drink *retsina* with this; I can't think of anything worse. You need, in my opinion, beer with this rich, oily, and fiery dish. I want lager and I want it cold!

2 large red bell peppers, seeded and sliced into 1/4-inch rings or 3 fresh pimientos, with stems
6 to 8 fresh hot chiles, preferably a mixture of red, green, and yellow, with stems
3 long Italian chiles, with stems
6 to 8 small boiling onions
20 large cloves garlic
1 large onion, cut into 1/2-inch rings
Fresh dill (see Note)
2 to 3 cups olive oil

Place all vegetables in a skillet (with a tight-fitting lid) large enough to hold them in a single layer. Lay dill on top and pour in enough olive oil to cover vegetables in pan.

Place over moderate heat. When oil begins to simmer, reduce heat to lowest possible setting, turn vegetables over once, cover, and cook until boiling onions are quite soft (45 minutes to 1 hour). If you have an electric stove, the lowest setting may not be low enough and you may need to use a heat diffuser.

When vegetables are done, remove from heat, leave covered, and serve when cool.

Serves 6

NOTE—6 flower heads of large mature pickling dill (usually available late summer or autumn) or 1/2 bunch baby dill (sometimes called bouquet dill*) tied together as for bouquet garni.*

Fried Eggplant with Yogurt
Turkey

Remember that not all heat comes from the genus *Capsicum*. Garlic, particularly raw garlic, can be hot indeed. This dish from my friend Leyla combines garlic with eggplant, bell peppers, and yogurt.

1 large eggplant
1/2 cup unbleached all-purpose flour
1/2 teaspoon baking powder
Pinch salt
1 cup (approximately) beer
1 tablespoon olive oil
Light-flavored vegetable oil, for frying
1 each medium green and red bell pepper, seeded and cut into 1-inch-wide strips
1 medium onion, cut into bite-sized pieces
1 cup (8 oz) plain yogurt
15 to 20 cloves garlic, minced
6 or 8 pitted black olives, for garnish
1 lemon, cut into 6 to 8 wedges, for garnish

Cut about 1/2 inch from top and bottom of eggplant. With a sharp knife, peel eggplant lengthwise in strips, making a

Continued

striped pattern of peeled and unpeeled areas, each about 1 inch wide. Cut eggplant cross-wise into 1/4-inch slices. Cover and set aside.

Mix together flour, baking powder, and salt. Whisking constantly, pour in enough beer to form a thin batter, as for pancakes. Add olive oil and whisk again.

In a large, heavy frying pan, heat about 1/2 inch of oil. When it is hot enough for frying but not smoking, dip a slice of eggplant into batter and fry on both sides until golden brown. If it seems to be browning too quickly, reduce heat, wait a moment, then fry another slice of batter-dipped eggplant. When temperature is correct, fry dipped slices of eggplant a few at a time, drain off excess oil, and set aside to keep warm.

Add peppers to oil and fry just until skin begins to blister. Drain and set aside. Then add onion and fry, tossing in oil, until pieces are heated through. Drain and set aside with egg-plant to keep warm.

In a blender purée yogurt and garlic until garlic is totally dissolved.

To serve, arrange slices of eggplant in a circle around the rim of a serving dish. Scatter onion and bell pepper over eggplant and drizzle yogurt-garlic sauce over all. Garnish with olives and lemon wedges. Serve at once.

Serves 6 as a side dish, 10 to 12 as a party appetizer

Hotter-than-Hell Sichuan Stir-Fry
China

The Chinese cuisine served in the United States has come a long way from the innocuous combinations served up in the chop-suey palaces of yesterday. For evidence, try this tingling tantalizing stir-fry. For a fire extinguisher, try Chinese beer; they are among the world's best brews.

Sichuan Savory Sauce (recipe
  follows)
12 to 15 very small slim dried
  red chiles
1/4 cup peanut oil
1/4 cup chicken broth
2 cloves garlic, thinly sliced
1 teaspoon slivered fresh
  ginger
2 medium onions, cut into bite-
  sized wedges

1/2 pound broccoli florets,
  blanched
1 each large green and red bell
  pepper, seeded and cut into
  thin strips
1/2 cup canned water chest-
  nuts, drained
1/2 pound snow peas, trimmed
2 medium tomatoes, cut into 8
  wedges
Steamed rice, for accompani-
  ment

Make Sichuan Savory Sauce.

Put chiles in a small bowl and cover with boiling water. Let sit until water cools. Drain. In a large wok over low heat, heat oil. Add drained chiles, reduce heat to lowest possible setting and simmer until soft (45 minutes to 1 hour).

Add broth and turn heat to high. When hot, add garlic, ginger, and onions, and stir-fry for about 1 minute. Add broc-coli and stir-fry until heated through but still crisp. Add remaining ingredients except rice and stir-fry until heated through but still crisp.

Spoon out excess liquid and discard. Add sauce and stir-fry to coat all vegetables. Serve with steamed rice.

Serves 6

Sichuan Savory Sauce

1/2 cup chicken broth
1/4 cup rice vinegar
1/4 cup dark brown sugar
1/4 cup soy sauce
1 1/2 teaspoons tomato paste
4 to 6 cloves garlic, minced
1 tablespoon grated fresh
   ginger
1/2 teaspoon dry mustard
1 teaspoon crushed dried hot
   chiles, or more to taste
2 tablespoons hoisin sauce
1 teaspoon cornstarch dissolved in 1 tablespoon water
   or chicken broth

In a blender purée all the ingredients except cornstarch mixture. Pour purée into a saucepan and bring to a boil. Immediately reduce heat to simmer and cook for 10 minutes, stirring occasionally to prevent sticking. Add cornstarch mixture and simmer until sauce is thickened and translucent. Set aside.

Chiles en Nogada
Mexico

I usually serve these stuffed chiles on Cinco de Mayo, Mexican independence day. It is altogether fitting, since the red, green, and white of the ingredients are the colors of the Mexican flag.

1 cup each grated sharp
   Cheddar cheese and grated
   Swiss cheese
1 cup ricotta
1 1/2 cups finely shredded
   cooked lean ham
1 tablespoon finely minced
   seeded fresh hot chiles, or
   more to taste
1/2 cup dried currants
1/2 cup slivered blanched
   almonds
1 tablespoon dark brown sugar
1/2 teaspoon ground cinnamon
1/8 teaspoon each ground
   cloves and ground cumin
Salt, to taste
Minced small fresh hot chiles,
   to taste (optional)
8 canned whole peeled green
   chiles
Oil, for coating pan
Whipped Cream Sauce (recipe
   follows)
2 tablespoons fresh pomegranate seeds, for garnish
1 tablespoon coarsely chopped
   cilantro, for garnish

In a large bowl mix together all ingredients except salt, fresh chiles, canned chiles, oil, sauce, and garnishes. Taste and adjust seasonings. Preheat oven to 350° F.

Drain canned chiles and separate them on a flat work surface. Run a finger inside each chile to open, being careful not to tear. Gently pack each chile with stuffing. Place stuffed chiles on a lightly oiled baking dish. Bake until cheeses have melted (no more than 10 minutes). Remove from oven and arrange on a serving platter. Make Whipped Cream Sauce.

To serve, spoon sauce over stuffed chiles. Garnish with pomegranate seeds and cilantro and serve immediately.

Serves 4 to 6

Whipped Cream Sauce

1 cup (1/2 pt) whipping cream
1 cup blanched almonds,
    ground to a powder
1 teaspoon sugar
1/4 teaspoon ground cinnamon
1/4 cup tequila

Whip cream until it holds peaks. Gently fold in almonds, sugar, cinnamon, and tequila.

Okra and Chiles
Tex-Mex Cuisine

Okra is a vegetable that needs to be cooked gently and quickly to retain its fresh crisp quality. It should be al dente. The cooking time for okra will vary greatly depending on size, age, and growing conditions.

2 tablespoons lard
1 1/2 teaspoons chili powder
1/2 teaspoon ground cumin
1/2 teaspoon mixed dried
    herbs (see page 13)
6 cloves garlic, minced
2 medium onions, sliced into
    rings
2 tomatoes, chopped
6 to 8 small fresh hot chiles,
    cut into thin rings
1 large bell pepper, seeded and
    cut into thin strips
1 pound okra, stemmed

Salt and coarsely ground black
    pepper, to taste
1/3 cup grated sharp Cheddar
    cheese
2 bacon strips, crisply fried
1 small fresh hot chile, seeded
    and cut into thin rings

Preheat oven to 350° F. In a large, heavy skillet, heat lard. When lard is hot but not smoking, add chili powder, cumin, herbs, and garlic, and stir rapidly for about 1 minute. Add onions and toss. Add tomatoes and stir to mix well. Stir in the 6 to 8 chiles, bell pepper, and okra. Reduce heat to simmer, cover, and cook until okra is tender but not mushy. Season to taste with salt and pepper.

Transfer mixture to a casserole or other heatproof serving dish. Sprinkle with cheese. Crumble bacon and sprinkle over cheese. Scatter seeded chile over top. Bake until cheese has melted and begun to brown (about 10 minutes). Serve at once.

Serves 4 to 6

Green Beans in Mustard Vinaigrette
Creole Cuisine

A mustard, garlic, and horseradish vinaigrette gives everyday green beans a zesty new dimension.

Mustard Vinaigrette (recipe
    follows)
1 1/2 pounds green beans, cut
    into lengthwise slivers
1 teaspoon capers, drained, for
    garnish
1 teaspoon chopped canned
    pimiento, drained, for
    garnish

Make Mustard Vinaigrette.
    Fill a large saucepan with water and bring to a boil. Add beans and cook until water returns to a boil. Remove beans with a slotted spoon, drain, and put into cold running water until cool. Bring pan of water to a boil again, add beans again, and boil until tender (about 3 minutes). Drain and place on a serving plate. Pour vinaigrette over and garnish with capers and pimiento. Serve hot or cold.

Serves 6

Mustard Vinaigrette

1 teaspoon dry mustard
1/4 cup olive oil
6 cloves garlic, finely minced
1 teaspoon prepared horseradish or grated fresh horseradish to taste
1/4 cup red wine vinegar
1 teaspoon sugar
1 tablespoon minced fresh parsley
1/2 teaspoon coarsely ground black pepper

In a small bowl mix dry mustard with oil, using back of a spoon to smooth any lumps. In a jar with a tight-fitting lid, combine mixture with remaining ingredients, and shake vigorously.

Leeks in Creole Vinaigrette
Creole Cuisine

Leeks, an outstanding vegetable on their own, are made even better by this zesty yet subtle Creole vinaigrette.

4 to 6 medium leeks
3 tablespoons red wine vinegar
1 teaspoon paprika
1 teaspoon Dijon mustard with seeds
1/2 teaspoon cayenne pepper
1/4 teaspoon sugar, or to taste
8 to 10 teaspoons olive oil
Salt and coarsely ground black pepper, to taste

Trim root end from leeks and trim off all but 4 to 6 inches of green tops. Split leeks in half lengthwise. Rinse well under cold running water. Fill a large saucepan with water and bring to a boil. Gently drop in leeks and leave until water returns to a boil. Drain immediately and place leeks under cold running water until they are cold. Refill pan and bring water to a boil. Add blanched leeks, reduce heat to simmer, and continue to cook until leeks are tender but not mushy (no more than 5 minutes). Test doneness by cutting off a bit of green and tasting it. Drain and soak in running water until cold. Drain and set aside.

In a medium bowl mix well with a fork, vinegar, paprika, mustard, cayenne, and sugar. With a fork or wire whisk, blend in olive oil, a few drops at a time, until a thickish sauce is formed. Season to taste with salt and pepper.

To serve, arrange leeks attractively on a serving plate and drizzle with vinaigrette. Refrigerate for at least 1 hour before serving.

Serves 4 to 6

Chorizo-and-Cheese Potato Pancake
Mexico

My great-great-ever-so-great-grandfather was Johan Wyss, the author of *Swiss Family Robinson*. I still have distant cousins in and about Bern, and on my first trip to Switzerland, they introduced me to *rösti*, a traditional potato dish of that region. Some years later while staying with a friend in Oaxaca, Mexico, I was amazed to be served for breakfast one morning a rösti, topped with perfectly prepared sunny-side-up eggs. Well, it wasn't quite a rösti. If anything, it was better: Sandwiched between the crisp golden outer layer of potato was a layer of zesty cheese, chiles, and chorizo. It was a grand way to start a day. This breakfast dish is traditionally served topped with fried eggs and accompanied with salsa in a bowl.

4 medium potatoes
2 or 3 links chorizo (see page 95)
1 medium onion, minced
6 to 8 cloves garlic
4 small fresh hot chiles, seeded and cut into thin rings

Continued

1/2 cup sliced mushrooms
1/4 teaspoon ground cumin
Oil, for frying
1/2 cup grated sharp Cheddar
*   cheese*
2 green onions, including tops,
*   minced*
1 teaspoon minced cilantro
Salt and coarsely ground black
*   pepper, to taste*

Peel potatoes and put into a pan large enough to hold them comfortably. Cover with water and parboil until a small sharp knife can easily pierce the outer 1/4 inch but meets with considerable resistance farther in (10 to 15 minutes). Drain, rinse in cold water, and set aside to drain.

Remove casings from chorizo, place meat in a heavy skillet over moderate heat, and sauté lightly (no more than 5 minutes). Add onion, garlic, and chiles, and sauté until soft (2 to 3 minutes). Add mushrooms and cumin and sauté until vegetables are tender (2 to 3 minutes). Remove chorizos and vegetables from heat and set aside.

Generously oil a large skillet, at least 9 inches in diameter, and put over high heat. Meanwhile, shred potatoes on the large holes of a grater. When pan is hot, add half of the shredded potatoes and distribute evenly. With the back of a large spoon or a spatula, pat potatoes down so that they are somewhat compressed and even. Reduce heat to medium and fry potatoes undisturbed for about 2 minutes.

Sprinkle surface of potatoes evenly with chorizo and vegetable mixture. Sprinkle with cheese, then green onions and cilantro. Season to taste with salt and pepper. Cover with the remaining grated potatoes. Make sure that potatoes are evenly distributed and all cheese is covered. With the palm of your hand, flatten and even potatoes. Cook until golden brown (about 5 minutes), then lift an edge with a spatula and check for doneness. Remove pan from heat and set on a flat work surface. Cover pan with a flat plate large enough to cover surface completely. Holding plate and pan firmly, invert and remove pan so that potato cake is browned side up on plate. Wipe any bits of food from pan, oil again, and reheat. Carefully slide potato cake, raw side down, into hot pan and cook until done (about 10 minutes). Slide onto a heated serving plate. Serve hot.

Serves 6

Hominy in Chile Sauce
Native American Cuisine

A food dislike is a perfectly valid emotion. You try it, you hate it, and you say, "Thank you very much. That was an interesting experiment and I think I'll pass on seconds." That is reasonable.

I hate hominy. There aren't many things that I don't like, but I will not willingly eat most people's potato salad or most people's pineapple-upside-down cake, I hate gin, and I hate hominy. I get a tight feeling in my throat when I smell the stuff. My parents, however, loved it and would have it when I wasn't home.

Hominy was developed by Native Americans. The dry kernels of corn were soaked in a solution of lye until they had swollen to more than twice their size. Then the lye was removed with fresh water baths, resulting in large, soft, tender kernels of corn that could be prepared in a number of ways.

I, of course, don't like any of them, but for those of you who enjoy the stuff, I think you will enjoy this recipe of Southwest Native American origins with a few white man's additions.

Hominy Chile Sauce (recipe follows)
1 can (29 oz) hominy, drained
1/2 cup each grated sharp Cheddar cheese and grated Swiss cheese
6 to 8 pitted black olives, thinly sliced
1 tablespoon chopped cilantro

Prepare Hominy Chile Sauce. Preheat oven to 350° F.

Stir hominy into sauce and pour into an ovenproof serving dish. Toss together grated cheeses and scatter over top of hominy. Add olives and cilantro over all and bake until cheese has melted and is beginning to bubble and brown (10 to 15 minutes). Serve hot.

Serves 4 to 6

Hominy Chile Sauce

1/4 cup lard
10 cloves garlic, minced
2 large onions, chopped
1 large bell pepper, seeded and chopped
6 small fresh hot chiles, cut into thin rings
4 large tomatoes, chopped
1/2 teaspoon mixed dried herbs (see page 13)
1 bay leaf
1/2 teaspoon each ground cumin and dried oregano
1 teaspoon sugar
2 tablespoons minced cilantro
1/2 teaspoon coarsely ground black pepper
1 can (6 oz) pitted black olives, drained
Salt, to taste
Crushed dried hot chiles (optional)

In a heavy skillet over high heat, heat lard. Add garlic and onions and sauté until lightly browned. Add bell pepper, fresh chiles, tomatoes, herbs, bay leaf, cumin, oregano, sugar, cilantro, and pepper. Stir and bring to a boil. Reduce heat and simmer, stirring occasionally, until a thick sauce is formed. Add olives and salt to taste. If you desire a hotter sauce, add crushed chiles a bit at a time, stirring and simmering for a few minutes after each addition.

VARIATION—Sauté 3 or 4 links of chorizo, cut into 1/2-inch pieces, and stir into hominy and sauce before baking.

Brussels Sprouts in Cheddar-Horseradish Sauce
England

In my travels in Great Britain, I discovered indigenous dishes that are candidates for membership in the Galvanized Gullet: delightful and zesty offerings whose depth of flavor comes from mustard or horseradish. This preparation of brussels sprouts, a British favorite, comes from Shipton-under-Wychwood, Oxfordshire. Be careful not to overcook sprouts.

Cheddar-Horseradish Sauce (recipe follows)
1 1/2 pounds firm brussels sprouts, well trimmed
Parsley sprigs and pimiento, for garnish (optional)

Make Cheddar-Horseradish Sauce.

Fill a large pan with water and bring to a boil. Add brussels sprouts and boil gently until a small sharp knife can readily pierce them (no more than 5 minutes).

Put brussels sprouts in a serving dish and drizzle with sauce. Garnish with parsley sprigs and pimiento (if desired).

Serves 4 to 6

Cheddar-Horseradish Sauce

2 tablespoons butter
2 tablespoons unbleached all-
  purpose flour
1 teaspoon dry mustard
2 cups milk
2 eggs, well beaten
1 cup grated sharp Cheddar
  cheese, preferably white
3 tablespoons prepared horseradish, or grated fresh
  horseradish, to taste
1 1/2 teaspoons minced fresh
  dill weed or 1/2 teaspoon
  dried dill weed
1 teaspoon chopped canned
  pimiento
Salt, to taste

In a medium saucepan over medium heat, melt butter. Add flour and mustard and stir briskly until a paste is formed. Do not let mixture brown; lower heat if necessary. Begin adding milk in a thin stream, whisking constantly. Never let it boil or simmer. Cook over low heat, stirring constantly with a whisk, until mixture is smooth and thickened (7 to 8 minutes). If sauce has lumps, purée it in a blender, and return to saucepan.

Pour half of the mixture into a small bowl and whisk to cool a bit. Whisking constantly, slowly pour beaten eggs into white sauce. When thoroughly incorporated, slowly pour egg mixture into white sauce in saucepan, over low heat, whisking continuously. Whisk until thickened (it may take as long as 20 minutes). If sauce forms lumps or curdles, purée in blender.

When sauce is thickened, smooth, and glossy, add remaining ingredients, stir to blend, and taste for seasoning. Add salt and more horseradish if desired. Set aside and keep warm.

Alu Ka Rayta
India

This is a variation on potato salad. The yogurt, fresh chiles, and a blend of fresh herbs take it out of the ordinary potluck fare.

4 to 5 medium potatoes, or
  1 1/2 to 2 pounds very small
  red-skinned potatoes
3 tablespoons light-flavored
  vegetable oil
1 teaspoon each cumin and
  anise seeds
1 medium onion, chopped
4 cloves garlic
3 small fresh hot chiles, preferably red, green, and yellow,
  cut into thin rings
1 cup (8 oz) plain yogurt
2 tablespoons minced fresh
  coriander
1 tablespoon minced fresh mint
1/4 cup minced fresh parsley
2 green onions, minced
Salt, to taste

If using medium potatoes, cut into 1/2-inch slices; if using red-skinned potatoes, leave whole. Cover potatoes with water and boil until tender but still showing some resistance when pierced with the point of a small, sharp knife (15 to 20 minutes). Drain and peel.

In a heavy skillet or wok over high heat, heat oil. Add cumin and anise seed and stir until they begin to crack and pop, almost like popcorn. Add onion, garlic, and chiles. Stir-fry until onions are translucent but not browned (2 to 3 minutes). Add potatoes and stir-fry until they are evenly coated with spice mixture and lightly browned (no more than 5 minutes).

Put into a serving bowl and add yogurt, coriander, mint, parsley, and green onions. Stir and season to taste with salt. Chill for at least 1 hour before serving.

Serves 4 to 6

Aviyal
India

When I assembled this recipe for stir-fried vegetables in Coconut Masala, I chose produce that was appealing and available at the time. When you make it, feel free to pick from whatever vegetables are fresh and abundant at the market or in your own garden.

Coconut Masala
   (recipe follows)
2 tablespoons peanut oil
2 tablespoons water
1 large carrot, cut on the
   diagonal into 1/4-inch slices
   and blanched
10 or 11 stalks broccoli, cut
   into 3-inch lengths and
   blanched
1 small yellow summer squash,
   cut into 1/4-inch slices
2 small slim dried red chiles
1 red bell pepper, seeded and
   cut into thin rings
2 small fresh hot chiles, seeded
   and cut into thin rings
6 green onions, including 3 to 4
   inches of green tops, cut into
   2-inch lengths
3 tablespoons minced fresh
   coriander

Make Coconut Masala.

In a large wok or skillet over high heat, heat oil and the water. Add vegetables, one at a time in the order given, and stir-fry each for 40 to 60 seconds before adding next one. Add coriander and toss. Spoon in masala, toss gently over high heat for about 1 minute, spoon into a bowl, and serve hot.

Serves 6

Coconut Masala

2 cups freshly chopped coconut
   (see page 12)
1 3/4 cups water
2 tablespoons each butter and
   peanut oil
2 tablespoons grated fresh
   ginger
6 cloves garlic, minced
1 medium onion, chopped
1 tablespoon crushed dried hot
   chiles, or more to taste
1 1/2 teaspoons ground
   coriander
1 teaspoon dry mustard
1 teaspoon ground cinnamon
1/2 teaspoon each ground
   turmeric, ground cumin, and
   fennel seed
1 1/2 teaspoons sugar
Salt, to taste

In a blender purée coconut and 1 1/2 cups of the water. Set aside.

In a heavy saucepan or skillet over moderate heat, melt butter with oil. Add ginger, garlic, and onion, and sauté until onion is translucent (2 to 3 minutes). Lower heat if necessary to prevent browning. Stir in remaining ingredients except the remaining 1/4 cup water and salt. Cook for about 1 minute.

Add the remaining water and cook over low heat, stirring constantly, for about 5 minutes. Add coconut purée, stir well, and cook for another 2 to 3 minutes, stirring to prevent scorching. If mixture appears too dry, add more water, 1 tablespoonful at a time, until a very thick sauce results. Season to taste with salt and add more dried chiles if desired.

"All cooks agree with
   this opinion,
No savory dish without
   an onion."
—Nineteenth-century verse

NOODLES, BEANS, RICE, AND BREAD

In this section you will discover my "diet downfall." I like a fresh loaf of sourdough French bread or a hot baked potato dripping with butter. And I like rice! Served forth in almost any way except as rice pudding, rice will lead me off the straight and narrow. So will beans, pasta, lentils, dumplings, potstickers, linguine with clam sauce, pasta with pesto, or tortillas—ah, yes, tortillas. There is nothing like a tortilla dripping melted cheese and salsa; a tortilla spilling minced onion, tomato, and chiles out the end; a crisp flour tortilla doing its best to wrap itself around guacamole, refried beans, salsa, chiles, lettuce, onion, garlic, and lots of freshly minced cilantro. Oh well, sweat pants are more comfortable than blue jeans anyway. Pass the starch, please.

Mee Krob
Thailand

For this famous dish, which combines crisp noodles with shrimp and pork, you will need Asian noodles made from rice or mung-bean flour; do not use noodles made from wheat flour. The appropriate kind are sold under a number of names, including dried *rice-flour noodles, rice sticks, rice vermicelli, cellophane noodles, bean threads, mung-bean-flour noodles,* and *long rice.* Frying noodles in hot oil is guaranteed to make any observer think you are a magician. When the oil is appropriately hot, slide in the noodles and watch them quadruple in size.

8 green onions, for garnish
1 small fresh hot red chile, for garnish
1/2 pound rice-flour or mung-bean-flour noodles
Light-flavored vegetable oil, for deep-frying
2 eggs, lightly beaten
1/2 pound lean pork, cut into 2-inch strips no more than 1/4 inch wide
1 pound cooked tiny shrimp
1 medium onion, chopped
8 cloves garlic, minced
1 tablespoon grated fresh ginger
1/2 tablespoon crushed dried chiles
1/4 cup black bean paste (see Note)
1/2 teaspoon shrimp paste (see Note, page 68)
2 tablespoons tomato paste
3/4 cup sugar
1/2 cup freshly squeezed lemon juice
1 tablespoon lemon rind, cut into thinnest possible slivers
3 small fresh hot chiles, preferably red, seeded and cut into thinnest possible slivers
1/2 pound fresh bean sprouts

Trim roots from green onions and discard. Cut off green tops, leaving 4 inches at white end. Holding each onion by white end, make into a brush: With a small, sharp knife, begin 1 inch from white end and slice through lengthwise; roll onion on a flat surface. Repeat cutting and rolling until it resembles a brush. Place in water and refrigerate until needed. Finely mince remaining green parts and reserve.

Cut flesh of red chile into a fringe and leave attached at stem end. Remove seeds. Reserve.

In a large saucepan bring 2 to 3 quarts of water to a boil and add noodles. Boil until just tender. These thin noodles will cook quickly (3 to 5 minutes). Drain and leave in a colander to dry.

In a large wok heat enough oil for deep-frying. When oil is hot but not smoking, drizzle in about 1 tablespoon of beaten egg with your fingers. It will congeal immediately. When it is lightly browned, remove with a slotted spoon and place on paper towels to drain. Repeat until all egg is used. Set aside.

Let oil become hot again and begin deep-frying noodles, a few at a time. If they do not puff up and become crisp almost immediately, you are probably frying too many at one time. Remove soggy noodles, let oil get hot again and try another, smaller batch. Remove noodles from oil with a slotted spoon as soon as they are golden brown and crisp. Set aside to drain on paper towels. Continue until all noodles are fried.

Remove all but about 1/4 cup of oil from wok. Over medium-high heat, add pork and shrimp and toss in oil for about 2 minutes. Add remaining ingredients, except bean sprouts, in order given. Stir-fry for about 1 minute after each addition. Reduce heat and simmer, stirring constantly, for 15 to 20 minutes.

To assemble, put fried noodles in a deep serving plate and spoon over shrimp and pork mixture. Toss very gently to avoid breaking noodles. Shape into a mound and place bean sprouts in a ring around it. Lay egg "lace" on top of noodle mixture. Set brushes of green onions around edge of dish, sprinkle the minced green onion tops over all, and place fringed red chile on top a cap.

Serves 6

NOTE—*Black bean paste is available at Asian markets.*

Kaeng Chud Woon Sen
Thailand

Fried or boiled, hot or cold, cellophane noodles are a delight. Boiled and served hot, they form the distinctive base for this typical Thai dish.

1/4 cup Chinese cloud ear mushrooms
2 ounces cellophane noodles
2 tablespoons peanut oil
1/4 pound lean pork, cut into very thin 2-inch-long strips
1 tablespoon shrimp paste or anchovy paste (see Note, page 68)
6 cloves garlic, thinly sliced
1 tablespoon finely slivered fresh ginger
1 large onion, cut into thin rings
6 cups light chicken broth
1 cup sliced fresh mushrooms
4 small fresh hot chiles, thinly sliced
3 tablespoons sugar
1/4 cup freshly squeezed lemon juice or more, to taste
Rind of 1/2 lemon, cut into thinnest possible slivers and blanched
2 tablespoons soy sauce
1/2 pound small peeled shrimp
6 green onions, including tops, cut into 3-inch lengths
2 eggs, lightly beaten
Salt, freshly ground black pepper, and cayenne pepper, to taste
1 tablespoon minced fresh cilantro, for garnish

Soak cloud ear mushrooms in warm water to cover for 1 hour. Cover cellophane noodles with boiling water and let sit for 30 minutes.

In a wok over high heat, heat oil until hot; sauté pork until well browned on all sides (3 to 4 minutes). Add shrimp paste and stir pork to coat thoroughly. Add garlic, ginger, and onion, and toss with pork for 1 minute. Set aside.

In a large pot bring broth to a boil. Reduce heat to moderate and add fresh mushrooms, chiles, sugar, lemon juice, lemon rind, soy sauce, and shrimp. Stir in pork and onion mixture. Drain cellophane noodles and cloud ear mushrooms, add to pot, and gently stir. Simmer for about 2 minutes. Add green onions and, stirring very gently, drizzle in beaten egg, a bit at a time. Season to taste with salt, pepper, and cayenne. As soon as egg is set, transfer to a serving dish and sprinkle with cilantro.

Serves 6

Hot Potstickers
China

The popularity of potstickers, among other Chinese dishes, shows how sophisticated American tastes for Chinese food have become. These spicy stuffed dumplings arrived with immigrants from the northern provinces of China.

1/2 cup unbleached all-purpose flour, plus flour for dusting
1/4 cup water, or more as needed for dough
1/4 cup peanut oil
Hot Potsticker Filling (recipe follows)
1 cup chicken broth

In a medium bowl mix together thoroughly with a fork flour, the water, and 1 tablespoon of the peanut oil. If dough is not soft and pliable, add more water, 1 teaspoon at a time, until dough is soft and comfortable to work with. Knead on a lightly floured surface until soft and glossy.

Form into a long, thin log 1 inch in diameter. Cut into 1/2-inch chunks. Place each piece on a lightly floured surface and flatten it with the palm of your hand. Then, using a lightly floured rolling pin, roll each piece of dough into a circle about 3 inches in diameter. When finished, stack rounds lightly and cover with a slightly dampened cloth to keep them from drying out while you make filling.

Make Hot Potsticker Filling.

Put about 1 tablespoon filling in the center of each round of pastry. Fold pastry in half and press edges together with thumb and forefinger. Then fold over edge to seal. Secure by either crimping with fingers or laying pastry on a flat surface and sealing with tines of a fork. Fill all rounds.

In a heavy cast-iron skillet over high heat, heat 2 tablespoons of the oil. Lay pastries in oil and fry undisturbed for 2 minutes. Pour in broth, reduce heat to simmer, cover, and cook until almost all liquid is absorbed (about 10 minutes). Remove lid, add the remaining oil, swirl in pan to cover all potstickers and continue to fry, uncovered, for about 2 minutes. Scoop from pan with a spatula and put on a serving plate brown side up.

Makes 2 dozen Potstickers

Hot Potsticker Filling

1/2 pound ground lean pork
1/2 cup minced cooked cabbage
1/2 cup minced onion
6 cloves garlic, minced
1 1/2 teaspoons finely grated fresh ginger
1 teaspoon crushed dried hot chiles, or more to taste
1/4 teaspoon five-spice powder
1 tablespoon brown sugar, or more to taste
1 tablespoon cornstarch
1 egg
2 tablespoons soy sauce
4 green onions, including tops, finely minced
1/4 cup minced fresh parsley
1/4 teaspoon coarsely ground black pepper, or more to taste
Oil, for frying

In a large bowl mix together thoroughly all ingredients except oil. Make a small patty and fry in a bit of oil to test for seasonings. Add more chiles, pepper, or sugar to taste and test again.

Steamed Chile Noodle
Chinese-American Cuisine

When this giant noodle is sliced on the diagonal and served hot with Asian sesame oil, chile oil, and soy sauce, it makes an excellent appetizer or side dish.

1 cup unbleached all-purpose flour, plus flour for dusting
1/4 cup water, or more as needed for dough
1 tablespoon peanut oil
2 green onions, including tops, finely minced
1/4 cup finely minced cooked lean ham
1 1/2 teaspoons finely minced fresh hot chile
Light-flavored vegetable oil, for moistening
Asian sesame oil, for accompaniment
Chile oil and soy sauce, for accompaniment (optional)

Mix well with a fork, flour, the water, and peanut oil. If dough is too dry, add more water, 1 teaspoon at a time, until a soft, workable dough is formed. Knead well on a lightly floured board. Divide into 4 to 6 equal pieces. Place each piece on work surface and, using as little flour as possible, roll out very thin, no more than 1/16 inch.

Try to keep as close to a rectangle as possible.

Sparingly sprinkle half of noodle surface with green onions, ham, and chiles. Fold in half and roll again to press ingredients into dough and to press halves of dough together. Turn dough over and roll again. With a sharp knife or pizza wheel, trim it into a rectangle. Put a few drops of vegetable oil on surface and spread evenly over surface. Turn dough over and oil other side. Roll up dough, jelly-roll fashion, in the direction that will produce longest noodle roll. Place on a plate and prepare remaining pieces of dough. When all are finished, put them in a Chinese steamer placed over boiling water in a wok or in a large pot. Cover and steam for 30 minutes.

To serve, place on a heated plate and slice on the diagonal into 1-inch chunks. Serve hot with heated sesame oil for dipping. Also offer bowls of soy sauce and chile oil (if desired).

Makes 4 to 6 large Noodles

Udon
Japan

Shiitake mushrooms, *udon* noodles, *nori* (sheets of dried seaweed), and *katsuobushi* (dried bonita flakes)—all unique to Japanese cuisine—are combined in this dish of noodles in a stock redolent with chiles and ginger. Good solid peasant fare, it is excellent for a cold day or for clearing the sinuses. Serve with chopsticks and additional black and cayenne pepper for diners to add if they want to make this fiery dish even hotter. Beer is a must to cool down this one.

3 large shiitake mushrooms
1 package (14 oz) udon noodles
6 cups light chicken broth
2 tablespoons katsuobushi (see Note)
6 cloves garlic, crushed
1 onion, quartered
1 tablespoon chopped fresh ginger
2 tablespoons crushed dried chiles, or more to taste
1 tablespoon sugar
3 sheets nori
Salt and freshly ground pepper, to taste

Continued

Oil, for coating pan
2 eggs, lightly beaten
3 green onions, finely chopped
  small
1 small fresh hot red chile,
  seeded and cut into thinnest
  possible strips
1 small fresh hot green chile,
  seeded and cut into the
  thinnest possible strips
1 cup tofu cubes (1/2 in.)
12 snow peas, stemmed and cut
  lengthwise into thin slivers

Soak mushrooms in warm water to cover for 1 hour. Drain and set aside. In a large saucepan bring 2 to 3 quarts of water to a boil and add noodles. Cook at a rapid boil until noodles are soft but not mushy (about 10 minutes). Drain, rinse in cold water, and set aside.

In a large pot, put broth, katsuobushi, garlic, onion, ginger, dried chiles, sugar, and 2 sheets of the nori, and bring to a boil. Reduce heat to low and cook for 45 minutes. Season to taste with salt, pepper, and more dried chiles. Cook for another 10 minutes.

Strain broth, return to pot, bring to a boil, and add noodles. Reduce heat and simmer for 5 minutes. Cut mushrooms into quarters. In a lightly oiled omelet pan, make eggs into two or three small rolled omelets. Remove to a flat surface and sliver finely. Crumble the remaining sheet of nori. Add eggs, nori, and remaining ingredients to noodles and broth. Stir gently and simmer for another minute before serving. Serve hot.

Serves 4 to 6

NOTE—*If katsuobushi is unavailable, you may substitute 1 cup fish scraps, often called* chowder scraps, *available from fish markets.*

Pasta e Fagioli
Italy

With red beans in the center and green pasta on the outside, this dish of Italian inspiration is a visual as well as a gastronomic masterpiece.

1 cup dried pinto beans
Red Sauce (recipe follows)
1 1/2 pounds vermicelli or
  angel's hair pasta
1 teaspoon olive oil
Green Sauce (recipe follows)

In a large saucepan cover beans with water and bring to a boil. Reduce heat to moderate and cook until beans are tender. You may have to add more water occasionally. Drain beans and set aside.

Make Red Sauce.

In a large pot of rapidly boiling water, cook pasta until just tender. Drain, return to pot, add olive oil, and cover. Leave until ready to assemble dish.

Make Green Sauce.

Add drained beans to Red Sauce and cook just long enough to heat beans thoroughly. Pile beans and sauce into center of a large serving platter. Use tongs to arrange pasta around edge of beans. Drizzle Green Sauce over pasta and serve.

Serves 6

Red Sauce

4 slices bacon
2 tablespoons olive oil
10 cloves garlic, chopped
1 large onion, chopped
1 tablespoon crushed dried
  chiles
3 small fresh hot red chiles,
  sliced into thin rings
1 large bell pepper, seeded and
  chopped
4 large tomatoes, chopped

1/2 teaspoon mixed dried
  herbs (see page 13)
1 tablespoon sugar
1/2 cup dry red wine
Salt and freshly ground black
  pepper, to taste

In a large, heavy skillet, fry bacon until crisp. Remove from pan and set aside. Heat olive oil in pan, then add garlic and onion. Sauté gently until onion is soft but not browned (2 to 3 minutes). Add remaining ingredients and bring to a boil, stirring frequently. Reduce heat to simmer and cook until a thick sauce results (about 45 minutes).

Green Sauce

1/2 cup butter
1 cup fresh basil leaves
1 medium onion, quartered
2 small fresh hot green chiles,
  chopped
1 cup grated mozzarella
1 1/2 teaspoons sugar
Salt and pepper, to taste

In a saucepan melt the butter but do not allow it to brown. In a blender purée butter and remaining ingredients. Return to saucepan used to melt butter and simmer for no more than 5 minutes.

Garbanzos con Chorizo
Basque-American Cuisine

When Basques began immigrating to California, they found that the eastern slope of the Sierra Nevada resembled the geography of their native Pyrenees. In this new land they herded sheep, as their forefathers had done for generations in the tall mountains between France and Spain. Like numerous other immigrant populations who have added to the rich texture of American culture, the Basques brought their cuisine with them and adapted it to accommodate its new environs. The end result may be seen in a number of robust yet subtle dishes such as this chickpea (garbanzo) and sausage stew.

1 1/2 pounds chorizo (see
  Note, page 95)
3 tablespoons olive oil
10 cloves garlic, chopped
3 medium onions, chopped
4 small fresh hot chiles,
  chopped
3 large tomatoes, chopped
2 stalks celery, chopped
1 scant teaspoon mixed dried
  herbs (see page 13)
1 tablespoon sugar
Salt, pepper, and crushed dried
  hot chiles, to taste

4 cups cooked chick-peas
2 tablespoons minced cilantro,
  for garnish

In a heavy skillet over medium heat, sauté chorizo until well browned on all sides. Prick them several times to prevent bursting. When done, set aside.

Add olive oil to pan and sauté garlic and onions until translucent but not browned (2 to 3 minutes). Add remaining ingredients except chick-peas and cilantro and cook over moderate heat, stirring occasionally, until a thick sauce is formed (30 to 45 minutes). Slice chorizo into 1/2-inch chunks and add with chick-peas to sauce. Simmer for 5 minutes before transferring to a serving plate. Sprinkle with cilantro.

Serves 6

New Orleans Red Beans and Rice
Creole Cuisine

Years ago I was a partner in a magnificent, grand disaster. The New Orleans House jazz club featured Victorian decor, New Orleans food and my partner's traditional jazz band. Our venture failed but New Orleans Red Beans and Rice survived.

Like jazz, red beans and rice is a New Orleans tradition: beans for the protein and rice to fill you up. It is also economical, which makes it appealing to struggling musicians. Red beans and rice holds such a firm place in New Orleans culture, and, therefore, in the hearts of New Orleans jazz musicians, that there is hardly a Dixieland musician who can play a sweet note without a good "bate" of red beans and rice under his or her belt. According to legend, the recipe that follows came from the kitchen of Louis Armstrong's mother and it evolved through the efforts of some of the great names in jazz: It is said that Billie Holliday's mama, Lou Waters, Bob Scoby, Kid Ory, and Turk Murphy all had a hand in it. The vocalist in our band, who was married to Bessie Smith's daughter, claimed that Bessie Smith herself helped create this tasty pottage.

Whether this is history or legend, here is not "a" but "the" recipe for New Orleans Red Beans and Rice. Serve it with corn bread, greens, and sweet, sweet jazz—and the saints may come marching in just to dish themselves up a plate.

4 cups small dried red beans or pinto beans (not kidney beans)
1 large onion, quartered
2 bulbs garlic, peeled and halved
1 bay leaf
1 tablespoon mixed pickling spices
2 cups long-grain white rice
Red Bean Sauce (recipe follows)
1 teaspoon oil or butter
Minced fresh parsley, for garnish (optional)

In a large pot put beans, onion, garlic, and bay leaf. Add enough water to cover beans by 3 or 4 inches. Put pickling spices in a large tea ball and add to pot. Bring to a boil and reduce heat to maintain a slow boil or simmer until beans are quite tender (at least 1 hour). Time will vary depending on condition of beans. Add more boiling water from time to time. When beans are tender, turn off heat and let them sit in water while you prepare rice (see Perfect Rice, page 141) and Red Bean Sauce.

Drain beans and add to sauce. Stir and simmer until both are hot (about 10 minutes).

To assemble, put fluffy rice in a ring around the outside of a large, deep serving platter. Pour beans into center. Sprinkle top with parsley (if desired).

Serves at least 12

Red Bean Sauce

1/4 cup bacon drippings or lard (drippings are traditional)
1 pork butt or boneless shoulder (2 1/2 to 3 lb), cut into thin strips 1/4 inch wide and 2 inches long
2 large onions, chopped
10 to 15 cloves garlic, chopped
6 large tomatoes, chopped
1 cup beef broth
4 small fresh hot chiles, cut into thin rings
2 large bell peppers, seeded and cut into thin strips
6 stalks celery, chopped
1 pound mushrooms, sliced
1/2 pound okra, cut into 1/4 inch rings
1/2 cup minced fresh parsley
1/2 tablespoon mixed dried herbs (see page 13)

3 tablespoons chili powder
2 bay leaves
3 tablespoons sugar
1/2 cup dry red wine
Salt, coarsely ground black
    pepper, and crushed dried
    chiles, to taste

In a dutch oven or other large, heavy pan over medium heat, melt drippings. Sauté pork until browned on all sides but not dry and hard (5 to 10 minutes). Add onions and garlic and sauté until onions are soft (2 to 3 minutes). Add tomatoes and stir. Cook for 2 to 3 minutes, then add remaining ingredients except seasonings. Bring to a boil, then reduce heat and simmer, stirring frequently until a thick, rich sauce is formed (1 1/2 to 2 hours). During last half hour of cooking, season to taste with salt, black pepper, and crushed chiles.

PERFECT RICE

Here is a way to make perfect rice every time, as told to me by my Chinese-Hawaiian first father-in-law. This method of cooking rice works no matter how much rice you are cooking or what size or shape pot you are using.

Put rice into a pot with a tight-fitting lid—the tight-fitting lid is essential. Cover rice with water to the level of your first thumb knuckle above the rice, cook uncovered until water is just level with surface of rice. Remove from heat, cover, and leave rice to steam for 45 minutes—no matter how much rice you use. Uncover, add a few drops of oil or a dollop of butter, and fluff with a fork. Cover and leave for an additional 10 to 15 minutes.

You may wonder what the difference is between Cajun and Creole cuisine. Both cuisines grew from the same cultural traditions, use the same ingredients, and are indigenous to southern Louisiana. The main difference is that Creole is primarily a restaurant cuisine, tamed up, domesticated, and formulized, whereas Cajun is still wild and untamed, a home cuisine or, as the natives say, "handmade cookin."

Dirty Rice
Cajun Cuisine

This recipe derives its name from the color and texture imparted by cooking the rice in a rich, flavorful pork liver stock. Don't let the name or the ingredients put you off.

1 pound pork liver
10 cloves garlic, minced
1 large onion, minced
1 tablespoon crushed dried
    chiles
1 tablespoon sugar
6 cups water
Powdered beef bouillon, to
    taste (optional)
2 cups long-grain white rice
1 tablespoon butter
1/2 cup minced fresh parsley
Salt and freshly ground black
    pepper, to taste

Chop liver into small pieces. Put in a large pot with garlic, onion, chiles, and sugar. Add the water and bring to a boil. Reduce heat to simmer, cover with a tight-fitting lid, and cook until liver is practically disintegrated (about 2 hours). Taste liquid; if it seems weak, enrich with powdered beef bouillon to taste.

Add rice, stir, and bring to a boil. Continue to boil until liquid is reduced to top of rice. Reduce heat to lowest possible setting. Add butter, cover, and let sit undisturbed for 45 minutes. Just before serving, add parsley and season to taste with and salt and pepper. Toss lightly and serve hot.

Serves 6 to 8

Persian Orange Rice with Almonds
Iran

Zesty yet refined, this creation displays as much artistry as the fine Persian carpets.

2 large seedless oranges
4 cloves garlic, minced
1 tablespoon grated fresh
  ginger
1 teaspoon (1/2 gram) saffron
1 tablespoon crushed dried
  chiles, or more to taste
1 tablespoon Madras-style
  curry powder
1/2 teaspoon ground cinnamon
3/4 teaspoon minced fresh dill
  or 1/4 teaspoon dried dill
1/4 cup frozen orange juice
  concentrate
3 tablespoons sugar
1/4 teaspoon anise seed
1/2 cup butter
1 cup light chicken broth
2 cups long-grain white rice
1 cup slivered blanched
  almonds
1/2 cup chopped pistachios
1/2 cup minced fresh parsley
Salt and coarsely ground black
  pepper, to taste

Peel oranges. Remove as much of white as possible from inside of rind by scraping gently with a sharp knife. Sliver rind as thinly as possible. Blanch rind and set aside.

Chop oranges. In a blender purée oranges, garlic, ginger, saffron, chiles, curry powder, cinnamon, dill, orange juice, sugar, and anise.

In a large, heavy skillet or casserole with a tight-fitting lid, melt butter. Gently sauté orange rind for 1 minute. Adjust heat to keep butter from burning. Pour in contents of blender and broth and simmer, stirring occasionally, for 5 minutes. Add rice and stir. Smooth top of rice and cook according to directions for Perfect Rice (see page 141).

Stir gently to fluff; add almonds, pistachios, and parsley, and fluff again. Season to taste with salt and pepper. Pile into a serving dish and serve hot.

Serves 4 to 6

Nasi Kuning Lengkap
Indonesia

You may serve this coconut-flavored rice just as it comes out of the pot, or you can make it into a one-dish feast. When served for special occasions in Indonesia, it is molded into a tower and topped with such additions as thin strips of marinated barbecued meat, chicken, shellfish, raw vegetables, cooked vegetables, eggs, peanuts, or toasted coconut. Try various combinations of your own.

1 whole coconut
1/4 cup peanut oil
1 large onion, minced
8 cloves garlic, minced
2 tablespoons each crushed
  dried hot chiles and grated
  fresh ginger
1 tablespoon ground turmeric
1 teaspoon ground cinnamon
1/2 teaspoon fennel seed
1/4 teaspoon ground cloves
1 tablespoon dry mustard
3 tablespoons sugar
3 cups long-grain white rice
4 green onions, minced
Salt and freshly ground black
  pepper, to taste

Open coconut and shred according to instructions on page 12. Set aside.

In a large skillet or casserole over medium-high heat, warm peanut oil. Sauté onion and garlic until onion is translucent but not browned (2 to 3 minutes). Add chiles, ginger, spices, mustard, and sugar, and cook over high heat, stirring constantly, for 2 minutes. Add rice and stir to coat evenly. Cook according to directions for Perfect Rice (see page 141) except when you first uncover pot, gently stir in shredded coconut and green onions. Season to taste with salt and pepper, cover again, and leave for 5 minutes before serving.

Serves 8

Arroz Verde
Mexico

This green rice is an excellent accompaniment for a wide variety of Mexican dishes. Try it with Chicherones con Salsa (see page 76), or any recipe from your own Latino repertoire.

2 large green bell peppers
6 small fresh hot green chiles
5 cups chicken broth
1 cup chopped fresh parsley
1 large onion, chopped
8 cloves garlic, chopped

1/4 teaspoon freshly ground
black pepper
1 1/2 teaspoons sugar
1/2 teaspoon dried oregano
1/4 teaspoon ground cumin
1/4 cup corn or light-flavored oil
2 cups long-grain white rice
Salt, to taste
1/4 cup minced cilantro

Roast bell peppers and chiles over a gas flame or under a broiler until skins blister. Turn to roast all sides. Wrap in a damp towel and leave for 5 minutes. Use towel to rub off scorched bits of skin. Stem, seed, and chop bell peppers and chiles. In a blender purée until smooth, bell peppers, chiles, 1 1/2 cups of the chicken broth, parsley, onion, garlic, pepper, sugar, oregano, and cumin.

In a large, heavy skillet or casserole with tight-fitting lid, heat oil. When oil is hot but not smoking, add rice and stir continuously for a few minutes to coat rice with oil, but not long enough to let it brown. Add vegetable purée and simmer, stirring occasionally, for 5 minutes. Add the remaining broth and bring to a boil. Reduce heat to moderate, add salt to taste, and continue cooking uncovered until liquid

is level with top of rice. Cover and reduce heat to lowest possible setting. Leave undisturbed for 30 minutes. Turn off heat and leave until rice is tender (15 to 20 minutes). Add cilantro and fluff with a fork.

Serves 6

The Cajuns say, "A day without rice is a day without eating." In some Chinese provinces a common greeting translates as, "Is your rice well?" whereas in other areas of China a young woman may be complimented with "She knows rice." "He shares his rice" is a Japanese expression that indicates one's philanthropic value. Argentines will sadly shake their heads when talking of a friend who has hit the skids and say, "Poor man, he has lost his rice."

Pre-Dune Fried Rice
Galvanized Gullet Contribution

Long before his *Dune, Dune, Dune,* and then some more *Dune* days, the late science fiction author Frank Herbert worked for a San Francisco newspaper. He knew a lot about advertising and public relations, and he invited me and my partner to his house to discuss publicity for our New Orleans House jazz club (see New Orleans Red Beans and Rice, page 140).

Now I am not particularly fond of science fiction, so Frank's talents in that direction were lost on me, but he turned out to be one of the finest practitioners of northern Chinese cooking that I have ever had the pleasure to cross chopsticks with. One of the wonderful dishes he served that night was this out-of-this-world stir-fried rice with chiles. The recipe calls for hoisin sauce. If it is unavailable, use 2 additional tablespoons of soy sauce. It's not the same, but it still makes a fine dish.

2 eggs, lightly beaten
1/4 teaspoon each ground ginger, five-spice powder, and sugar
1/8 teaspoon cayenne pepper
Oil, for coating pan
1/2 medium onion
1/4 cup peanut oil
4 cloves garlic, very finely minced
1 teaspoon finely grated fresh ginger
4 cups cooked long-grain white rice
3 tablespoons soy sauce
3 tablespoons hoisin sauce
6 snow peas, steamed and slivered lengthwise into fine threads
6 small fresh hot chiles, seeded and cut into paper-thin rings
1/2 cup cooked lean ham, very finely slivered
2 green onions, including the tops, sliced into paper-thin rings
Salt and freshly ground black pepper, to taste

In a small bowl beat together eggs, ground ginger, five-spice powder, sugar, and cayenne. Using a brush or paper towel dipped in oil, lightly oil an omelet pan. Heat pan over medium heat. Pour in half the egg mixture and form into a rolled omelet. Set aside. Repeat with the remaining egg mixture. Using a sharp knife, sliver omelets and set aside. Slice onion into thinnest rings possible. Cut rings in half once. Set aside.

In a large wok over medium-high heat, warm oil. Add garlic, fresh ginger, and onions, and toss until just heated through (no more than 1 minute). Add rice. Mix together soy and hoisin sauces and add to rice. Stir-fry until rice is evenly coated with sauce.

Add remaining ingredients, including slivered omelet, and toss gently. Cover and let sit without heat for 5 minutes. Toss gently before serving.

Serves 6

BREAD

Salsa Loaf
Family Recipe

This bread is good hot or cold, by itself or as an accompaniment to a meal. It is made by the sponge method, a process of preparing dough for kneading that can take from one to three hours, depending on the temperature of the room and the age of the yeast. The whole recipe requires four to eight hours. Incidentally, you do not have to preheat the oven when making most yeast breads.

1 cup lukewarm water
1 package active dry yeast
1/4 cup sugar
4 cups unbleached all-purpose flour, plus flour for dusting
1/4 cup light-flavored vegetable oil, plus oil for coating pan
1 teaspoon salt
1 cup mild or hot chunky salsa, commercial or homemade (see Salsa Son-of-a-Gun, page 157)
2 tablespoons minced cilantro
4 cloves garlic, minced
1 egg white, lightly beaten (optional)

In a large bowl mix well the water, yeast, and sugar. Add 1/2 cup of the flour, mix, and leave in a warm place. Mixture will become frothy and begin to bubble. Add another cup of flour, the 1/4 cup oil, and salt. Beat well and leave until bubbling and spongy (1 to 3 hours). When mixture is light and spongy, begin adding the remaining 3 cups flour, stirring well after each cup is added. When dough is soft and workable, turn out onto a lightly floured surface and knead thoroughly for about 15 to 20 minutes (see On Kneading, page 146).

When dough is ready, roll out into a rectangle about 1/2 inch thick.

Spread salsa over surface of dough, leaving a 1-inch border all around. Sprinkle cilantro and garlic over salsa. Starting with long edge, roll dough jelly-roll fashion. Pinch length of seam to make a seal. Place seam side down, and wrap roll around itself like the shell of a snail. Set on an oiled baking sheet.

If you want a glossy finish, brush surface with egg white. Leave in a warm place until doubled in bulk (1 to 4 hours).

Time will depend on temperature and humidity of room. Bake at 350° F until loaf is well browned and sounds hollow when tapped lightly (45 minutes to 1 hour).

Makes 1 large round loaf

SALSA LOAF WITH CHEESE
Omit cilantro and garlic. After spreading dough with salsa, sprinkle 1/2 cup of Swiss or mozzarella cheese over surface.

SALSA LOAF WITH CHEESE AND ONIONS
After spreading dough with salsa, sprinkle with 1/2 cup grated sharp Cheddar cheese, 1/2 cup grated Swiss cheese, 1/2 cup minced onion, and 1 teaspoon finely minced fresh dill.

Yewollo Ambasha
Ethiopia

Although an Ethopian specialty, this delicious loaf with its unusual combination of spices is not unlike the *pain d'épice* unique of Dijon, France.

2 packages active dry yeast
2 cups lukewarm water
1/2 cup sugar
1/2 cup butter
2 tablespoons ground coriander
1 teaspoon each ground carda-
  mom and crushed fenugreek
  seed
1/2 teaspoon freshly ground
  black pepper
2 cloves garlic, minced
1/2 cup minced onion
1 tablespoon finely grated fresh
  ginger
1/2 teaspoon each ground
  cinnamon and cayenne
  pepper
1/4 teaspoon ground nutmeg
1/8 teaspoon ground cloves
2 tablespoons paprika
1 teaspoon salt
5 to 6 cups unbleached all-
  purposed flour, plus flour
  for dusting
Oil, for coating pan
Melted butter, for crust (op-
  tional)

In a large bowl mix yeast, the water, and 1 tablespoon of the sugar and let sit while you melt butter. While the butter is cooling, add remaining ingredients, except flour, and oil, to bowl with yeast. Stir well, and add butter. Add 1 cup of the flour, stir well, and leave until bubbling and spongy (1 to 3 hours). When mixture is quite active, begin adding the remaining 4 to 5 cups flour, stirring well after each 1/2 cup. The goal is a soft dough. When enough flour has been added, turn out onto a lightly floured surface and knead well (see On Kneading, following).

Pinch off a small piece of dough about the size of a golf ball and set aside. Form remaining dough into a round shape and place on a lightly oiled baking sheet. With a sharp knife, make a shallow cut in the form of a cross, no more than 1/4 inch deep, across top of loaf. Shape small piece of dough into a ball and set in middle of cross. Let loaf sit in a warm place until doubled in size. Bake at 350° F until crispy and golden brown (50 to 60 minutes). Slide loaf onto a wire rack. If a soft crust is desired, brush with optional butter and wrap with a clean cloth (see On Slicing Hot Bread, page 149).

Makes 1 large round loaf

ON KNEADING
When the flour, water, and yeast have become a soft, workable dough, turn out onto a lightly floured surface. Now using the heels of your hands, you need to knead, and knead, and knead.

When I'm teaching, to illustrate just how much time it takes to knead properly, I put a bit of food coloring on a piece of dough. When the food coloring is completely incorporated into the dough, it is fully kneaded. My students are usually surprised to find kneading takes as long as 20 minutes.

When making yeast breads, the major difference between failure and success is insufficient kneading. However, you must also be careful not to work too much flour into the dough. Keep the work surface very lightly floured and your hands only lightly dusted with flour. If they become too sticky, wash off all the dough, dry thoroughly, and pat with flour again. The dough should be soft and elastic with a satiny sheen.

Chile Corn Bread
Family Recipe

Corn bread at our home has always been a glorious gastronomic experience: light, crumbly, and moist, usually dripping with butter and honey, but occasionally containing other ingredients. Sometimes my mother would fold chunks of very ripe avocado or cheese into the batter. One thing she would not use is milk; for almost all baking, milk is not necessary unless you have someone in the family who really needs the extra calories.

2 cups yellow cornmeal
1/2 cup unbleached all-purpose flour
2 teaspoons baking powder
2 tablespoons chili powder
1/4 cup sugar
Salt, to taste (optional)
1/4 cup light-flavored vegetable oil, plus oil for coating pan
1 cup water
2 eggs, separated

Preheat oven to 350° F. In a bowl beat well all ingredients except egg whites. In a seperate bowl, beat whites until they are high and fluffy and form peaks. Fold gently into corn batter. Oil a 10-inch cast-iron frying pan and pour in batter. Bake until top is well browned and bread is light (40 to 50 minutes). Bread is done when a skewer inserted into center comes out clean.

Makes 1 round loaf

SALSA-BACON CORN BREAD—Just before baking, put 1 cup hot chunky salsa (commercial or homemade, see Salsa Son-of-a-Gun, page 157), by tablespoonfuls, on surface of bread; crumble 3 strips crisply fried bacon and sprinkle on top.

Chile-Cheese Corn Bread
Family Recipe

This variation on the family favorite incorporates sautéed vegetables and cheese.

1 tablespoon light-flavored vegetable oil
3 small fresh hot chiles, cut into thin rings
1 medium onion, cut into thin rings
6 cloves garlic, minced
1/2 cup each grated sharp Cheddar cheese and grated mozzarella cheese
2 tablespoons minced cilantro
1 tablespoon chili powder
1/2 teaspoon sugar
Salt, to taste (optional)

1 recipe Chili Corn Bread, (see preceding recipe)
Oil, for coating pan

Preheat oven to 350° F. In a skillet over medium-high heat, heat oil and add chiles, onion, and garlic. Sauté until soft but not beginning to brown (2 to 3 minutes). In a large bowl toss together the remaining ingredients except Chile Corn Bread and oil for coating pan. Prepare cornbread batter and pour into an oiled 10-inch cast-iron frying pan. Spread sauté vegetables on top of batter and sprinkle with cheese mixture. Bake until top is well browned and bread is light (40 to 50 minutes). Bread is done when skewer inserted into center comes out clean.

Makes 1 round loaf

Injera
Ethiopia

This Ethopian millet bread has the texture of a tortilla. It can be used as both a serving dish and an eating implement, as when served with an Ethiopian stew (*wat*) such as Sik Sik Wat (see page 62).

1 cup millet
1 cup boiling water
2 cups unbleached all-purpose
   flour
1 1/2 teaspoons baking powder
1/4 cup sugar
1/4 cup peanut oil
Salt, to taste
1 cup (approximately) cold
   water
Oil, for coating pan

Put millet in a large bowl and pour the boiling water over it. Let millet sit until the water is cool, then purée in a blender until a smooth paste results. Put paste back into bowl and add remaining ingredients except the cold water and oil for coating pan. Gradually add the cold water, stirring constantly, until batter is the same consistency as for pancakes. The amount will vary greatly, depending on quality of millet.

Heat a large skillet, omelet pan, or griddle, and lightly oil. Surface should not be as hot as it would be for cooking pancakes. Injera should set, not brown. Pour enough batter in pan to coat surface and make a cake about 1/8 inch thick and 9 inches in diameter. Cook over lowest possible heat until surface is dry. If the bottom browns, reduce heat before baking next Injera. As each bread is finished, set on a large plate and cover with a damp cloth. Serve hot.

Makes 6 to 8 breads

Saint Gyles Faire Gingerbread
England

During the late Middle Ages and the Renaissance in England, gingerbread was sold at all great country fairs, each of which had its own recipe. The merchants at any given fair were licensed to sell breads made only from that particular fair's recipe. In my travels in England I have collected over 50 of these gingerbread recipes. They range from light fluffy cakes resembling those we are familiar with in the United States to gummy steamed puddings. All are delicious whether or not they resemble anything we have experienced. This recipe for soft, chewy gingerbread—with the texture of a drop cookie—comes from the fair in Oxford, named after Saint Gyles.

Saint Gyles was the patron saint of beggars and thieves, who were not allowed inside the gates of most cities. Therefore, all fairs named in honor of Saint Gyles were held just outside the walls. The fair at Oxford continues today, though you won't find the goats, pigs, or sheep of yesteryear. Like almost all fairs in England today, it is nothing more than a carnival with rides and shooting galleries. And you have to make do with caramel corn and cotton candy instead of wonderful heady gingerbread.

1 cup dark molasses
1 cup dark brown sugar
1 tablespoon cider vinegar
1/2 cup butter
1 teaspoon baking soda
2 tablespoons ground ginger
1 tablespoon ground cinnamon
1/2 teaspoon anise seed
1/4 teaspoon ground cloves
Pinch salt
3 cups unbleached all-purpose
   flour
Oil, for coating pan

Preheat oven to 350° F. In a large bowl mix well all ingredients except flour and oil for pan. Begin working in flour until it is all incorporated. Hands are the best tool. If necessary add water, a spoonful at a time, to give dough a workable consistency. Work until well blended, then drop by tablespoonfuls onto a lightly oiled baking sheet. Bake until golden brown (about 20 minutes). Remove from pan to cool. When bread is cool, texture should be slightly chewy, not crisp.

Makes about 3 dozen
Gingerbread

Basic Pastry
Family Recipe

Pastry is a personal matter. This is my favorite recipe for a good basic pastry (if you have one you like better, use it). Lard makes the best texture but butter tastes better; combining the two gives you the best of both worlds. If you do not have lard, you may substitute margarine for both the lard and butter, but do not use all butter—it is too soft.

1/3 cup lard
1/3 cup butter
1 1/2 cups unbleached all-purpose
   flour, plus flour for dusting
Pinch of salt
4 or 5 (approximately) table-
   spoons water

With a pastry blender, cut lard and butter into the 1 1/2 cups flour and salt until mixture is powdery. Using a fork, mix rapidly while gradually adding the water to form a soft dough. Turn out onto a lightly floured board and knead dough sparingly, just until it is no longer sticky and will hold together in a ball. Roll out to about 1/8 inch thick and use to line an 8- or 9-inch pan.

Makes one 8- or 9-inch Pie Pastry

ON SLICING JUST-BAKED BREAD
If you are going to eat bread hot from the oven, do not slice it. Just tear off chunks and stuff it into your mouth, with or without butter. If you try to slice hot bread, it will squash and become doughy. If you want to be able to slice a loaf with ease, coat the top of the baked bread with melted butter or margarine, then wrap loaf in a clean cloth and leave until cool. This makes a soft, tender crust that will slice easily. If you want a crunchy crust, let bread cool uncovered on a rack.

CHAPTER THIRTEEN

ACCOMPANIMENTS

The recipes in this section are for a variety of tasty, zesty accompaniments for hot foods. Some accompaniments, such as pickles, can stand alone as nibbles or snacks. Others, such as salsas, mustards, horseradishes, and chutneys, are designed to be served with and enhance other dishes.

ON MAYONNAISE

Have you given mayonnaise any serious thought lately? No? Well, you really should, you know. After all, when something is that good and only requires a little elbow grease, the least you can do is think about it for a while. According to legend, Caesar gave it quite a lot of thought, and so did Cleopatra, and Alexander the Great, Thomas Jefferson, and Mary Queen of Scots.

According to the dictionary, the word *mayonnaise* is French. A different origin is recorded in a story that concerns "Mary, Mary, quite contrary," or Mary Queen of Scots, who, it is said, are one and the same person. We are told that Mary's personal physician invented mayonnaise as a cure for seasickness—mariner's malady or *mal de mer,* which, when corrupted by the English and Celtic tongues, became mayonnaise. (Personally, I can't think of anything less likely to make me feel better when bobbing across the English Channel in a royal barge than a nice oily spoonful of mayonnaise.)

One of my favorite stories says that Caesar, while trekking across the deserts in hot pursuit of Pompey, took time out, right there in the middle of the sand, to invent mayonnaise as a quick energy food for his legions. Perhaps you prefer the story that it was mayonnaise, not her Nile-green eyes and full-blown body, that bound Caesar to Cleopatra.

Another tale declares that, during Alexander's conquest of Persia, his chefs put eggs in the leather bags used to carry olive oil: The thick oil was meant both to cushion the eggs, preventing them from breaking, and to seal the pores of the shells and retard spoilage. The story says that a few of the eggs broke in the oil, anyway, and after a day's jostling in a wooden-wheeled cart, the result was mayonnaise.

My favorite of all mayonnaise stories is true and it happened in London. A friend was so impressed by my just whipping up a bowl while we were chatting over tea that she asked for the recipe. The next morning she called me in tears. She had made batch after batch, she said, and none of them had worked. Did I think that, perhaps, she wasn't boiling the egg long enough?

Basic One-Egg Mayonnaise
Family Recipe

Making mayonnaise is mostly a flexible process; you can vary the ingredients and some of the procedure and you will still produce a fine sauce. However, there is one absolute: you must add the first half of the oil no more than 1/2 teaspoon at a time, mixing thoroughly between additions. This seems to take an interminable time. But just as you are about to give up in despair, voilà, the mixture gets thick and really does look like mayonnaise. At this point, you may begin adding the oil faster.

Which oil you use is up to you; I have used peanut oil, corn oil, safflower oil, and generic oil with equal success. Some people insist on olive oil, but I think it's too heavy. When I want the flavor of olive oil but not the heaviness, I use a blend.

The recipe calls for an egg, but you may use just the yolk or just the white and still get a perfect mayonnaise. Alter the flavorings depending on how the mayonnaise will be used. If it is for a fruit salad, add a little more sugar. If it is for a tuna salad, you probably want more mustard and less sugar.

To mix the mayonnaise, you may use a fork, wire whisk, hand rotary beater, electric beater, or blender. The ingredients may be chilled or at room temperature. However, once made, it must be refrigerated for safe storage; covered, it will keep in the refrigerator for at least one week.

1 egg
1 teaspoon freshly squeezed
lemon juice or cider vinegar
1/4 teaspoon sugar
Salt, to taste
1/2 teaspoon dry mustard
2 cups vegetable oil

In a deep bowl thoroughly blend together egg, lemon juice, sugar, salt to taste, and mustard. Begin adding oil, 1/2 teaspoon at a time, beating well between each addition. When mixture begins to thicken, you may add oil 1 teaspoon at a time; as it continues to thicken, add oil 1 tablespoon at a time. After it is thick, taste and adjust seasonings.

Makes about 2 cups

Aioli de Provence
France

You don't have to fly to Provence to have perfect aioli for your artichokes. Just use this simple recipe for a zesty, velvet-smooth sauce that has various uses—it is also excellent with asparagus and broccoli, or as a topping for omelets.

6 to 8 cloves garlic
1 recipe Basic One-Egg Mayonnaise (see page 152)

Mince garlic very finely. Before making Basic Mayonnaise, put 1/2 cup of the oil in a blender with minced garlic and purée. Set aside. Continue as for basic mayonnaise. When mayonnaise has thickened and plain oil has been incorporated, begin adding oil-garlic mixture.

Makes about 2 cups

VARIATION
Blend 1/3 cup minced fresh parsley, 1/4 cup minced fresh mint leaves, 1/2 cup minced fresh basil leaves, or 2 tablespoons Dijon mustard with the 1/2 cup of oil and the garlic.

FLUFFY AIOLI
Separate egg used to make Basic One-Egg Mayonnaise. Follow directions using only yolk of egg. When aioli is finished, beat white and gently fold in.

CAPSICUM MAYONNAISE
In a blender purée 4 cloves garlic, minced; 3 small fresh hot chiles; and 1/2 cup of the oil used to make Basic One-Egg Mayonnaise. Add to mayonnaise at end of preparation.

HORSERADISH MAYONNAISE
Mix 1/2 cup prepared horseradish, or freshly grated horseradish to taste, with 1/2 cup of the oil used to make Basic One-Egg Mayonnaise. Add to mayonnaise at end of preparation.

Aaron's Salsa Mayonnaise
Family Recipe

My younger son came up with this version. It is good with cold meats and cold boiled potatoes, as a sandwich spread, and as a dip for celery and other raw vegetables.

1/2 cup Basic One-Egg Mayonnaise (see page 152)
1/2 cup mild or hot chunky salsa, commercial or home-made (see Salsa Son-of-a-Gun, page 157)
6 cloves garlic, finely minced
2 tablespoons finely minced onion
1 teaspoon finely minced small seeded fresh hot chile

In a bowl mix all ingredients together well.

Makes about 1 cup

Dana's Chutney Mayonnaise
Family Recipe

Devised by my daughter, this mayonnaise goes well with cold ham, cold meat pies, or pasties. Try it with minced ham or chicken, onion, and lettuce in pita bread or a flour tortilla.

1/2 cup Basic One-Egg Mayon-
naise (see page 152)
1/2 cup mango chutney
1/4 teaspoon cayenne pepper
1/2 teaspoon finely grated
fresh ginger

In a blender purée all ingredients until smooth. Refrigerate for a few hours before using.

Makes about 1 cup

Firehouse Mustard
England

Mustard and horseradish are used often in England to create sauces and side dishes guaranteed to add interest to any meal. This mustard is particularly good with cold ham.

3 tablespoons dry mustard
1/2 teaspoon each cayenne
pepper and grated fresh
ginger

1 tablespoon dark brown sugar
1/4 cup cider vinegar, or to
taste

In a bowl mix together mustard, cayenne, ginger, and sugar. Gradually add cider vinegar, stirring constantly until mustard is the desired consistency.

Makes about 1/4 cup

Pub Mustard
England

This is extremely good with cold meats, cold meat pies, and pasties—the foods served in an English pub. Use brown beer for this mustard, not the darker porter, stout, or Guinness.

1/3 cup dry mustard
1 teaspoon sugar
Salt, to taste
1 teaspoon malt vinegar, or
more to taste
1/4 cup (approximately) brown
beer, or to taste

In a small bowl mix together mustard, sugar, and salt to taste. Add vinegar and begin stirring with a fork. Gradually pour in beer, stirring constantly. When mustard is a thick paste, or the consistency you desire, mix well, cover, and set

aside for 30 minutes. Check it for consistency. You may find that after it sits you will want to add a bit more beer. Add more salt and vinegar if you want a zestier, piquant flavor.

Makes about 1/2 cup

Packwood Ranch Mustard
Family Recipe

The ranch hands on my family's Packwood Ranch loved to spread this mustard liberally on cold beef or cold chicken pie.

3 tablespoons mustard seed
1/3 cup dry mustard
1 teaspoon sugar
1/4 cup cider vinegar, or to
taste

In a blender or with a mortar and pestle, crush mustard seed. Put in a bowl with dry mustard and sugar. Stirring constantly, add enough cider vinegar to make into a spreadable paste.

Makes about 1/2 cup

Wine Mustard
California

This heady concoction is an excellent accompaniment to cold meats and sharp cheeses.

1/3 cup dry mustard
1 teaspoon ground turmeric
3 cloves garlic, pressed
1/4 cup cream sherry, or to taste

In a bowl mix together mustard, turmeric, and garlic. Add enough cream sherry to form a paste.

Makes about 1/2 cup

Soy Mustard
Hawaiian-Japanese Cuisine

This mustard is excellent with sushi, sashimi, dim sum, and with noodles and cold meats of just about any origin.

1/3 cup soy sauce
1 tablespoon grated fresh ginger
2 tablespoons dry mustard
2 tablespoons sugar
6 cloves garlic
1/4 teaspoon coarsely ground black pepper

In a blender purée until liquefied all ingredients except black pepper. Strain. Add pepper and stir.

Makes about 1/3 cup

Vinegar Horseradish
England

When using fresh horseradish in a recipe, it is best to make only the quantity you are going to use that day or the horseradish loses its zap. I make fresh horseradish by two methods: with vinegar and with cream. Both are quite good; it's just a matter of preference.

1/2 cup grated fresh horseradish
1/4 cup cider vinegar, or more to taste
1 teaspoon sugar, or more to taste

In a blender purée all ingredients until smooth. If you want a thinner mixture, add more vinegar, 1 teaspoon at a time. Add more sugar to taste.

Makes about 1/2 cup

HORSERADISH CREAM
Substitute 1/4 cup or more heavy cream for vinegar.

Dill and Horseradish Sauce
England

This sauce is exceptionally good with beef and whitefish. In my opinion it will absolutely destroy salmon, but then there are very few things I like with salmon other than salmon.

1/2 cup Basic One-Egg Mayonnaise (see page 152)
3 tablespoons prepared horseradish or grated fresh horseradish, to taste
1/2 tablespoon minced fresh dill
1/2 teaspoon sugar

In a bowl mix together all ingredients and let sit overnight before using.

Makes about 1/2 cup

Sterling's Easy Sauce Diablo
Family Recipe

An invention of my older son, this sauce is very good with beef, hot or cold.

1/4 cup soy sauce
2 tablespoons catsup
1 tablespoon dry mustard
1 1/2 teaspoons sugar
4 cloves garlic, finely minced
1/8 teaspoon cayenne pepper
1 1/2 teaspoons olive oil

In a bowl thoroughly mix together all ingredients.

Makes about 1/2 cup

Good Husband and Huswife,
    when summer is done,
Go look to thy larder
    that waste be there none.
Let salt, spice and brine
    do their work best,
Eat fresh what you may,
    then pickle the rest.
—Thomas Tusser, 16th century

Môlho de Pimenta e Limão
Brazil

Serve this hot and zesty chile and lemon sauce with pork, chicken, or beef. It is especially good with grilled foods.

6 pickled hot chiles, minced
1/2 onion, minced
1 tablespoon minced garlic
1/2 cup minced green onions,
    including tops
1 tablespoon minced cilantro
1/2 cup freshly squeezed lemon
    juice
1 teaspoon sugar

In a bowl combine all ingredients and stir. Let sit at least 1 hour before serving.

Makes about 1 1/2 cups

Capsicum-Ginger Glaze
Family Recipe

This is an excellent marinade or glaze for a variety of meat or poultry dishes.

1/4 cup frozen orange juice
    concentrate
1 medium onion, chopped
4 cloves garlic, chopped
2 tablespoons grated fresh
    ginger
3 small fresh hot chiles, seeded
1/4 teaspoon ground cinnamon
1/4 teaspoon freshly ground
    black pepper
1/4 cup Rhine wine
1/4 cup light-flavored vegetable
    oil
Cayenne pepper, to taste
(optional)

In a blender purée all ingredients. Pour into a saucepan over high heat and bring just to a boil, whisking constantly. Reduce heat to simmer and continue whisking for about 5 minutes. If you want a hotter sauce, add cayenne. Strain.

Makes about 1 cup

Berberé
Ethiopia

A hot, hot, hot seasoning paste, this Ethiopian lava is used as a base for many dishes as well as for an accompaniment. Serve with Sik Sik Wat (see page 62) and use in Kifto-Stuffed Chiles (see page 20). It will keep for several weeks if refrigerated.

6 to 8 tomatoes, coarsely chopped
2 tablespoons grated fresh ginger
6 to 8 fresh hot chiles, finely minced
1/2 teaspoon each ground coriander, ground cardamom, ground fenugreek, ground nutmeg, and ground cinnamon
1/8 teaspoon ground cloves
2 large onions, minced
8 to 10 cloves garlic, minced
1 tablespoon salt
1/2 cup dry red wine
2 cups paprika
5 tablespoons cayenne pepper
1 teaspoon coarsely ground black pepper
1/4 to 1/3 cup vegetable oil
2 to 3 tablespoons sugar
2 tablespoons minced cilantro

Put all ingredients in a saucepan and cook over medium heat, stirring constantly, until a thick sauce results (15 to 20 minutes). Transfer to a jar or small crock for storage.

Makes about 2 1/2 cups

Hot Teriyaki Sauce
Japan

I was first introduced to teriyaki by my Chinese-Hawaiian first husband. The marriage didn't last but my love of teriyaki has. This sauce makes a fine marinade, glaze, or dipping sauce for fish, meat, or fowl.

1 cup soy sauce
1/4 cup smoky Asian sesame oil
1/4 cup cream sherry
1/3 to 1/2 cup brown sugar
6 cloves garlic, finely minced
1 1/2 teaspoons grated fresh ginger
1/2 teaspoon dry mustard
1/2 teaspoon crushed dried hot chiles
1/4 teaspoon coarsely ground black pepper

Put all ingredients into a glass jar with a tight-fitting lid and shake well. Refrigerate overnight. Shake the jar occasionally. The next day, strain through a fine mesh sieve.

Makes about 1 3/4 cups

Salsa Son-of-a-Gun
Family Recipe

I always have this chunky salsa on hand. The recipe makes a fairly hot salsa. It could be hotter. For those seeking a lifetime membership in the Galvanized Gullet, add more crushed dried hot chiles. For a salsa that is not so hot, buy milder chiles and remove the seeds. For a salsa that is not hot but retains the chile flavor, substitute 1 pound of bell peppers for the 1 pound of chiles and add crushed dried hot chiles a little at a time until desired hotness is obtained. The recipe yields four quarts. You may can the salsa, freeze it, or keep it in the refrigerator. The salsa keeps in the refrigerator for up to two weeks. If you want to can it, follow the instructions in the U.S. Department of Agriculture's

Continued

publications on canning or the canning instructions in any standard cookbook.

8 pounds ripe tomatoes, finely chopped
1 pound fresh very hot chiles, chopped
12 to 15 cloves garlic, chopped
8 to 10 large onions, finely chopped
1 bunch celery, finely chopped
1/4 cup light-flavored vegetable oil
1 cup distilled vinegar, or more to taste
1/2 cup sugar, or more to taste
1/2 cup minced cilantro
1 1/2 teaspoons freshly ground black pepper
Salt, to taste
Crushed dried hot chiles, to taste (optional)

In a blender purée 1 cup of the chopped tomatoes with as many chiles as can be accommodated. Continue until all chiles have been puréed. Pour purée into a large pot. Add the remaining tomatoes and remaining ingredients except salt and dried chiles.

Cook over high heat for 10 minutes, stirring frequently to avoid scorching. Reduce heat to moderate and cook, stirring occasionally, until salsa is somewhat thickened (about 45 minutes). Season to taste with salt, more sugar or vinegar, or dried chiles (if desired). Cook for at least 10 more minutes after making any additions.

Makes about 4 quarts

Salsa Cruda
Mexico

On my most recent trip to Mexico, I encountered *salsa cruda,* or fresh uncooked salsa. It is served throughout Mexico: from glass bowls set in larger bowls of cracked ice in posh restaurants catering to the tourist trade, and in a paper cup in truck stops and markets. No matter how it's presented, salsa cruda is great; despite its volcanic quality, it adds a light freshness to Mexican foods.

5 large ripe tomatoes, chopped
6 small fresh hot chiles, chopped
4 cloves garlic, minced
1 large onion, finely chopped
4 green onions, including tops, finely chopped

1/3 cup minced cilantro
1/4 teaspoon coarsely ground black pepper
1 teaspoon sugar
Salt, to taste

In a blender purée tomatoes, chiles, and garlic. Pour into a bowl and add remaining ingredients. Refrigerate at least 1 hour before serving.

Makes about 3 cups

Salsa Diablo
Family Recipe

This salsa has a smooth texture. If you want it hotter, add cayenne to taste. If you don't want it so hot, remove seeds from chiles or use milder chiles. If you want it only mildly hot, use bell peppers instead of chiles and gradually add cayenne to achieve desired hotness. The hot chile oil can burn, so be careful while transferring batches of this sauce. Do not touch your hands to your face until you have washed them very well. Salsa Diablo keeps for about two weeks in the refrigerator, or it may be frozen.

1 can (46 oz) tomato juice
1 pound fresh very hot chiles,
  chopped
4 large onions, chopped
6 cloves garlic, chopped
1/3 cup minced cilantro
1/4 cup sugar
1/3 cup distilled vinegar
1/2 teaspoon coarsely ground
  black pepper
Salt, to taste
Cayenne pepper, to taste
  (optional)

Put all ingredients in a large
pot and bring to a boil. Reduce
heat and simmer for 30
minutes. Let cool somewhat.
Purée in a blender until
smooth, in several batches if
necessary. Pour purée in pot
and simmer over low heat,
stirring frequently to prevent
sticking, until sauce thickens
(30 minutes).

Makes about 2 pints

PICKLES AND CHUTNEYS

Most condiments grew from the
need to preserve, or pickle, a
portion of the autumn harvest
for the lean months ahead. Wet
pickles were foods placed in a
liquid with added preservatives.
Dry pickles were made by
repeatedly rubbing a mixture of
dry herbs, spices, and salts
into the surface of the food
until enough of the mixture
was incorporated to ensure
preservation.

Salt was almost always an
essential element for both wet
and dry pickling. The kind of
clear, refined, high-quality salt
required for preserving was
very expensive. Therefore, it
was important to choose only
good-quality meat for pickling,
a practice that gave rise to the
expression "worth its salt."

Gastronomy has taken
pickling a long way. We have
myriad techniques for making
pickles, preserves, conserves,
chutneys, and sauces that are
used for their special charac-
ters, not just because they will
keep. Here is a selection of hot
ones.

NEVER store pickles or other
foods with a high vinegar
content in metal containers.
They can become toxic.

Crown and Treaty Pickled Onions
England

During one attempt in the mid-
sixteenth century to negotiate an
end to the Civil War, Charles I
and his entourage rode from
the royalist stronghold in
Oxford to meet with represen-
tatives of Parliament, who came
from Westminster. They met at
an inn in Uxbridge. A treaty
was signed but it didn't stick.
What did stick was the name,
for the inn has been called the
Crown and Treaty ever since.
These wonderful pickled onions
originated at the Crown and
Treaty. They will be ready to
eat in about three days, but
will keep in a cool place for
months.

2 pounds small boiling onions
  (each 1 in. diameter)
12 small dried red chiles
1/2 cup salt
1/4 cup sugar
1 tablespoon mixed pickling
  spices
4 cloves garlic, crushed
1 tablespoon salt, or to taste
1 quart (approximately) cider
  vinegar

Continued

Peel onions. Put onions and chiles in a bowl with the 1/2 cup salt and enough water to cover. Stir and let sit overnight.

The next day, drain onions and chiles and rinse in fresh water. Put salt, sugar, pickling spices, garlic, and salt to taste in a saucepan and add 2 cups cold water. Bring to a boil, then reduce heat to simmer. Cook for 15 minutes. Let cool.

Pack onions and chiles into sterilized jars or a small crock. Pour spice liquid over, then add enough vinegar to cover. If using jars, screw down lids and store in a cool place. If using a crock, cover and place in refrigerator.

Makes about 2 quarts

To peel boiling onions quickly, drop into rapidly boiling water and leave for about 1 minute. Drain, rinse in cold water, and peel with a small sharp knife.

Royal Standard of England Hot Mustard Pickle
England

The Royal Standard of England is reputed to be the oldest pub in the country, though, of course, lots of pubs claim that honor. Oldest or not, the Royal Standard is a good pub in a beautiful building just outside the town of Beaconsfield. The beer is good, and the excellent lunchtime buffet includes these pickles.

You can eat them right away or refrigerate for up to three weeks. Do not freeze.

1 small cauliflower or 1/2 large
* cauliflower*
2 medium green tomatoes,
* chopped*
2 large onions, chopped
2 cucumbers, grated
1 cup salt
1/4 cup unbleached all-purpose
* flour*
1/2 cup sugar, or more to taste
1/2 cup dry mustard
1/2 cup butter
2 cups vinegar, preferably malt
1 tablespoon ground turmeric
1 tablespoon capers, drained
1 teaspoon celery seed
Salt, to taste

Separate cauliflower into smallest possible florets. Cut any that are larger than your thumbnail into smaller pieces. Put florets in a large bowl, add tomatoes, onions, and cucumbers, and sprinkle with the 1 cup salt. Toss, then cover with cold water. Let sit in a cool place for at least 2 hours but do not refrigerate.

When ready to make pickle, drain vegetables and rinse in cold running water. Put into a large pot, cover with water, and place over high heat. When water boils, remove from heat and drain. Rinse vegetables in cold running water and drain again.

In a large saucepan, mix together flour, sugar, and mustard, and add butter. Cook over moderate heat, stirring constantly, until butter is melted and a paste is formed. Slowly add vinegar, whisking, until thick. Add remaining ingredients, lower heat to simmer, and cook, stirring occasionally, for 5 minutes. Remove from heat and add to drained vegetables. Toss to coat evenly. Pack into jars or crocks and refrigerate.

Makes about 1 1/2 quarts

Pickled Chiles
Cajun Cuisine

These pickled chiles will be ready to use in about three weeks; after that, they will start to lose their crispness. If you are a macho type who loves to crunch on hot chiles, these will be fine for that game about two weeks after you make them. I like to use these chiles when they are quite soft, after a month or two. I cut them up for burritos and quesadillas. You need a sterilized one-pint jar with a ring-and-dome lid to make these pickles; the recipe can be multiplied to fill more jars.

2 cups small fresh mild or hot
    chiles
6 cloves garlic
1/3 cup light-flavored vegetable
    oil
1 fresh dill flower head (see
    Note, page 123) or
    1/2 teaspoon dried dill
1/2 teaspoon sugar
1 1/2 cups (approximately)
    distilled vinegar

With a sharp knife, make a slit in side of each chile. Put chiles into sterilized pint jar. Add garlic, oil, dill, and sugar. Fill jar with vinegar, put on ring and lid, screw down, and shake. Leave in a cool place.

Makes one 1-pint jar

Kimchee
Korea

Kimchee is the Korean form of coleslaw but with the addition of fire and lightning. Traditionally, it was put into sealed clay pots and buried in the ground to ferment. Today, the vegetables have to sit overnight in salt in a bowl, then for a week in jars until ready to eat. Serve kimchee as you would pickles or chutney, to accompany cold meats or as a fiery snack.

1 medium head napa cabbage,
    cored and thinly sliced
2 large onions, cut into thin
    rings
1/2 cup salt
10 cloves garlic, coarsely
    chopped
2 tablespoons slivered fresh
    ginger
1 1/2 teaspoons crushed dried
    hot chiles
1 teaspoon sugar

Put cabbage, onion, and salt in a bowl, knead gently with your hands to incorporate salt, and leave overnight.

The next day, rinse well under cold running water, then drain. Rinse and drain again. Add remaining ingredients and knead to mix thoroughly. Pack into glass jars or small ceramic pots. Add enough water to reach top of ingredients. Leave at least 1 week in a cool, unrefrigerated place.

Makes about 2 quarts

Pickled onions, chutney, and mustard pickle are traditionally part of an English "ploughman's lunch," which usually consists of a chunk of good bread and a piece of English farmhouse cheese. All this and a pint of good brown ale are enough to keep one ploughing until dinnertime.

Quick and Easy Cheatin' Chutney
Family Recipe

Every larder should include chutney. This sweet, hot one is a good accompaniment for Indian food, and it can be made in about one hour. The pickled vegetables used in this recipe are available in most supermarkets.

1 cup orange marmalade
1 cup hot mixed pickled vegetables, very finely chopped
1 cup raisins
1 teaspoon crushed dried hot chiles
1 cup dark brown sugar
1 cup cider vinegar
1/2 teaspoon ground cinnamon
1 tablespoon grated fresh ginger
4 cloves garlic, minced

In a saucepan over high heat, bring all ingredients to a boil, stirring constantly to prevent sticking. Reduce heat to simmer and cook until much of liquid has been reduced and chutney is thick and the consistency of jam (45 minutes to 1 hour). Stir frequently.

Makes about 3 cups

Jamaica Inn Chutney
England

The Jamaica Inn sits alone on the isolated wastes of Bodmin Moor in Cornwall. It was here in this lonely hospice that the wan (aren't they always wan?) heroine of Daphne du Maurier's novel of the same name met with terror night after cold, gray wind-torn night. Less than a mile away down a narrow, rutted dirt road lies Dozmary Pool, reputed to be the lake into which Sir Bedivere lobbed Excalibur after Arthur died.

Inside the inn today you are greeted with a large crackling fire ready to chase away the chill of the moor. Like most good English country inns, the Jamaica Inn serves a buffet lunch. Mackerel, Cornish pasty, steak and kidney pie, or ploughman's lunch is accompanied with this sweet-and-sour, hot and zesty chutney. It is traditionally served with cold meats and is particularly good with cold sliced ham or cold meat pies.

3 pounds apples, with skins, finely chopped
3 pounds onions, chopped
3 cups raisins
3 cups dark brown sugar
2 cups malt vinegar
2 tablespoons mixed pickling spices
1 tablespoon grated fresh ginger
1/2 to 1 teaspoon crushed dried hot chiles
1/2 teaspoon ground cinnamon

Put all ingredients in a large pot and bring to a boil. Reduce heat and simmer, stirring occasionally, until thick and glossy (about 2 hours). Let chutney cool in pot. Pack into a bowl, crock, or jars; cover and store in refrigerator.

Makes about 2 quarts

"Thou shalt be . . . stewed in brine, smarting in lingering pickle." *Antony and Cleopatra,* Act II, Scene V.

ACCOMPANIMENTS

CHAPTER FOURTEEN

FIRE EXTINGUISHERS

If you are a fancier of hot foods, then you know that heat has many levels. There is the zip of garlic and onion, whose tastes linger for hours though the harshness dissipates quickly. There is the sweet burr of ginger and the growing glow of mustards. There is that incredible explosion in the sinuses caused by horseradish, which makes its appearance like a nova, then fades almost as quickly. Capsicums (the chiles), on the other hand, definitely have staying power—so much so that sometimes it is necessary to put out the fire.

Sometimes even the most ardent lovers of hot foods occasionally find it necessary to cry uncle, wave the white flag, and put out the fire. How to do that? The recipes in this section help. Over generations, people who eat fiery foods have learned certain tricks. Trick number one is that, in most cases, water does not help. Beer is much better. The best choice is a flavorful brew with a good balance of hops and malt. I would not select a stout or porter to put out the conflagration, nor would I choose a low-calorie beer. A beer that is light in color, not calories, is an ideal fire extinguisher.

Something sweet is better still. In cuisines where capsicum is a predominant ingredient, desserts are either exceedingly sweet—sweet beyond the average tolerance—or they consist simply of fruit, which is one of the finest fire extinguishers available. When serving a dinner that is based on one of the cuisines designed to bring a significant conflagration to the palate, I almost always end the meal with a platter of chilled fruit.

Indian, Southeast Asian, and African cuisines call for a variety of sweet chutneys and condiments to accompany a meal of hot dishes. Small Mexican restaurants and market stalls serve hot foods with a form of guacamole without chiles, a mild salsa cruda, and the ubiquitous lime. I find fresh limes with food wherever I go in Mexico. Sucking on a quarter of a fresh lime and then drinking some good beer puts out the fire nicely.

Leyla's Ice Yogurt and Cucumber
Turkey

The first fire extinguisher I ever learned about must be attributed, like so much of my

culinary knowledge, to my friend Leyla. The ice for this dish should be fine enough that it is merely small crystals that cool the tongue and palate.

2 large cucumbers, peeled and grated
1 cup (8 oz) plain yogurt
2 cups crushed or shaved ice

In a medium bowl mix all ingredients together well and serve immediately.

Makes about 3 cups

Yogurt Ice
Middle East

Despite their religious and military disagreements, Richard Coeur de Lion and Saladin held each other in high regard. It is said that once, when Richard lay quite ill and in a delirium, Saladin kept a fleet of runners busy supplying the ailing king with ices to reduce his fever. The image that comes to mind when one hears this legend is sherbet; however, a chilled delight of fruit and yogurt like this one is more likely.

A handsome way to present this dish when you prepare it with such sturdy-skinned fruit as oranges, lemons, pineapples,

and small melons is to scoop the fruit carefully out of the skins and use the shells to serve the Yogurt Ice.

3 cups chopped fresh or canned fruit
2 cups (16 oz) plain yogurt
1/2 cup sugar

In a blender purée fruit. In a large bowl mix puréed fruit with yogurt and sugar and put into a freezer. Stir every 15 to 20 minutes to ensure that ice sets smooth and creamy and fruit is evenly distributed. Do not freeze solid.

Makes about 3 cups

Persian Mast Va Khiar
Iran

This almost-frozen yogurt, flavored with fresh herbs, makes a delightful fire extinguisher to accompany Middle Eastern dishes.

1 large cucumber, grated
1/4 cup minced red bell pepper or fresh pimiento
2 green onions, including tops, minced
1 tablespoon minced fresh dill or 1 teaspoon dried dill

1 tablespoon minced fresh
  cilantro
1 teaspoon sugar
1 tablespoon freshly squeezed
  lime juice
1 cup (8 oz) plain yogurt
Dill or cilantro sprigs, for
  garnish (optional)

In a medium bowl mix all
ingredients together thoroughly
and put into freezer. Stir every
10 minutes for 45 minutes to 1
hour. Mixture should not freeze
solid, but should just begin to
form crystals.

Mound into a serving dish
and garnish with dill sprigs (if
desired). Serve immediately.

Makes about 1 1/2 cups

Minted Yogurt Cooler
Family Recipe

Cool, refreshing, and easy to
make, this yogurt with mint is
great with curries.

1/2 cup chopped fresh mint
  leaves
1 teaspoon sugar
1 tablespoon freshly squeezed
  lime juice
1 cup (8 oz) plain yogurt
Mint sprigs, for garnish
  (optional)

In a blender purée all ingredients until mint leaves are
incorporated. Pour into a
serving dish and chill for at
least 1 hour before serving.
Garnish with mint sprigs (if
desired).

Makes about 1 cup

The Ultimate Fire
Extinguisher
Family Recipe

This is a marvelous fire extinguisher and a grand centerpiece
for a fancy dinner party or
buffet table. Using jagged-cut
melons, skewered fruit, and
Minted Yogurt cooler for
dipping, you can create a show
stopper. The fruits listed here
are only suggestions; choose
what is available, letting Mother
Nature and your imagination be
your guides.

1 large watermelon
1 large cantaloupe
1/2 honeydew melon
1/2 casaba melon
1 box strawberries
2 large seedless oranges
4 limes
2 cups seedless grapes
3 or 4 mint sprigs, for garnish
2 recipes Minted Yogurt Cooler
  (see preceding recipe)

Jagged-cut watermelon so that
it becomes a long oval serving
dish. You should remove only
about one fourth to one fifth of
the total bulk when making the
"lid."

Jagged-cut cantaloupe in half
to make two dishes. Remove a
small slice from bottom of
watermelon and cantelope half
so that they will sit firmly.

With a melon baller or a
sharp teaspoon remove meat
from all melons. Wash strawberries but leave on stems. Leave
peel on oranges and slice into
thin rings. Cut each lime into 6
wedges. Toss all fruit together
gently and put into hollowed-
out watermelon shell. Thread
some of the fruit alternately
onto short bamboo skewers and
arrange around edge of watermelon shell. Garnish with mint.

Put Minted Yogurt Cooler
into cantaloupe shells. When
serving, place a cantaloupe
shell at each end of watermelon. Provide extra skewers.
Guests may dip skewered fruit
into yogurt or gather fruit of
their choice for dipping.

Serves 12 or more

Agua de Fruta
Mexico

In Mexico, fruit waters are sold at small restaurants and market stalls. They are made simply by mincing fresh fruit and letting it sit in ice water for a few hours before serving. The result is subtle in flavor and color. In Mexican market places a fruit-water stand is a welcome haven displaying 5-gallon jars filled with chunks of ice and pastel liquid, the outsides of the jars wet with rivulets of condensed moisture.

Do not expect Agua de Fruta to be like fruit juice. It is not as intense or sweet. It is cool and refreshing, tasting lightly of the fruit from which it is made, and it's a wonderful fire extinguisher. Appropriate fruits are watermelon, pineapple, strawberries, Persian melons, peaches, cantaloupe, or any other tropical fruit.

6 cups minced (not puréed)
  fresh fruit
1 gallon cold water
Several large chunks ice

Put fruit into a large glass jar or pitcher. Add the water and stir. Let sit at room temperature for 2 hours. To serve, add chunks of ice.

Makes 16 cups

Put-out-the-Fire Salsa Cruda
Mexico

Most salsas add fire. This one is designed to put it out.

4 large tomatoes, minced
2 large bell peppers, seeded
  and finely chopped
1 large cucumber, finely
  chopped
6 green onions, including tops,
  minced
1/4 cup minced fresh parsley
2 tablespoons minced cilantro
1 medium sweet red onion,
  minced
1/4 cup freshly squeezed lemon
  juice
1 teaspoon sugar
Salt, to taste

In a large bowl mix together all ingredients and refrigerate for at least 2 hours before serving.

Makes about 2 cups

Gewürztraminer Sherbet
Galvanized Gullet Contribution

This is a most elegant and delightful refresher. One of the few people I have ever met who had a tolerance for hot food equal to mine was a wine maker. Joel and I met one hot summer afternoon at a California winery. He and other close friends shared a picnic I brought. The Cajun Boudin (see page 96) put the others under the table, but Joel scarfed up chunk after fiery chunk saying only, "Yes, it's a little warm." That afternoon he eagerly joined the Galvanized Gullet and gave me this recipe for a superb fire extinguisher based on Gewürztraminer wine.

I always like to envision guests at Joel's house asking, "This meal is delicious. Did you make it yourself?" And of course, he could answer, "Yes, all of it," since he had made the wine as well.

1/2 cup sugar
1 bottle fine Gewürztraminer
2 egg whites
1 cup (1/2 pint) whipping
  cream

In a large bowl stir together sugar and wine until sugar has dissolved. Put into freezer and leave until slushy but not frozen solid. Stir every 20 minutes or so to ensure that sherbet sets evenly. When it has reached a thick but not solid consistency, beat egg whites until quite stiff but not dry. In a separate bowl beat cream until stiff. Gently fold egg whites and cream together, then very gently fold mixture into partially frozen wine. Scoop into individual sherbet glasses or leave in a large serving dish and refreeze until set but not solid.

Makes about 4 cups

Orange-Ginger Freeze
Family Recipe

The flavors of orange and ginger complement each other perfectly. Served between hot dishes, this refreshing freeze cleanses the palate.

1 cup (8 oz) yogurt
1 cup orange marmalade
1 1/2 teaspoons finely grated fresh ginger
3 egg whites

In a blender purée yogurt, marmalade, and ginger until smooth. Transfer to a bowl, set in freezer, and leave until it is thick but not solid. Stir every 10 to 15 minutes so that mixture sets evenly and does not become ice. When it is thick, beat egg whites until stiff and gently fold into orange-yogurt mixture. If it becomes too liquid, return to freezer until it resets but is not solid. Serve immediately.

Makes about 2 1/2 cups

Cottage Cheese Refresher
Family Recipe

Cottage cheese makes an excellent vehicle for all sorts of culinary creations. Here it is blended with the flavors of fresh herbs to cool down the palate and ready it for the next conflagration.

2 cups (16 oz) small-curd cottage cheese
2 stalks celery, very finely minced
1/4 cup finely minced fresh parsley
1/4 cup finely minced fresh mint
2 tablespoons finely minced cilantro
1 medium bell pepper, seeded and finely minced
1 fresh pimiento, seeded and finely minced (optional)
1 teaspoon sugar
Pinch salt

In a large bowl mix together all ingredients and refrigerate at least 2 hours before serving.

Makes about 2 1/2 cups

CHAPTER FIFTEEN

BEER

Learning the complexities and subtle variations of the world's fine brews can be a pasttime equally as rewarding as learning to enjoy the products of the vintner's art. For those who like it hotter, this would be altogether appropriate because beer is a highly effective liquid fire extinguisher. I can't imagine serving wine with most Mexican, Indian, Chinese, Thai, Hawaiian, or Japanese food. Beer can also be an excellent companion to many American foods usually enjoyed with wine. Wine is truly a delight and the perfect accompaniment to many meals, but not all.

People who know of my love of good beers will often ask me which is the best. That's like asking what is the best food, poem, painting, dance or song. Beer, like anything else, fortunately, comes in a variety of styles suited to a variety of needs and uses. Usually I prefer fuller-flavored, top-fermented British brews, or the complexities of a good hoppy Mexican or Belgian beer, or my own San Francisco steam. But not always. If I have just finished mowing the lawn on a swelter- ing California afternoon, or cleaning the unventilated attic, I can't think of anything less appealing than a nice dark, flat, tepid pint of Oxfordshire's Old Hooky. What I want is a very cold glass of lager; pale, light- flavored and effervescent. However, when solving the world's problems on a chill evening in my favorite Oxford pub, The Turf Tavern, or partici- pating in a song fest at The Blue Anchor in Cornwall, a glass of cold lager would be most inappropriate. Then I want a pint of delicious, full- flavored Tanglefoot or Spingo, and I want it served at a cool, not cold, temperature that lets the rich flavor develop to its fullest.

Originally all beers were "top fermented." When fermentation takes place at higher tempera- tures, the yeast stays on the top of the fermentation vessel. The result is a fuller- flavored brew. The effect of higher temperatures is compa- rable for wines. Red wines are fermented at higher tempera- tures than white wines, and the result is a not a better, but a bigger, wine, with more com- plex flavors.

There is a drawback to top fermentation: it's harder to maintain quality control. Some- times it is unbelievably deli- cious and, at other times, it may have all the charm of a pair of old gym socks.

England has a strong tradi- tion of top-fermented brews. The major styles are bitter, mild, and pale ale. Forty per- cent of all beer consumed in England is bitter, only 20 percent is lager style, and the remainder is divided between mild, pale ale, bottled strong ale, and stout.

A word of warning to any of my fellow Americans who may be planning a trip to Merry olde England and wish to spend an evening or so enjoy- ing the delights of the English pub: please, do not embarrass yourself by asking for "a glass of bitters." Bitters are an added flavoring in some mixed drinks. You are going to have a hard time gagging down a pint pot of bitters. However, you will probably enjoy trying a pint or half pint of "bitter," which is a generic term for one style of English beer. Being quite heavily hopped, it usually has a more or less bitter flavor, which gives it its name. It is full-bodied, malty and low in carbonation and is usually between 3 and 5.5 percent alcohol by volume. You are probably used to beer that is 3.5, and you are definitely used to a pint being 16 ounces. But be aware of this; in England a pint is 20 ounces, so watch it.

"Mild" is a distinctive draught brew, very rich in both flavor and color though not having the characteristic bitter bite of a "bitter." Many milds have a rich, smooth, velvety taste and texture, and they are experiencing a renaissance after several decades of quiet popularity. They run from 2.5 to 3.5 percent alcohol.

In true British fashion, "pale ale" is not pale at all, but a deep amber color. When created it was paler than the other brews of the time which were porters and stouts. However, in the rapidly proliferating brew pubs and micro breweries of America, pale ale is pale indeed, light golden in color, unlike its British namesake.

I would like to shatter the American myth that English beer is served warm. It is not served warm. It is served at cellar temperature, which is usually pleasantly cool but not chilled. This allows the full complexity of flavors to come through.

Whereas almost all British brews are top fermented, only a few continental brews are: the Trappiste brews produced in a few Belgian abbeys and the Netherlands; Klösch, produced in the region around Cologne; and Dusseldorfer, found in Dusseldorf, Munster, and a few north Rhineland towns.

Almost all other beers made on the continent today are lagers or bottom-fermented brews. The word *lager* means "stored," or "iced," and the method is relatively recent given the long history of brewing. After all, many archaeologists and geographers believe that grains were first domesticated for brewing, not baking.

For centuries, brewing was a touch-and-go business, its product often turning out to be cloudy or sour. This was often attributed to "beer witches." After millenia of sour beer, folks started noticing that beer brewed in winter or stored in cool caves didn't go sour as often and was frequently clear and pleasant looking. Some time around the beginning of the fifteenth century, a few of our more brilliant ancestors started thinking that, just possibly, it wasn't witches or the devil, but rather temperature that determined the quality of beer. They started experimenting with making beer in caves and, sure enough, more of the beer was good more of the time.

Some few truly enlightened brewers even went so far as to cut ice from rivers and lakes in winter, store it in caves or pack it in straw, and then use it to cool beer brewed in summer. When fermentation takes place at lower temperatures, the yeast eventually settles to the bottom of the cask, thus eliminating the need for skimming the beer before it's sold.

Until the invention of mechanical refrigeration, bottom-fermentation, or lagering, continued to be carried on almost exclusively in regions that had a ready supply of ice. With refrigeration, lagering became the dominant style of brewing throughout the world. People were anxious to have beers that, although somewhat diminished in their complexity of flavors, were more consistent in their quality.

People often ask if I prefer lager or pilsener. This is an inaccurate distinction. All pilseners are lagers, since they are bottom-fermented beer. However, the term *pilsener* refers to those beers brewed in the style developed in the town of Pilsen in Bohemia.

Another misunderstood term is *bock*. The famed dark beer from Einbeck was widely acclaimed and, therefore, widely exported. In the days before either pasteurization or refrigeration, the alcohol content was fortified so that it could survive its travels. Thus it was known not only for its fine flavor but also for its strength. Like all good things, Einbeck beer was soon widely imitated. In Bavaria, where the accent is quite different, it became known as *Oanbock* and this gradually became simply *bock bier*.

No matter where a *bock-style* beer is produced it tends to be somewhat stronger than other beers of the region. The strongest commercially produced beer in the world is *doppelbock*, or double bock, brewed in northern Bavaria. It has an alcohol content of 13.2 percent by volume. Like all pilseners, all bocks are lagers, since they are also bottom-fermented.

In the United States, the term *bock beer* came to describe color rather than strength. It was traditional for breweries to totally drain their vats once a year in order to give them a thorough cleaning. This was usually done in the early spring. The last beer drawn from the vats was darker than the normal brew, having collected sediment during the year. It was bottled as bock. A few breweries today produce a bock beer which, though darker and somewhat richer in flavor than their normal product, is not any stronger. You can usually find it on the market around April.

San Francisco is the home and place of origin of America's only indigenous brewing style. Steam beer, of delicious fact and wondrous legend, grew out of the needs of a frontier society. Gold miners, adventurers, and frontiersmen had a great thirst. Unfortunately, the hot, dry California climate was not particularly favorable to the production of beer by traditional methods. Breweries in the east had access to ice to cool their lagering tanks, but brewers in California did not. Steam beer is a delightful compromise between top and bottom fermentation, producing a rich and full-bodied brew similar in character to English bitters, but with a thick, creamy head produced by natural fermentation. Although the beer is highly effervescent, it is not gaseous like many American lagers.

There are several theories as to the origin of the word *steam* in the name. It does not mean that the beer is served hot and steaming. It is possible that originally the breweries were operated by steam power. My favorite theory is that old Pete Steam invented the process; however, as much as I love folk legends, I must admit it probably is not so. Most likely the name came from the head of steam that was released when a keg was tapped. The steam formed because the beer was fermented naturally in the keg, like champagne.

There were dozens of steam beer breweries in the San Francisco Bay Area from its invention during the gold rush until Prohibition, and by the 1930s, my father had sampled the wares of most of them. However, the Anchor Brewing Company is the only one that reopened after that American phenomonon, Prohibition. In 1965, even Anchor went onto the endangered species list when bankruptcy threatened to close its doors. But miracles often occur in strange places. Who would have thought that the son of a washing machine manufacturer would be the one to save a San Francisco tradition from extinction?

Fritz Maytag bought the company and headlines like "FROM SUDS TO SUDS" and "MAYTAG SAVES STEAM FROM A REAL SUDSING" were splashed across San Francisco newspapers. The little brewery soon climbed out of the red and well into the black, and Anchor Steam can be enjoyed across the country and around the world. Maytag rightly assessed that the public was ready to look more favorably on a brew that went beyond the dimensions of standard American brewing.

My father satisfied his love of good beers with Tuborg, Ritterbrau, Asahi, Dos Equis, Guinness and, of course, Anchor Steam. Today I wouldn't have room to list even a portion of the fine imports available, let alone the production of brew pubs and micro breweries. And Anchor Steam Beer, like California's premium wines, is taking its place among the great brews of the world. I found a delightful bit of cross-cultural exchange recently when I walked into my favorite pub in Cornwall, The Blue Anchor, a tiny establishment that still brews its own excellent beer. The brewer was wearing a T-shirt that read, "ANCHOR STEAM BEER, made in San Francisco since 1896."

As excellent and historic as good old steam beer is, it's no longer the only game in town. In 1978 the law in some states changed to allow the consumption of beer on the premise where it was brewed. Shortly thereafter, California had her first two brew pubs. Currently, brew pubs and micro breweries, each producing their own distinctive brew, are springing up at a phenomenal rate, particularly in the northwest. America is in the delightful grip of a flavor renaissance. Americans now expect—no, we demand—an ever-expanding culinary horizon. We eagerly explore taste frontiers that leave the meat and potatoes of yesteryear far behind. The tingling tantalizing delights of hot hot foods are only one direction in which this renaissance is taking us. As in the exploration of space, we now know that our culinary explorations can go where no man has gone before. And when we get there not only will the food be exciting, but also there will be myriad good brews with which to wash it down.

INDEX

BIOGRAPHICAL NOTE

Geraldine Duncann's family roots go far back into California's past. "When my white ancestors came to California before the Gold rush, my Paiute Indian ancestors were there to greet them," she explains. Her culinary roots extend back to the multicultural kitchen at the family cattle ranch in the San Joaquin Valley. Early in her life she was exposed to such exotic foods as oysters steamed in beer, a method that Jack London had taught her father. After leaving home, her knowledge of North African, Ceylonese, Oriental, and Polynesian foods was gleaned from her associations with some excellent cooks from other countries.

Duncann's formal training was in art, at the California College of Arts and Crafts in Oakland. But her main interest soon became focused on the study of food. She has taught classes on the origins of cuisines at the University of California Extension in Berkeley, in New Orleans, and abroad in Oxford and Dijon. In her extensive travels throughout the world, Duncann is an indefatigable collector of recipes, cooking lore, and interesting people: "The best apple pie I have ever eaten was made by a ninety-year-old political activist who got the recipe from Henry Miller. The best Chinese food I have ever tasted was cooked by Frank Herbert." From the bottom of

the Grand Canyon to the Swiss Alps, from Oaxaca to the Louisiana bayous, she has had the good fortune to make close friends, many of whom delight in sharing their extensive culinary knowledge with her.

Duncann's international rovings in search of unusual food have led to a career as a food and travel writer. Her columns have appeared in the *San Francisco Examiner,* the *Los Angeles Herald examiner* and in other newspapers through The Food Package syndicate. Her articles have been published in *The International Review of Food and Wine, Motorland,* and a number of in-flight magazines, and she has served as food editor for *Old*

West, a historical journal. Six of her recipes were included in the 1985 edition of *The Best of Food and Wine,* published by *The International Review of Food and Wine.*

When not writing or cooking, Geraldine Duncann pursues her many other interests, which range from California's wines and mines to the spinning and weaving of the Orkney Islands; from the ancient stone circles of forgotten Celtic cultures to the contents of the Museum of Modern Art; from scuba diving and sailing to set and costume design and singing American and British folk music. She currently lives in Ashland, Oregon.

101 PRODUCTIONS COOKBOOKS

Softcover Titles

The Art of Cooking for Two
  by Coralie Castle & Astrid Newton — $9.95

Barbecue & Smoke Cookery by Maggie Waldron — $8.95

Bread & Breakfast by Linda Kay Bistrow — $10.95

The Calculating Cook by Jeanne Jones — $8.95

Coffee by Kenneth Davids — $10.95

The Ethnic Vegetarian
  by Shanta Nimbark Sacharoff — $8.95

Fifteen Minute Meals by Emalee Chapman — $8.95

Flavors of Hungary by Charlotte Slovak Biro — $10.95

Flavors of India by Shanta Nimbark Sacharoff — $8.95

Flavors of Japan by Delphine & Diane J. Hirasuna — $8.95

Flavors of Mexico
  by Angeles de la Rosa & C. Gandia de Fernández — $8.95

Flavors of Northern Italy by Violeta Autumn — $8.95

From Sea & Stream by Lou Seibert Pappas — $8.95

Greek Cooking for the Gods by Eva Zane — $10.95

Grill It In! by Barbara Grunes — $10.95

Home & Grill by Barbara Grunes — $10.95

Juice It Up! by Pat Gentry — $10.95

Kabobs on the Grill by Barbara Grunes — $10.95

Eggplant Mediterranee by Sotiris Kitrilakis — $11.95

The Hors d'Oeuvre Book by Coralie Castle — $10.95

Kitchen Tools by Patricia Gentry — $8.95

More Calculated Cooking by Jeanne Jones — $8.95

The New Harvest
  by Lou Seibert Pappas & Jane Horn — $9.95

One Pot Meals by Maggie Gin — $8.95

Pasta International by Gertrude Harris — $8.95

The Portable Feast by Diane D. MacMillan — $8.95

Real Bread by Maggie Baylis & Coralie Castle — $10.95

Secrets of Salt-Free Cooking by Jeanne Jones — $10.95

Some Like It Hotter by Geraldine Duncann — $10.95

Soup by Coralie Castle — $10.95

The Tea Lover's Treasury by James Norwood Pratt — $9.95

Vegetarian Gourmet Cookery by Alan Hooker — $10.95

Hardcover Titles

Diet for a Happy Heart by Jeanne Jones — $17.95

Teatime Celebrations by Patricia Gentry — $15.95

101 Productions and *California Culinary Academy* cookbooks are available from your local bookseller, or directly from The Cole Group, Inc., 4415 Sonoma Hwy., Santa Rosa, CA 95409. For a free catalog of all our cooking titles, call (707) 538-0495.

PRICES SUBJECT TO CHANGE WITHOUT NOTICE